DOWN
THE
DORDOGNE

DOWN
THE
DORDOGNE

BY

MICHAEL BROWN

SINCLAIR-STEVENSON

LONDON

First published in Great Britain by
Sinclair-Stevenson Limited
7/8 Kendrick Mews
London SW7 3HG

British Library Cataloguing in Publication Data
A CIP catalogue record for this book is available from the British Library.
ISBN: 1 85619 064 1

Typeset by Phoenix Photosetting, Chatham
Printed and bound in Great Britain by
Butler & Tanner Ltd, Frome and London

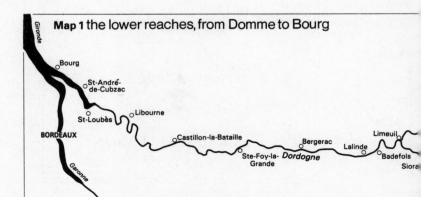

Map 1 the lower reaches, from Domme to Bourg

TO
JOAN AND DENIS

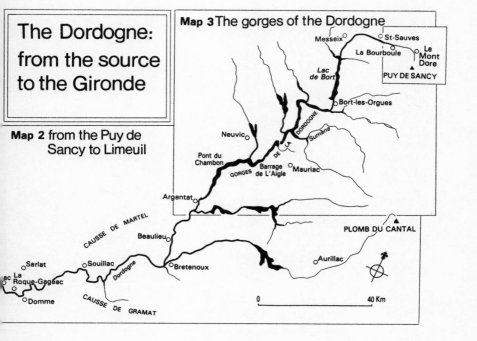

The Dordogne:
from the source
to the Gironde

Map 2 from the Puy de
Sancy to Limeuil

Map 3 The gorges of the Dordogne

Messeix
St-Sauves
La Bourboule
Le
Mont
Dore
Lac
de Bort
PUY DE SANCY

Bort-les-Orgues

Neuvic

Pont du
Chambon

Barrage
de L'Aigle
Mauriac

GORGES
DE LA DORDOGNE
Sumène

Argentat

CAUSSE DE MARTEL

PLOMB DU CANTAL

Beaulieu

Sarlat
Souillac
Dordogne
Bretenoux
Aurillac
ac La
Roque-Gageac

Domme

CAUSSE DE GRAMAT

0   40 Km

CONTENTS

1: THE PUY DE SANCY 1

2: THE ROAD TO BORT-LES-ORGUES 31

3: THE FLIGHT TO VAYRAC 57

4: BACKWARDS TO BEAULIEU 81

5: INTO THE CAUSSE 95

6: CHATEAUX COUNTRY 127

7: A BRUSH WITH LE TROISIEME AGE 151

8: THE PEN AND THE SWORD 165

9: A LA RECHERCHE DES GORGES PERDUES 197

Epilogue: ONE MORE TIME 215

CHAPTER 1

THE PUY DE SANCY

From the top of the Puy de Sancy you can see, on a clear day, all the way to the Alps. The day I was there it was hot and windy; the sky overhead was a clear blue but a haze reduced visibility. Even so, the view was superb. The Puy is the highest point of the Massif Central (6186 feet) and, because there are no nearby peaks tall enough to get in the way, there is an enormous all-round panorama. I felt as though I were inside a huge inverted bowl, the sky above forming the base, the rim being the circular indigo haze where earth and sky met at the horizon: for the first time I understood what is meant by the welkin.

Twenty miles to the north, the breast-shaped Puy de Dôme with its radio mast nipple was clearly visible; to the north-east I looked down the Vallée de Chaudefour to Lac Chambon, sparkling in the sun; further round, range on range of mountains stretched eastwards until lost to view; to the south I could see another lake, Lac Chouvet, and beyond it, thirty miles away, the unmistakeable hammer shape of the Plomb de Cantal – after the Puy de Sancy itself, the highest point of the Massif (6084 feet); westwards, green foothills merged gradually into the plain.

The Puy de Sancy is an extinct volcano which erupted over 300,000 years ago. Relatively speaking, this is quite recent, for the whole region is volcanic, the earliest eruptions dating from sixty million years ago. Underlying the volcanic lava and debris are crystalline and granite rocks that belong to the primary period 600 million years ago. It is a weird and fascinating landscape quite unlike the Alps or the Pyrenees, consisting for the most part of the gentle rounded slopes of extinct volcanoes, craters, often filled by lakes and strange shaped volcanic plugs, such as those of Tuilière and Sanadoire, which can clearly be seen to the north-west, near the Lac de Guéry.

The jagged summit of the Puy de Sancy is unusual and due to a pelean type of eruption in which a lava dome formed over the chimney of an earlier eruption, sealing it. This created a build-up of gases culminating in a second huge explosion that wrecked the original dome and produced great clouds of gas called *nuées ardentes*. The remnants of the summit and crater of the original volcano are covered by the lava outflow of the later eruption and this, combined with 300,000 years of erosion by glaciers and extremes of weather accounts for the broken outline of the mountain. The Puy de Sancy is one of three ruined volcanoes that together form the Mont-Dore Massif, the others being the Banne d'Ordanche (4962 feet) and the Puy de l'Aiguiller (5002 feet), both of which lie to the north.

The top of the Puy de Sancy is a splendid place to see and appreciate this strange, moon-like landscape. It must have been a nightmarish scene some sixty million years ago when the first eruptions took place: the earth's crust racked by gigantic convulsions, cracking and heaving and pock-marked with mountainous blisters; day turned to night by a black pall of gas and volcanic ashes, the stygian gloom lit up by colossal explosions as molten magna spurted hundreds of feet into the air, like some titanic primordial orgasm, and bombarded the surrounding slopes with huge rocks: a hellish vision worthy of the palette of Hieronymous Bosch. But sixty million years ago there were no human beings to observe the scene, and even if there had been, no living thing could have survived for long in that hostile environment.

I was not alone on the summit. Far from it: all around me were French holiday-makers enjoying themselves, some were stretched out in the sun, others sat admiring the view and each other; there were all ages from tiny tots to *grandpères* and *grandmères*. It was certainly not what I had expected when I first planned my assault on the Puy. Of course, having looked at the map, I knew that there was a *téléphérique* that would take me to within two hundred metres of the summit but after that I had imagined myself following a path like those I had climbed in the Pyrenees, winding up through woods to emerge on grass covered slopes, intersected by streams and freckled with wild flowers. Instead I found myself in a queue of fellow tourists scrambling up a steep stony path on a bare dusty ridge, down which wound another line of satisfied customers, like two columns of industrious ants. Looking around me I realised I was overdressed for the part: most people were scantily clad in T-shirts and shorts and wore trainers. I felt a bit of an idiot in my Rohan bags and heavy walking boots. At the top a narrow space of fifty feet long and thirty feet wide was crammed with sightseers. In the middle was a *table d'orientation* which I had to fight to get near and where it was impossible to stay for long because of the pressure of newcomers. Of course I should have guessed it was going to be like this when I arrived at the foot of the mountain and saw the car park: it was enormous. Lines of cars stretched in a great curve and there were many large coaches as well. Near the station for the *téléphérique* there was a restaurant and several bars; it was not a place to come in July to savour the peace of the mountains.

My reason for being on the Puy de Sancy was not to climb the mountain but to look for the source of the River Dordogne, down which I planned to travel to its confluence with the Garonne, near Bordeaux, some three hundred and fifty miles away. The Dordogne starts life as two small streams, the Dore and the Dogne, which unite on the flank of the mountain not far from the car park. The Dore rises quite close to the summit so, having taken my fill of the view, I set off down another steep track on the side opposite to the one I had come up. It was covered with loose scree and quite difficult, or so I thought and I was glad of my boots, until a boy of twelve galloped past wearing trainers. Soon after I struck the GR4e, one of those well-marked trails commonly found in French mountains. I continued down this well-beaten path for a short way until the slope became less severe and a spongy grass replaced the bare rock. Suddenly to my left I saw a trickle of brown water: it was the start of the Dore. I followed the growing stream, which ran between banks of buttercups and other wild flowerss, until it reached the edge of a precipice, over which it plunged, out of sight. There was another splendid view from the head of the waterfall down to the car park, a thousand feet below, and on down the narrow valley of the Dordogne to the spa town of le Mont-Dore, where I was to spend the night.

I didn't feel that it was necessary to search out the precise source of the Dogne, which lay somewhere to my right, but continued on down the track. Although wide and easy to follow, it was still steep and I was constantly surprised at how easily I was overtaken by young Frenchmen and their girls wearing singlets and running shorts. The path was badly eroded, which is hardly surprising considering the number of people using it, and there were parts that were fenced off so that they could be repaired by planting coarse grass. After climbing and walking for over three hours I was beginning to feel rather tired but at last I came out on a grassy slope near the foot of the Cascade de la Dore, which I could see falling in a long thin jet, from the ledge that I had left more than two hours ago, into a nearby gulch, where it disappeared from sight.

A short scramble up to my right brought me to a boulder-strewn watercourse. Ahead of me, but protected by a wire fence, I saw, beneath a concealing screen of trees, the exact spot where the Dore and the Dogne meet. I knew it was the right place because, with typical French thoroughness, each stream had a little notice identifying it. Ignoring the INTERDIT sign, I climbed over the wire and stood on a rock in the middle of the stream taking photographs. It was a good moment and only slightly marred by the fact that the long hot summer had already reduced the new-born river to a mere trickle.

I walked alonside the Dordogne for a little way until it disappeared into a culvert that ran under the car park. My mission for the day accomplished, I sat down at a café for a well-earned cup of tea and a *crêpe aux myrtilles*, to the accompaniment of jazz from a two-piece band consisting of a mouth-organ and a guitar.

Although it was only another two and a half miles down to le Mont-Dore, I felt I had walked far enough for one day, so I caught the bus which dropped me at the beginning of the town, just round the corner from my hotel. I was staying at the Hôtel Mouflons, named after a hardy species of mountain goat whose rams have huge, curling aggressive-looking horns. I know because there was a pair of stuffed mouflons in the vestibule of the hotel.

Le Mont-Dore is a small but attractive spa town wedged into a narrow but picturesque valley which culminates in the vast natural amphitheatre dominated by the Puy de Sancy. To the east rise the steep slopes of the Puy de l'Aigle and to the west those of the Capucin; both are thickly wooded. To the north the valley opens out until blocked by the massif of the Puy Gros, which deflects the Dordogne westwards.

The town is tiny with a population of only 2,300. It is U-shaped,

opening to the north, with two main arteries: the Avenue Jules Ferry on
the west side is a continuation of the road from La Bourboule, the next
town down the valley, while the Avenue de General Leclerc on the east
leads to Clermont Ferrand. The whole of le Mont-Dore is squeezed
between these two roads in a space only 320 feet wide and half-a-mile
long.

At the south end of the spa is a bustling market-place and close by, on
the right bank of the Dordogne, the small but attractive municipal
gardens and the casino. The heart of the town is the Place de Panthéon,
dominated by the forbidding classical façade of the *Etablissement
Thermal* but otherwise surrounded by the town's smartest hotels and
bars. Between the Place de Panthéon and the municipal gardens are
narrow streets of shops and restaurants. This small area comprises the
active centre of le Mont-Dore: to the north is the railway station and, on
the outskirts, a large campsite, while to the south are some horrific
modern chalets built of dark wood and the local basalt, chiefly serving
the winter skiers.

I had come up to le Mont-Dore on the train that morning from Brive,
after saying good-bye to my wife. Sybil and I had spent the last three
days at the Auberge du Vieux Chêne, Champs-sur-Tarentaine, which
we used as a base to reconnoitre the Mont Dore region before I set off
on my long walk. Now Sybil was on the auto-train on her way to
Boulogne and I was on my own. The idea of a journey down the
Dordogne had been gestating in my mind for some years, ever since I
read *Two Summers in Guyenne*. The author, Edward Harrison Barker,
made a similar trip at the end of the nineteenth century, when this part of
France was unknown territory to most Frenchmen, let alone a solitary
English traveller. So remote was the Auvergne in those days that many
of the people that Harrison Barker met spoke only patois and, because
he was a stranger, assumed that he must be French: they had no concept
of any country other than France, which in itself was a foreign land to
them.

I was fascinated by Harrison Barker's account of his adventures and
decided to emulate him, although I knew I could not follow his exact
route: after all he spent two years in the region and stayed for several
months at Beynac, exploring the area much more thoroughly than I
could possibly hope to do.

7

Originally, I had meant to travel down the Dordogne during my holidays, so that the whole journey would have been spread over some years, but in May 1989 I unexpectedly found myself made redundant and decided that, now I had the opportunity, I might as well complete the walk in one go. I finished my job as Art Director at Hamish Hamilton on June 24th and the very next day Sybil and I left for three weeks holiday at our house near Villeneuve-sur-Lot, at the end of which we drove up to Champs-sur-Tarentaine. So, although I had been thinking about this journey for some years, I had very little time to plan the actual trip. During my last week at Hamish Hamilton, I rushed round London looking for a suitable rucksack. I also bought a pair of Rohan bags and a jacket, both of them with pockets and zips in the unlikeliest places, some large-scale maps, two pairs of thick socks and a Swiss army knife. I already possessed a good pair of Austrian walking boots, so now I had most of the essentials. For the rest, my equipment consisted of spare clothes, a towel and toilet bag, a plate, knife, fork and spoon, a portable radio, so that I could listen to the World Sevice, a torch and some medicaments. On top of these I also took a Michelin *Green guide to the Auvergne*, a Michelin *Red Guide to Hotels and Restaurants* (I was not intending to live rough), a *Logis* hotel guide and volume two of the Penguin edition of *Remembrance of Things Past*. I have been trying to finish Marcel Proust's masterpiece ever since I was given the whole set of twelve volumes in the old Scott Moncrieff edition for my twenty-first birthday and this seemed an ideal opportunity to make some progress. My idea was to tear off each page as I read it and to dispose of it in an appropriate manner.

By the time I reached le Mont-Dore, it had become clear to me that my choice of rucksack was a mistake: it was too small and hung too low on my back, putting a great strain on my shoulders. So, the morning after my ascent of the Puy de Sancy, I combed the town looking for a new one. Eventually, I found what I was searching for, a frame rucksack made by a Canadian firm, McCann, which sat on my hips and projected above shoulder level, giving a much better weight distribution. Instead of opening from the top, it had a central pocket, unzipped from the back, surrounded by large pockets, top and bottom, and two more on either side. This made it much easier to divide the load and to find items afterwards.It was certainly a big improvement on the first one but still very heavy. The metal frame was a bit uncomfortable but I solved this problem by lashing the English rucksack, which was well padded, to the back of the new one. It was also useful to have a spare rucksack with me to use as a day-sack if I stayed somewhere for more than one night.

Having solved the rucksack problem I decided that, as there was still an hour or so to go before lunch, I would visit the *Etablissement Thermal*. It seems highly likely that the therapeutic qualities of the waters of le Mont-Dore were known to the Gauls and perhaps to earlier peoples: what is certain is that the Romans built a temple and thermal baths here in the second century AD and the surviving ruins show that they covered a much greater area than the buildings that exist today. After the departure of the Romans, le Mont-Dore declined into an obscurity which lasted until the seventeenth century. We know from Madame de Sevigné that it was during the reign of Louis XIV that patients began to return to take the waters, although as there was no road to the village only the most intrepid or the most desperate undertook the rigorous journey. It was not until 1787, when M. de Chazerat, the *Intendant* of the Auvergne, built a new road and started work on the first thermal baths since Roman times, that le Mont-Dore became a fashionable watering place. The fame of Doctor Michel Bertrand and the visit by the formidable Duchesse de Berry, who led a failed insurrection against King Louis Philippe in the Vendée, established its reputation. In 1890, Monsieur M.E. Camut began the almost total reconstruction of the old baths into the grandiose edifice I was about to enter.

Seen from the outside the *Etablissement Thermal* is far from inviting. Built of the local dark basalt in an austere classical style, it looks more like a prison than a sanatorium but the moment I crossed the threshold I found myself in a different world. I was standing in a vast hall, running parallel to the façade, and covered by painted groin vaults, supported by marble corinthian columns. The painting of the vaults looked as though it was influenced by murals found at classical sites such as Pompeii or Herculaneum. On the side opposite the entrance each vaulted bay contained a large semi-circular apse, painted a terra-cotta colour and oulined by an arch composed of alternate blocks of grey and white marble.

Placed within the apse were palm trees planted in large wooden tubs. Leading off this vestibule was a second, tunnel-vaulted hall. Here too

9

the ribs of the vault were made up of alternating white and grey marble and were supported by marble corinthian columns but between the rib arches the roof had a coffered ceiling with glass panels, giving a dappled light which, playing over the striped arches, was quite dazzling.

At the far end of the hall was an arch surmounted by a lunette containing a wall painting depicting an imaginative reconstruction of the roman baths. A flight of steps led up to a baldachino, flanked by two columns from the original roman baths, inside which was a fountain of warm, bubbling water, the so-called Source César.

I was fascinated by this florid architectural setting which created a world of pure fantasy like an Alma-Tadema painting or a film set for a Babylonian epic by D.W. Griffith. To the right of the entrance was a ticket office. Visitors are not allowed to wander round the *Etablissement* on their own, so I bought a ticket and joined a guided tour. The diminutive guide, dressed in a long white coat and full black beard, looked suspiciously like Toulouse-Lautrec. He obviously considered himself something of a wit and kept the party in fits but I was bored by his commentary which was little more than a publicity exercise extolling the amenities of the *Etablissement* and the therapeutic qualities of the waters, whereas I was only interested in the architecture. However, I was in a minority of one and the rest of the audience hung on his every word. The French do take their health very seriously, which accounts perhaps for the popularity of spa towns like le Mont-Dore, which are to be found all over France, all of them with their regular *clientèles*. Eventually, our party reached another large hall dominated by a corinthian column from the original roman baths. Here were rows of desks at which patients sat with rubber tubes stuck up their noses. By now I had had enough: I managed to slip away and, taking a last look at the extraordinary Byzantine vestibule, made my escape.

After this salubrious tour I was badly in need of a drink, so I dropped into a nearby bar and ordered a beer. On the way in I chanced to see a notice advertising a simple meal of chicken and chips and a desert, which I thought I might try, but when I inspected the printed menu I could not find it. Next to the bar, and part of the same establishment, was a proper restaurant where I assumed I could get my chicken and chips. I asked the formidable lady who guarded the cash register at the entrance if there was room for me: '*Bien sur*', and I was ushered in. As soon as I sat down I realised I had made a mistake: the restaurant was rather smart in the steak-bar mode with black, buttoned leatherette benches, walls covered in dark red hessian, polished wooden tables with table mats depicting engraved scenes of le Mont-Dore and waitresses in black-watch tarten waistcoats; definitely not my kind of place: I like simple family restaurants with plain white tablecloths and freshly cooked local food. Worse still, when the menu arrived, it was printed (always a bad sign) and contained in a pompous leather cover. I scanned the contents but there was no sign of my chicken and chips. Desperately I searched for a regional dish at a price I could afford but the menu consisted mainly of expensive steaks, although there was a rather dull *menu touristique* at 110 francs. In the end, I ordered a *fruits de mer*.

The food was a long time coming but at last the waitress arrived and set down a circular stainless-steel stand bearing a plate covered with six succulent oysters, six langoustines in a wine glass, twelve clams and a whole crab! Confronted by this feast I decided to enjoy myself and to hell with the expense, so I ordered a half-bottle of Sylvaner to wash it down. The oysters were delicious with a heady whiff of the sea that I found remarkable considering that the ocean was hundreds of miles away. I worked my way steadily through this crustacean cornucopia and, in for a penny in for a pound, followed it by a *tarte aux myrtilles*. The *addition*, when it came, was 250 francs but by then I was past caring. Nevertheless, I determined not to make the same mistake again this trip – nor did I.

The afternoon was exceedingly hot and I was feeling sleepy so I went back to my hotel and rested. Later that afternoon, when the worst of the heat was over for the day, I decided to go up to Station Sancy and walk back to le Mont-Dore following the Dordogne. I took the coach up to the *station* and from there studied the Dore waterfall, and the gulch into which it disappears, through binoculars, trying to find a path down closer to the Dore than the one I had taken yesterday, but I could not see one. Turning my back on Station Sancy, I set off for le Mont-Dore.

The Dordogne passes in a culvert under the car park and emerges to flow for a short way alongside the highway. The first stretch was not at all attractive, the bed of the stream being littered with plastic sacks and other rubbish. I followed its course, walking along the road for a while until I came to an Auberge de la Jeunesse. Here, where the Dordogne parted company from the road, I crossed a small bridge into a hayfield and continued walking along the left bank until the watercourse was hidden from sight by a screen of scrubby trees and bushes. I scrambled down the steep bank to the bed of the stream and made my way along it, using large boulders as stepping stones. Eventually, the size and number of the rocks and the overhanging branches made progress so difficult that I was forced to clamber back up though the undergrowth to emerge blinking into the evening sunlight.

The Dordogne had now completely disappeared into a deep, tree-covered natural cutting, but at this point I picked up a marked path leading to le Mont-Dore, roughly following the course of the stream. For most of the time I was walking through fields of long grass, carpeted with wild flowers; to my left, long-horned, red cattle grazed on the nearby hillside below thick woods; it was a tranquil scene. Soon afterwards I saw the Dordogne again, where it left the cutting. From then on the stream was always in sight. Sometimes the Dordogne curved a long way away but always it returned again, even crossing my path. At last, after about an hour's easy walking I reached the outskirts of le Mont-Dore and soon afterwards I was sitting outside a cafe enjoying a well-earned beer.

One of the sights of le Mont-Dore is the *Grande Cascade*, a waterfall that plunges a hundred feet down a cliff face at the edge of the Plateau de Durbise, south-east of the town. Next morning I set off up the steep path that leads to the *cascade* (I prefer the French word whose second syllable seems to echo the stream's dying fall). The lower slopes of the cliff were thickly wooded and there were only occasional glimpses of the torrent, although I could hear it quite clearly, tumbling over the rocks. There were wild flowers amongst the trees and, from time to time, small streams strayed across my path. To begin with, I found it hard going but after a while I got my second wind and the rest, if not easy, was reasonable. After about an hour's steady climbing, I reached a clearing. Directly ahead of me was a great black cliff from the top of which fell a narrow column of water that ricochetted from a tumble of huge boulders in front of me, refracted droplets creating a shimmering rainbow. A rickety wooden bridge that crossed the stream offered a distant view of the cascade but by scrambling over the boulders I was able to get a better view of what was indeed an awe inspiring sight. A kind French girl took a photograph of me as I took up my 'silent on a peak in Darien' pose.

I was surprised to find that the path did not stop here but continued up the cliff, the last section consisting of a wooden stairway clamped to the rock face. The cliff is of great interest to geologists because it reveals several layers of volcanic strata, starting at the top with porphyritic trachyte and, in descending order, a sandy tuffa, interspersed with felspar, clinkstone, basalt, scoria, a volcanic slag, more basalt, mixed with felspar and finally a bed of basaltic tuff.

At the top I found a grass covered plateau from which there was a bird's eye view of le Mont-Dore, looking very small and vulnerable below, and to the left the valley stretching southwards to the Puy de Sancy. A path led along the cliff edge to the point where the mountain stream flowed over a ledge into space. I looked down but did not linger. The hypnotic compulsion to plunge into the *cascade* was almost irresistible; instead I walked away from the cliff up a delicious little valley through which murmured the mountain stream. To start with there were a great many French infants, all full of energy, despite their long climb, but soon I was on my own. It was an idyllic spot, the sun glinted on the surface of the stream which flowed over a series of small waterfalls between grassy banks, thick with wild flowers. I was furious that I had not brought a picnic with me, although I did have some water, fruit and raisins. I found a shady spot under one of the few trees on the plateau and stretched out among the wild flowers. I wish I were a better botonist: being able to identify wild flowers is something that all self-respecting long-distance walkers are supposed to be able to do but, although I can recognize the odd alpine, like gentians and aquilegia, for the most part I am very ignorant. Architecture is more in my line.

After half an hour or so, I set off again up a stony path that led I knew not where, hoping to reach a viewing point with an even better panorama: instead, the path grew increasingly steep and difficult and at the end of it was a busy main road. Frustrated, I retraced my steps to the cliff top, admired the view one last time and set off down.

I reached the Hôtel Mouflons just after one o'clock and barely had time to shower, change and grab a quick beer at the bar before catching a coach to St-Nectaire. Sybil and I are addicted to romanesque architecture and the day before I had spotted that there was a coach tour to the mountain village, famous, of course, for its cows' cheese but also for a beautiful romanesque abbey which contains some unique medieval treasures.

The coach was driven by an attractive and very composed lady of about thirty-five who gave a running commentary as she did so. It was a little alarming to begin with to see her steering nonchalantly round the sharp mountain bends, talking non-stop all the while, but her obvious competence and confidence soon lulled my fears and I sat back to enjoy the magnificent scenery. We took the D36 out of le Mont-Dore, winding up, via the Col de la Croix-St-Robert to the Plateau de Durbise. We were, in fact, on the same road that I had reached that morning fom the *Grande Cascade*. From there we descended to Lac Chambon and then passed the brooding red ruins of the Château de Murol, which, standing on a hill above the village of the same name, dominates the landscape for miles, appearing and disappearing from view as the road twists and turns.

As we approached St-Nectaire, our driver gave us a potted history of the abbey and told us what to look out for. She was scathing about the priest in charge whom she accused of bias against coach parties. According to her he was a dragon who kept the church's treasures well-guarded and spoiled the visit by his constant surveillance. I immediately found myself taking the side of the *abbé*, in his efforts to protect a unique heritage against a stream of uncomprehending gawpers; but in these matters I confess I am an unreconstructed elitist.

St-Nectaire belongs to a group of romanesque churches with common characteristics found in the Auvergne, of which the best known, apart from St-Nectaire itself, are Orcival and Issoire. Built of the local black basalt they have an austere beauty, accentuated by their isolated mountain settings. St-Nectaire is no exception; standing aloof on a small hill, Mont Cornidore, overlooked by the thickly wooded slopes of the Puy de Mazèyres, it looks impressively severe.

The coach was parked outside the abbey and we were told firmly that we had an hour to look round. I went first to the west end, but it is exposed to the worst of the bitter winter weather and was bare and devoid of interest, so I strolled down the north side to the east end, which is nearly always the best place from which to view a romanesque church. From here I could see the apse of the choir, with its three semi-circular chapels, and two smaller chapels projecting from the east walls of the transepts. Above them rose the solid block of the crossing tower. My eyes were led upwards via the pilasters and sloping roofs of the chapels to the roofs of the choir and transepts, which are on a level, and from there to the sloping shoulders of the crossing tower, a feature peculiar to Auvergnat churches, that mark the transition to the crowning feature, a two storey octagonal tower, capped by a shingle-tiled, pointed roof. The decoration is very restrained, being largely confined to the choir apse and consisting of dwarf columns, with leaf capitals, on either side of the central window, surmounted by a broad band ornamented with a repeating pattern of eight-pointed stars inscribed within circles. This extreme plainness meant that I could appreciate the clear lines and simplicity of form of the building all the better and I found the whole ensemble very satisfying. Entering the abbey, I was immediately struck by how small it is: the height of the nave is forty-nine feet and the total length of the building only 124 feet, and yet, despite the large number of visitors milling around, the dark coloured stone and simplicity of forms imposed a sombre gravity on the scene.

Immediately inside the west end is a narrow narthex, succeeded by a short, four-bay nave. Simple stone columns support the arches of the arcade, above which is a gallery, with twin-arch openings, surmounted by a pointed, tunnel vault. But I did not linger here; instead, I found myself drawn inexorably towards the choir, flooded with light from sixteen windows. Here, behind the altar, are six columns, clustered in a half circle, that support the semi-dome above. All of them have richly carved capitals illustrating scenes from the Bible. Altogether, there are twenty-two such capitals, most of them in the choir, and at a height where they can easily be seen. They constitute one of the abbey's chief glories.

Before entering the church, I had bought a guide to the capitals so that I could study them in detail. As I walked round, looking now at a capital, now at the guide book, the priest in charge approached me and asked if I needed any help in identifying them. It turned out that he was the author of the guide – Abbé Marcel Chabosy; what is more, he offered to inscribe my copy, which he did with a flourish. I got the impression that, far from being hostile to visitors, he was a lonely man and only too glad for an opportunity to talk.

Probably the most famous of the carvings is an ass playing a lyre, but the six capitals in the choir show, starting with the first column on the left, the arrest of Jesus with Judas kissing him and the healing of Malchus's severed ear; the flagellation and the apparition of Jesus before doubting Thomas. The next capital depicts the Transfiguration. Christ is carved on the angle and on either side of him are Moses and Elijah holding scrolls bearing the words: 'Let us pitch three tents here.' The three tents, looking more like churches, are shown at the base of the capital while Saint Peter, who is on Christ's right hand, points them out. On the left hand of Christ, the disciples James and John are shown fast asleep. Another face of the capital illustrates the miracle of loaves and fishes, while the final side shows a man clinging desperately to a column and being threatened by soldiers in chain mail. This is thought to represent the right to sanctuary.

The third column relates the life of Saint Nectaire. There is a particularly good scene showing the saint making the devil, disguised as a boatman, ferry him across the Tiber. Satan rages but an angel forces him to do the saint's bidding.

Capital four has scenes from the Apocalypse: a winged horseman brandishes three spears as he exterminates mankind. The damned recoil before him but on the other face of the capital the elect are saved by an angel with spread wings who carries the book of judgement and a pair of scales.

The Day of Judgement itself is the subject of the fifth capital: Christ sits in judgement, holding the instruments of his Passion. Two angels sound the last trumpet summoning all to judgement. The elect are on Christ's right hand and on the left four of the damned weep as they are led away . . .

The final capital shows the Resurrection. On one side Christ rises from the tomb. Alongside lie two sleeping soldiers, wearing chain mail tunics and conical helmets. On the other side, Christ, carrying the cross, descends into hell to rescue Adam and Eve. Adam clutches at Christ's robe while the devil looks on, powerless to prevent him. All the capitals are carved with great spirit and show great skill in composition, given the limited space available. The scene of the descent into hell, in particular, is remarkable in its handling of a complex subject with a great many figures.

Time was short so I reluctantly turned from my contemplation of the capitals to look at the abbey's treasures which are displayed in the north transept. Notre-Dame du Mont Cornadore is a wooden, twelfth-century statue of the Virgin seated on a throne with the Infant Jesus sitting on her knee. Mary's head is too big in proportion to her body and she has enormous hands that stretch protectively round the Christ child. In his left hand Jesus holds a copy of the New Testament. Mother and child stare fixedly ahead of them. Mary wears a dark-blue cloak, with gold fleurs de lys that were added in the fifteenth century, over a dark red robe. The statue served as a reliquary and there is a secret drawer at the back.

The treasury also contains a reliquary arm, covered with repoussé silver, alleged to have belonged to Saint Nectaire himself, and two beautiful book covers of Limoges enamel, mounted on wood. The finest of them shows Christ triumphant on the cross, with angels in the superior corners and the two Marys below. This scene is surrounded by a richly patterned border, inset with precious stones. But the most remarkable exhibit is the bust of Saint Baudime, one of Saint Nectaire's companions who helped him evangelize the Mont-Dore region in the third century. The hands and head are cast in brass and the body made of wood, covered with gold and copper repoussé work. The saint's hair is arranged in stylised curls across his brow and his moustache and beard are lightly suggested by a pattern of tiny holes punched with an awl. His robe was once studded with huge jewels but these were stolen, according to the guidebook, by the 'infamous Thomas gang' in 1907. But what sets the bust of Saint Baudime apart are the extraordinary eyes. Made of horn, with large black pupils, they stare ahead with a blank gaze that is quite hypnotic in its power, so that it is difficult to tear your own eyes away. This fine piece is also a product of the twelfth century Limoges workshops.

By now it was time to go. I raced back to the coach and was embarrassed to find, when I climbed on board, that I was the last and that the driver was waiting for me before starting. We set off down the hill and stopped at the bottom outside the entrance to a grotto. The attraction here proved to be thermal waters with the peculiar property of turning objects to stone. I was not excited by the prospect of looking at petrified shoes and bottles so having established that the visit lasted an hour I slipped away and walked back up the hill to the abbey. By now most of the tourists had gone and as the *abbé* had also disappeared, I was able to study the rest of the capitals undisturbed.

At five o'clock the coach left the grotto on the homeward journey. On the way we stopped at Lac Chambon, formed about thirty thousand years ago by the eruption of one of the most recent volcanoes of the region – the Puy de Tartaret. The gigantic convulsions that accompanied the birth of the new volcano caused a huge landslide that formed a natural dam, creating an immense lake that covers an area of 144 acres, although it is only forty feet deep. As we approached, the blue surface of the lake seemed to be covered by large, exotic butterflies. On closer inspection, they turned out to be the coloured sails of windsurfers. We stopped by a stretch of sandy shoreline to admire the view, which indeed was lovely, the steeply wooded mountain slopes rising sheer from the sky-blue waters. Most of the tour party made their way to the water's edge and tramped along the shore but I took refuge from the heat in a handy café, where a friendly Irish barman served me a delicious ice-cold beer.

We returned to le Mont-Dore at 6.30 p.m. after a very enjoyable trip. The volcanic scenery of the Auvergne is magnificent and, not for the first time, I found myself thinking how lucky the French are to live in a country with such a variety of landscapes. No wonder so few of them feel the need to travel abroad for their holidays with such riches on their doorsteps.

I liked le Mont-Dore and would happily have stayed there longer: certainly I had by no means seen all there was to see locally, but, if I was going to to make my journey down the Dordogne, it was time to move on, so the next morning I paid my hotel bill, collected some washing from the *blanchisserie*, paid a visit to the *bureau de Poste* and set off. It was nearly ten o'clock.

The main road to La Bourboule, the D130, runs alongside the left bank of the Dordogne and by now I knew it was very busy, so I decided to follow a minor road on the right bank and cross a bridge back on to the left bank when I got near to La Bourboule. Either way, the distance was not great – a mere seven kilometres (just over four miles) – but I was glad of this: it gave me a chance to get used to my pack and break myself in gently.

After a careful look at my map, I found a little road, starting at the station, that leads to the hamlet of les Marais, where the road swings westwards to La Bourboule. Feeling somewhat unwieldy, I started walking. The road led through le Queureuilh, the less salubrious end of le Mont-Dore. On my left was the Dordogne, partially hidden by verges overgrown with tall weeds; not that I wished to look too closely, for it was soon obvious that all the sewers of le Mont-Dore run into the river and just here it is an unhealthy-looking muddy brown. To the right was a small block of council flats, as bleak and cheerless as any equivalent building in Britain. Further on was a mini-supermarket and some small workshops.Soon afterwards, I reached les Marais, one *alimentation* and a few houses, where I turned left for La Bourboule. I had not gone very far when I saw a turning to the left that crossed the railway line and then the river to join the main road on the left bank.It was not long before I realised that in changing roads I had made a bad mistake. I had imagined that by now the D130, which winds down from le Mont-Dore, would have reached the flat valley bottom and I would have avoided the dangerous bends with cars hurtling round them. Not a bit of it. I was still quite high up and progress was every bit as difficult as I had feared. I had to be constantly on on the alert to avoid being run over. In theory you are supposed to walk on the same side as on-coming traffic so that you can see and be seen, but from time to time I was forced to cross the road, (not that easy with a heavy pack on your back), so that I could see further round a blind bend. On either side were thick woods; to the left the road hugged the mountain's flank but on my right the ground fell away. Far below, through a dense screen of trees, I could just make out the Dordogne imprisoned in a narrow ravine. Gradually I tacked my way to the bottom of the hill, where the going was easier. I was now out in the open, walking down a narrow valley, dominated to the north by the bald summits of three extinct volcanoes, the flat topped Puy Gros (4862 feet), nearest to le Mont-Dore; la Banne d'Ordanche, which looms over La Bourboule; and between them the smaller le Tenon. The road ran level along the valley but I was glad to see that there was also a footpath beside the river, newly emerged from its gully, so I no longer needed to worry about the traffic. I reached the outskirts of La Bourboule and shed my rucksack outside a church in the middle of the spa. As I did so, the clock struck twelve. The first leg of my journey was over: it had taken just two hours.

At first sight La Bourboule seemed bigger than le Mont-Dore, although the population is almost the same. Compressed within a narrow valley, less than a mile wide, the town straggles along both sides of the Dordogne, which here is more of a feature than at le Mont-Dore. The active centre, round the *Grands Thermes*, is less than two miles long by a quarter of a mile wide. I started looking for a hotel and to begin with approached a couple of *Logis* but both looked too expensive. I always judge French hotels by their menus and these did not look interesting or good value to me. Then, right in the middle of the town, just opposite the *Grands Thermes*, I saw the Hôtel de la Poste et Europe, an old fashioned hotel with a mansard roof, dormer windows and pale blue metal shutters. The hand-written menu was displayed in a vine root frame and, although hard to decipher, seemed interesting.

I left my rucksack in the vestibule and went inside. I was welcomed by *le patron* who looked disconcertingly like Groucho Marx, although his grey moustache was real. He offered me two rooms, one at only sixty francs and asked if I was going to eat at the hotel. I said yes and this seemed to cheer him up. He was even more cheerful when I insisted on a room with a shower, lifting me into a more expensive price bracket: he had obviously taken me for an impoverished hiker.

It was a pleasant room, long and narrow but with plenty of space between the bed and table. The wallpaper had little flowers, outlined in blue against a white background and the furniture was painted ice-blue. The window, at the far end, looked out over fish-scale slate roofs to trees growing on the lower slopes of the valley side. The shower was in a cupboard and a key had to be found to open it. As far as I could see, it didn't work, so I had a quick wash and went down to lunch. *En route* I told *le patron* about the shower. He expressed amazement that there should be a problem and said he would see to it.

Entering the dining room, I was taken aback to find a large room full of people, an impression accentuated by the diners being reflected in large wall mirrors that made a big room look enormous. There must have been a hundred people there altogether, sitting close together at long tables. They were served by two young waitresses, who moved amongst the tables with great good humour, exchanging badinage with the diners as they did so. Even allowing for the fact that these were set meals, their ability to cope was remarkable. Many of the residents helped out by refilling their own water jugs and fetching more bread. Indeed the atmosphere was very jolly with lots of animated chat between tables. There were a great many children and it was clear that this was a cheap hotel for holiday families *en pension*. I sat at a table with a couple drinking cider with their meal, whom I correctly deduced came from Normandy-Rouen, in fact. While I was waiting for my lunch, I took a closer look at the dining-room's extraordinary decor. Where there were no windows or mirrors the walls were covered with a chequered pattern with small squares of black, dark blue, light blue and magenta and this dazzling design extended all over the ceiling as well. Small tricolours, left over from the *quatorze juillet* celebrations, were strung across the room, adding to the festive atmosphere. Lunch arrived without my having to order: not great cuisine by any stretch of the imagination but perfectly acceptable, especially after my trek that morning. In the middle of my meal, the waitress arrived to explain that the shower did work and I must manipulate it *so* . . .

The weather was far too hot to go trapesing round the town, so after lunch I retired to my room for a siesta. When I got up I felt like a shower. Over the years I have stayed in a great many modestly priced French hotels and can claim to be something of an expert on the odd arrangements of their showers; indeed, I must have spent many hours trying to mop up floods of water that have surged over inadequate ledges as the result of blocked-up plug holes; but this shower was the most bizarre I have ever encountered. It was, as I have said, in a cupboard, the door being set flush into the wall of the room. I opened the door and was confronted by folding plastic doors that looked like frosted glass. I pulled the doors to one side to reveal the taps and shower head on the right inside wall. As soon as I turned the taps on water sprayed into the room and I quickly turned them off again. The trick, I discovered, was to get into the cupboard, closing first the outer door, then the folding doors behind me. This revealed an alcove on the left-hand side, into which I squeezed; from here I was able to manipulate the taps in safety, before stepping under the jet. To get the right temperature I had to turn the cold tap on as far as it would go. This produced scalding hot water, which I tempered by turning the hot tap on a mere fraction to produce just enough cold water, more than a fractional turn converted the red-hot stream to icy-cold.

After all these excitements I needed another rest.

My morning's trek had convinced me that my pack, though comfortable enough, was far too heavy, so I unpacked it and spread the contents all over my bed, on which I sat trying to decide what items I could discard. Proust was one of the first casualties. Volume II is 1169 pages long and even printed on thin bible paper it is weighty: I tore out pages 325–1169, leaving myself with a hundred pages (I had already got to page 225), which I thought would last me for some time. Since I was still in the Auvergne, a Michelin *Green Guide to the Dordogne* went out as well, together with a thick sweater, which in temperatures of over thirty degrees celsius, I felt I did not need, a spare pair of slacks and a shirt. When I left Hamish Hamilton, Dr. Black, who looks after the ailments of Penguin staff, gave me a first aid kit in a neat leather bag. I went through this carefully and threw out some sea-sick pills, which I didn't think I'd need on the Dordogne and, since I am not a junky, a packet of hyperdermic syringes and needles; nor do I suffer from insomnia, so out went the Mogodon. There were also some Augmentin tablets for 'upper respiratory tract infections with purulent nasal discharge and/or sputum, boils or infected lacerations with associated raised temperature'. I decided that were I unfortunate enough to contract such an infection, I would rely on a French doctor to cure it and I dumped these too.

By now it was late afternoon and the worst of the heat was over, so I ventured outside. My hotel stood right in the middle of the north side of the Boulevard Georges Clemenceau, La Bouboule's chief artery and the lively hub of the town. Here were several large hotels and numerous bars and cafés. On the other side of the boulevard was the *Grands Thermes*, a much more attractive building externally than the *Etabliss-ement* at le Mont-Dore. Its long, low, white-painted façade and taller wings, surmounted by silver domes, reminded me distantly of an imperial palace designed by Lutyens to impress the natives with the dignity and might of the British Raj. To the left of the *Grands Thermes* was a large open space, shaded by the inevitable plane trees where all day long there were games of *pétanque*. Behind the park and the *Grands Thermes* ran the Dordogne, crossed by several bridges. On the other side of the river was a less important thoroughfare and some axial roads, lined with more hotels, stretching a short way uphill. On this side too was a much larger playground – the Parc Fenêstre.

After my tour of the *Etablissment Thermal* at le Mont-Dore, I had no desire to visit the *Grands Thermes*; instead, after sitting in a café for some time over a pot of tea, writing my postcards, I went on a modest excursion up to the top of one of the local beauty spots the *Rocher des Fées*. This outcrop of the Banne d'Ordanche, lay close at hand, just at the back of my hotel. The ascent was easy, with flights of steps at frequent intervals, and took less than half an hour. From the top there was a good view over the town and, to my left, of the valley down which I had plodded that morning. I could see the road clearly and follow the course of the Dordogne until it was hidden by the tree-covered ravine below the hill leading up to Mont-Dore. To my right the view was limited by the shoulder of the Banne d'Ordanche.

I shared my table at dinner that evening with a black Frenchman from Guadeloupe, Monsieur Alex, who was very anxious that I should understand that Guadeloupe was administratively a part of France and not a colony. He had come from Guadeloupe to La Bouboule for the *cure* and was staying for three weeks, all at the expense of French Social Security – what would Mrs Thatcher have said!

He was a great admirer of the British Royal family and of Mrs. Thatcher – the French always are – and although I tried to disabuse him by explaining that Mrs. T was not at all keen on the National Health Sevice, his faith remained unshaken. It was a desultory conversation: we had little in common and I found him hard to understand. Later I discovered that the people of Guadeloupe are notorious for not pronouncing their Rs, rather as Cockneys swallow their vowels, so that even the French find their speech difficult.

After dinner, I wandered up to the Parc Fenêstre. To my surprise it looked like an English landscaped park with winding paths, large areas of green grass, a boating lake and some magnificent trees, including some giant sequoia, judiciously planted at focal points. The park was full of holiday families, the parents slumped in deck-chairs, digesting dinner, while their offspring ran shrieking in all directions, all of them enjoying in their own ways the last of the sunshine, which cast a golden glow over the scene.

Next morning, I went to the *bureau de poste* and bought a large cardboard box for my rucksack rejects. On the way back I dropped off my first film to be developed at a shop offering a two-hour service. Before I could pack my things I had to construct the box, which was supplied flat with instructions. It took me some time to work out what went where, not helped by the instructions being in French, but eventually I solved the mystery, packed the box and returned to the *bureau de poste*, where I posted it to Sybil.

When I went to collect my film, I found to my horror that it was completely blank. I had lost all the pictures I had taken of the source of the Dordogne and of the *Grande Cascade*. I was devastated.

At first I couldn't think what to do but, once the first shock was over, I realised that there was nothing for it, I would have to return to le Mont-Dore. If I stayed an extra day at the Hôtel de la Poste et de l'Europe, I could go up next morning by train, carrying just my day-pack. It meant I would have to go to the top of the Puy de Sancy again but this time I could take the *téléphérique* both going up and down and, of course, I now knew exactly where to find the source.

Monsieur Guillaume, the *patron* was delighted to accommodate me for another day so, that settled, I decided to take the *télécabine* from the Parc Fenêstre to the Plateau de Charlannes, another beauty spot, thirteen hundred feet above the town. As the *télécabine* rose there were superb views of the town below and, as we got higher, of the valley beyond. To my surprise I was confronted at the top by a wide tarmac road and a thick forest. For some reason I had expected to see a green park like the Parc Fenêstre. I set off along the road, which skirted the forest, in the company of twenty-odd exuberant French schoolboys and their harassed *moniteur*. To my relief, the school party soon peeled off to the left and entered the woods. I continued along the road for another five minutes until I reached the brink of a hill, where there was a vast panorama of the heavily-wooded country west of La Bourboule. Somewhere down there, hidden in a ravine was the Dordogne. I tried to work out the route I would have to follow on the next stage of my journey but it was all too far away and I gave up.

Turning aside I entered the wood, following a track which I guessed, from a map I had studied before setting off, would lead back in a wide circle to the *télécabine* station. I was soon deep in the forest. It was very dense and there were no views, only the narrow diminishing perspective of trees, a wedge of clear blue above and bright splashes of pink foxgloves in the verges. Mixed in with the foxgloves were tall yellow gentians, whose roots are used to make a popular local liqueur. At one time, the production of this liqueur threatened the gentian with extinction but now, within the *parcs regionals*, the flowers are protected.

An hour later I was still deep in the woods and beginning to wonder where the path was leading me. The sight of occasional signposts, marked Ski 2000, reassured me slightly but I was starting to get really worried when I saw ahead of me the same schoolboys I had last seen nearly two hours ago. To my relief their *moniteur* confirmed that I was on the right path for the *télécabine* station; even so it was nearly twelve o'clock before I reached it. I managed to catch the last *télécabine* down, to arrive back at the hotel just in time for lunch.

The afternoon was so incredibly hot that I felt completely enervated and, after a siesta, spent most of the time until dinner sitting in a café imbibing cooling drinks. All round me people were complaining of *la chaleur*; inert forms were slumped in chairs and parents and children quarrelled peevishly. Late that evening, when it at last began to cool down, I crossed the boulevard to the park and watched the *pétanque* players. The teams were obviously *ad hoc* arrangements of holiday makers staying at the same hotel and the differences in skill were only too apparent. The experts strutted to their marks to play their *boules* or, if it was not their turn, organized the rest of the team, pointing out where the next *boule* should be aimed and clucking with ill-concealed fury when, as usually happened, it missed. There were different games going on throughout the park but in the middle of this intense rivalry I was touched to see a young father instructing his six-year old daughter in the mysteries of *pétanque*. I was not too sure of the finer points myself and was tempted to ask him to teach me as well. Later in my trip, when I had gained in confidence, I would probably have done so but, before I could overcome my English reserve, it was the little girl's bed time and, hand-in-hand, they left the park.

Above the clicks of the metal *boules* and the shouts and groans of the players, I could hear the steady thump of a brass band. Following the sound of music I found a small appreciative crowd surrounding a pretty, cast-iron bandstand. It was a German band as was immediately apparent by their dress: the men wore black corduroy knickerbockers supported by broad braces over spotless white shirts and the girls mauve cotton skirts, with lace hems and matching scarves with blue fringes. Their music was typically aggressive, especially a spirited rendition of the *sabre dance* but seemed to go down well with the French audience. Despite the belligerency of the brass, my stroll through the park left me feeling pleasantly relaxed and after a nightcap at a café I went to bed and fell instantly fast asleep.

There was no sign of life in the hotel when I left at seven o'clock next morning, so I went to a café for my *petit déjeuner*. I arrived at the station in good time to catch the 7.42 a.m. to le Mont-Dore, to discover that this train runs on Saturdays only. Rather than wait over an hour for the next train, I decided to walk. This time I followed the minor road along the right bank of the Dordogne and found it much more agreeable. Just before I reached the point where I had turned off on my journey down, I had a good view of the river, which had been hidden from me on the other road. At Le Queureuilh, opposite the housing estate, I spotted a footpath that led under a railway bridge, alongside the Dordogne and up into the station yard. I then crossed a bridge and walked through the big campsite on the left bank of the river. It was criss-crossed with electric cables supplying power for the campers' fridges and television sets.

It was market day at le Mont-Dore and I bought a slice of *jambon de pays*, some tomatoes, peaches, plums and bread for a picnic. The walk had taken only sixty-five minutes and I was not at all tired but I did not fancy walking up to Station Sancy, so I hired a taxi. The driver was very friendly and told me that there was an easy promenade from the top of the Puy de Sancy to le Mont-Dore, via a plateau called Le Capucin, with superb views all the way. It sounded good and I decided to try it.

But first I went and photographed the source of the Dordogne all over again and then took the *téléphérique* up the Puy de Sancy. On the way I met an English couple, instantly recognisable by their Christopher Robin hats and sensible shoes. They were both in their seventies, retired and mad about birds. They complained that they had not seen many interesting birds in the Auvergne and we agreed that the Pyrenees was the place to find them.

I climbed to the summit of the Puy and had myself photographed and then, at 11.30 a.m., I set off on the walk to le Mont-Dore. At first all went well. The path was clearly marked and followed a ridge giving fantastic views, on one side down into the Mont-Dore valley, on the other down the southern flank of the mountain to the blue waters of Lac Chauvet. I had not gone far when the path, now little more than a goat track, started to climb steeply up the narrow edge of a beetling crag. I am no *mouflon* and looking down the sheer precipice into the depths below made me feel decidedly queasy, however I managed to divert my thoughts by admiring the wild flowers that grew profusely on these steep slopes, especially the splendid yellow gentians, standing rigidly to attention while all about them dipped and swayed in the warm wind.

I had been clambering up and down the ridge for about half an hour when I came to a crossroads. On my right a track led down the Val de Courre to the Station Sancy; ahead, as far as I could see, lay the route via Le Capucin. At first the path seemed clear enough but somewhere I must have gone astray because half an hour later it petered out and I found myself crossing a desolate moorland. The going was soft on wet, spongy turf and heather and I had to take care to stop my feet sinking into the brackish pond between the sods. I paused to take my bearings. Looking back I was surprised to find that I had already descended a hundred feet or more; in front of me was a featureless landscape, except for a line of tall blue poles stretching into the distance. I had no desire to struggle back uphill again so I decided to see where the poles led. Another half hour of difficult walking over uneven ground brought me to the edge of a bluff. Below me was a large black chalet with SKI CLUB DE FRANCE painted on the roof and chairs and tables set out invitingly on a terrace. By now I was feeling quite tired and very thirsty: I scrambled down the scree and sank thankfully into a chair. Two ice-cold *pressions* went down in quick succession – never did beer taste so good.

Feeling better, I asked the waiter where I was. Apparently this was Station de Chastreix-Sancy and it was roughly a mile due west of the path I should have been following. To get back on the right route I would have to climb back up the scree at a point where a herd of cattle could be clearly seen grazing at the edge. Here I would find a stream that I must trace back to a line of ski-poles (for that is what the blue poles were), which in turn would lead me back to the ridge.

Fortified by the beer, I struggled back up the scree, found the cows and then the stream. If anything the terrain here was even more difficult, bracken and peat, interspersed with small streams, bogs and barbed wire fences, on one of which I tore my pants. After plodding steadily upwards for half an hour, I was feeling very hungry. I looked at my watch and saw that it was 1.30 – time for a little something. There was not much shade in that barren landscape but I managed to find a place under a large rock and set about demolishing my picnic.

It was getting hotter all the time and when I started off again I found it hard going. To my dismay the ski-poles soon came to an abrupt end and there was still no sign of a path. By now it was 2.30 p.m. and I was beginning to worry about being lost in the mountains. I had seen no-one for an hour-and-a-half, I was not sure where I was and I was afraid that there might be bad weather on the way. My fears were based, quite irrationally, on my experiences of the Pyrenees, where clouds tend to drive over from Spain about midday, cloaking the peaks in an impenetrable mist. My imagination working overtime, I saw myself, my leg broken, lying huddled in the shadow of a rock, while lightning flashed, thunder growled and rain thrashed my helpless body; the alarm raised, mountaineering rescue teams combed the mountain slopes, in vain; years later bleached bones on the mountain-side. . . .

Enough of this: the only thing to do was to make my way back to the ski-station. But all to soon I realised that I had missed my way again. I was beginning to despair when I saw another line of ski-poles, bearing the words Ski-2000. They went on further uphill but by then I had had enough. I reasoned that if I followed the poles down I would eventually come off the mountain, however long it took, and, once I knew where I was, I reckoned I could find a way to get back to La Bourboule.

I set off again and soon afterwards the moorland was left behind to be replaced by firm turf, covered with big boulders and occasional twisted shrubs. For a while I was not sure if I was on the right track, the path sometimes climbing as well as descending but, because of the change in terrain, I felt I must be lower down than the spot where I had my lunch, so the general trend was in the right direction. At last, to my enormous relief, I saw below me another ski-station chalet at the end of a tarmac road, but when I got nearer my heart sank – it was shut up and empty. At that moment a *deux chevaux*, containing a young couple and their baby, appeared. Seeing that the chalet was closed, they were about to do a U-turn when I rushed towards the car and managed to make them stop. They were very kind: the young woman squeezed into the back of the car, along with the picnic and the baby, while I sat in the front. Then they drove me down to a road junction (it only took five minutes), where I read the magic words: La Bourboule 9 kilometres.

I later discovered that the ski-station was called Station de la Tour Chambourguet, which lies about a mile north of the Station de Chastreix-Sancy, although it had taken me over two hours to get there. I was now on a minor road, the D213, which led into La Bourboule from the south.

It was 3.30 p.m. when I started the last stage of the journey. The road descended steadily through the Bois de Charbonnière, a beautiful forest that was clearly a favourite picnic spot, for it was full of parked cars and family groups, sitting over the remains of their picnics or playing games under the trees. Further down I forked left onto the D18 which skirted the Bois de Charlannes, where I had walked only yesterday, although, after today's adventures, it seemed an age ago. The last half-mile was agony: I was extremely tired by now and my left little toe was giving me hell, but I plodded on and at last, just after 5 p.m., I limped into the Parc Fenêstre, sank down at the nearest café and ordered my third and best beer of the day.

CHAPTER 2

THE ROAD TO BORT-LES-ORGUES

When I woke up next morning, it was raining. I had made up my mind that it was time to move on, so this came as something of a blow and when Monsieur Guillaume (we were good friends by then) told me after breakfast that he had a spare room, if I wished to stay another night, I was sorely tempted. But I had already packed my rucksack, so I paid my bill, made my farewells and left.

I was anxious not to quit La Bourboule by the main road which climbs out of the town, on the north side of the river, in a series of tight bends, round which cars screech at terrifying speed. I certainly didn't fancy negotiating these hazards wearing my heavy pack.

Half-a-mile west of the La Bourboule is a small dam holding back the Dordogne and creating a picturesque lake. A careful look at the map showed me that there was a footpath on the south side of the lake, leading through the Bois de Charlet to the dam, at which point I could cross back to the main road, thus avoiding the worst of the bends.

At the start there was a stiff climb out of the town on a minor road but this lasted only ten minutes and then I found the path. By now the rain had stopped and I was able to take off my waterproof. The track led down through a beech forest, where it felt pleasantly cool and shady. Soon the path divided, the right-hand track going down towards the lake. After yesterday's experiences I had developed a horror of going downhill and having to climb back up again, especially wearing a heavy pack, so to begin with I followed the upper route. I had not gone very far when I realised that the lower path ran along the shore of the lake and that I would have to descend anyway to cross the dam, so I retraced my steps and went down. It was very agreeable walking by the lake which, although small, looked very attractive with its screen of trees reflected in the still, green waters.

I came to the dam and started to cross. Half way along I stopped to look over the down-river side: the surface of the Dordogne was covered with a thick, dirty foam, clearly there was a serious pollution problem here too, and the water level was very low, presumably because the authorities were holding the waters back in this period of drought. It was

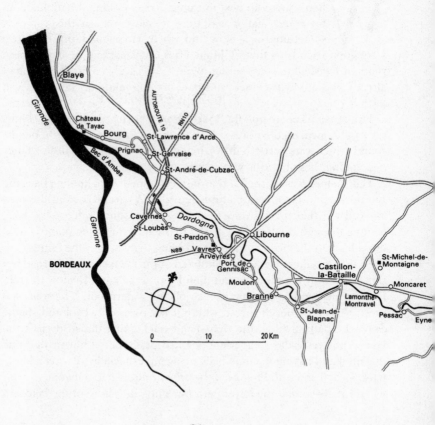

a disturbing contrast to the serenity of the tree-shrouded lake on the other side of the dam.

The main road proved to be every bit as difficult as I had feared. I tacked from side to side, wherever the verge was widest, listening carefully for cars at blind corners or crossing over to see round them, and all this time I was climbing from 2781 feet to 2794 feet, which may not sound much but was nevertheless hard work. Luckily, I did not have far to go before I reached a side turning, leading uphill to my next destination – St-Sauves d'Auvergne. It took only fifteen minutes to reach the

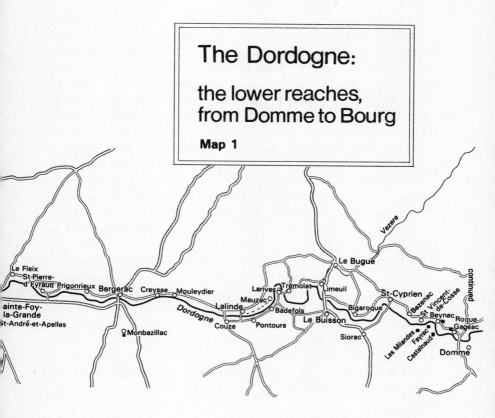

The Dordogne:
the lower reaches, from Domme to Bourg
Map 1

village but by this time I was sweating profusely in the hot sun. I made straight for the bar of the Hôtel de la Poste and ordered a Heineken.

Although I had not come very far that morning, I felt quite tired. It was some way to the next village and I didn't fancy walking in such intense heat, so I asked if the hotel had a spare room and, fortunately, they did. I had a quick shower, which here meant crouching uncomfortably on a ledge at one end of the bath, changed and went to lunch. The restaurant was full, most of the diners coming, I think, from a big campsite that I had passed at the foot of the hill. I had an excellent sixty franc lunch of *hors d'oeuvres, lapereau aux cèpes* and *tarte aux myrtilles*, with a half bottle of local rosé, after which I returned to my room, where I slept, washed some pants and listened to Robert Powell reading *A Tale of Two Cities* on the World Service.

Later I emerged to look round the village. The hotel is on the west side of a small irregularly shaped *place*. Opposite is a strange gateway which stands isolated, leading nowhere in particular. Harrison Barker thought it romanesque because of the strange mask-like heads carved above the entrance arch, but to me it looked like rustic Renaissance. The moulding and bases of the round-headed arch were clearly late gothic in style but on either side were bizarre, elongated pilasters, supporting a narrow entablature, which looked similar to those found on some Jacobean buildings in England. The area between the head of the arch and the entablature was divided into three rows decorated with carved heraldic shields and stylised flowers and leaves, interrupted by an empty niche. Above them were four blank, round-headed arches on chunky columns, containing grotesque bearded faces. At the top there were some minute figures, some of them wearing ruffs and doublet and hose, suggesting a late sixteenth- or early seventeenth-century date. This extraordinary jumble of styles points to local workmen trying to copy the latest Renaissance fashion (by then not so new!) and failing lamentably. It is believed that the gateway was built of stones from the ruins of the castle of Châteauneuf, which once stood here but of which no trace remains.

St-Sauves certainly occupies an ideal site for a castle at the top of a red sandstone outcrop, dominating an important crossroads where the road from le Mont-Dore meets the north-south highway from Clermont Ferrand to Mauriac. The view from the south end of the village is impressive: looking south-eastwards I could see the Mont-Dore range of volcanoes, culminating in the sharp-edged peak of the Puy de Sancy, while immediately below was the busy road from La Bourboule along which I had struggled that morning.

Turning my back on the view, I went to look at the church. The east end has a small romanesque apse but its chief external feature is a fine three-stage tower with a tall slate spire. The church is built of the usual black basalt but here it alternates with a lighter stone, giving a striped pattern which combined with two large openings in the third stage, makes the tower look almost frivolous in this dour mountain setting, reminding me of the striped cathedrals of Italy. Sadly the exterior of the nave is plastered, ruining the effect. Inside it was deliciously cool. The most interesting part here was the choir with its semi-dome, below which, at eye level, were six blank arches whose capitals were decorated with carved geometrical and leaf motifs.

It was now almost time for dinner but it was still so hot that I didn't feel hungry, so I contented myself with an omelette and a glass of wine, followed by a couple of beers in the bar before I paid my bill and turned in.

I left St-Sauves at a 7.15 next morning. I was making for the village of Messeix, over nine miles away, and I wanted to walk in the cool of the morning before the sun got too high.

I should explain that after La Bouboule the Dordogne disappears into a deep gorge through which it flows for fifteen miles until it reaches the lake of Bort-les-Orgues. The terrain changes too: the volcanic uplands, with their rich pastures, are replaced by crystelline rocks and granite, dating from the primary era, some six hundred million years ago. The soil here is thin and stony, poor farming land which has meant that the Corrèze has always been one of the poorest parts of France. Indeed it was not until the end of the nineteenth century, with the introduction of the first fertilizers, that yields rose for the first time above subsistance levels.

The farms are all on the plateau, as are the roads, for the gorges themselves are inaccessible. There are no routes along the bottom and no crossing until you reach the Gorges d'Avèze, seven miles west of

St-Sauves, where the road zig-zags down to the bottom and up the other side on its way to the village of Avèze, some miles away on the left bank. Messeix is quite near this crossing and I had decided to spend the night there and explore the Gorges d'Avèze the next day. I had no intention of trying to force my way along the bottom of the gorge. Harrison Barker tried and had to give up and he was a much more intrepid traveller than I am. Here is his description of his attempt:

> 'It became more and more difficult, then quite impossible, to keep along the bank of the stream. What is understood by a bank disappeared, and in its stead were rocks, bare and glittering, on which lizards basked, or ran in safety, because they were at home, but which I could only pass by a flank movement. To struggle up a steep hill, over slipping shale-like stones or through an undergrowth of holly and brambles, then to scramble down and to climb again, repeating the exercise every few hundred yards, may have a hygienic charm for those who are tormented by the dread of obesity, but to other mortals it is too suggestive of a holiday in purgatory.'

The morning was overcast and cool. I looked back towards le Mont-Dore and saw an evil-looking red glow in the sky. The top of the Puy de Sancy was hidden by swollen black clouds: the omens were not good. I plodded steadily upwards from St-Sauves (2657 feet) to the hamlet of Choriol (2969 feet). The Dordogne was less than a quarter-of-a-mile away on my left, hidden from view in its narrow ravine, but its course was clearly marked by the thick screen of trees covering the cliff top on the far side of the gorge.

Not far from Choriol I took a short cut along a farm track that cut across a long bend in the road. This gave me the chance to take a closer look at the land: it was very stony with only a thin covering of earth and bracken grew thickly on the verges, a sure sign of poor soil. At Choriol I passed two handsome barns built of undressed, red ironstone and roofed with those heavy stone slabs that, because of their rounded lower edges and the way they overlap, are called fish scales. Sadly, beautiful farm buildings like these are rare today, most fish-scale roofs having been replaced by corrugated iron.

The road continued upwards to the highest point (3015 feet), marked by a *télécommunications* pylon. I was not finding the landscape here particularly interesting: for the most part it was rough pasture land, dotted with trees and occasional thickets. In the distance a low line of hills ran parallel to my line of march.

With little to distract my attention, I was free to ponder what I was doing here. Nowadays, it is unfashionable to travel for its own sake; instead, the travel-writer makes a journey of self-discovery. Leaving behind the superfluities of modern living, he subjects himself to the rigours of the desert or the rain forest. The more arduous and dangerous the expedition the better; only by accepting such challenges and overcoming them can the veneer of civilisation be stripped away and the true man revealed. Unfortunately, I could not see myself in this role. If you don't know yourself by the age of 58 you never will. Not that there wasn't room for improvement, but I didn't think a two-month trip down the Dordogne was going to affect my character much, one way or the other. Nor was I willingly embracing discomfort. True, I had set myself the challenge of travelling down the Dordogne under my own muscle power, but I did not intend to push myself. Nor was I going to live rough; I was aiming to stay at a comfortable hotel each night and to eat well. Of course, I could have done the same trip by car but that would not have been so interesting. I like walking; it gives you time to observe small details and to notice gradual changes in the landscape. There are also more opportunities to stop and talk to people than if you are sealed inside a car. So here I was, after forty years in publishing, with the freedom to wander through one of the most beautiful parts of France, indulging my love of history, architecture, good food and wine, and I intended to make the most of it.

The main snag was my pack which, despite my clear out, was still very heavy. The weight was better distributed than before, the top of the pack now being level with the top of my head, but, although this was fine while I was on the march, it was very difficult to put on and take off. As soon as I slipped the strap off one shoulder, the thing became unwieldy and threatened to drag me off balance and this made me reluctant to stop. By now, however, I had worked out a technique to deal with the problem: I had become adept at spotting low walls, flights of steps, park benches, in fact anything at the right height on which to stand the bottom of the frame while I eased myself out of the straps.

It was not yet nine o'clock and I had covered nearly five miles, so I was feeling quite tired. I was walking through a small wood where, at intervals, there were stacks of logs on the roadside. One of these was the right height and I stopped for a rest. Soon afterwards, I felt some spots of rain, although not enough to persuade me to stop and put on my waterproof. Ahead of me I could see black rainclouds and a rainbow. I pressed on and shortly reached the first of three hamlets: Chomadoux, Bogros and La Mine, none of which had any shops, or even a bar. At Chomadoux a baker's van was driving slowly through, sounding its horn and stopping every so often for the locals to buy baguettes and pastries.

Just before Messeix it started raining quite hard. I stopped under a tree at a picnic site, with permanent tables and seats, a good place to take off my pack. It was on the corner of a road leading down to the Gorges d'Avèze. The rain didn't last long and I continued up a steep little hill to Messeix. I had walked nine miles and it was 11.00 a.m.

I found a bar near the church, and when I had finished my beer, asked if there was an hotel in the village.

'*Non, Monsieur.*'

It was a blow.

I asked where the nearest might be found and was told at St-Sauves or Bourg Lastic. I was certainly not going to retrace my steps and Bourg Lastic lay five miles to the north, away from the river. The only alternative was to walk to Tauves, over twelve miles away to the south, on the main road from La Bourboule to Bort-les-Orgues, but this meant descending into the Gorges d'Avèze and climbing up the steep cliff road on the far side and, after my morning's trek, I was doubtful that I could manage it.

I wandered aimlessly round the village, wondering what to do, and ended up at the church, hoping to find the *curé*; but it was locked. Outside the church a group of local women was talking animatedly. Most of them looked like farmers' wives, short and solidly built with wide hips and sturdy legs. Amongst them a taller figure stood out, a slim lady of a certain age, dressed in a light, summer two-piece, who wore her hair drawn back from her forehead and fastened on the nape of her kneck. In England she would have been a vicar's wife and head of the local W.I.

Choosing my moment, I interrupted the conservation and

explained my predicament. Immediately, as I had expected, the slim
lady took charge and started to interrogate the others, trying to find
somewhere for me to stay. Alas, in vain. The trouble was, she
explained, that Messeix, like so many others, is a dying village. Once,
there was a coal mine that gave the locals work (hence the hamlet
called La Mine that I had passed through) but a few years ago this
had been closed down and now the young men and their families had
all left the village. When the mine was working, there was enough
trade to support a small hotel but this had not survived the closure.
Eventually someone remembered that there was an *auberge* at a
hamlet called La Guingette, about seven miles away, south of the
Dordogne. I was not keen on walking that far and it meant missing
the Gorges d'Avèze, but there was no help for it, so, after telephon-
ing the *auberge* to book a room and warmly thanking the slim lady and
her friends, I departed.

I had walked less than half-a-mile when a white car drew up
alongside me. The driver wound down his window and asked me if I
were making for La Guingette. When I said yes, he asked me if I
would like a lift. Despite the fact that I had vowed not to hitch-hike, I
did not hesitate to accept his offer. After all, he had asked me, not the
other way round, and I had walked far enough for one day. I
struggled out of my pack, stowed it in the back and sat in the front
passenger's seat. The name of this knight-errant was Pierre de la
Brosse and he was the slim lady's husband. Apparently, he had
arrived home just after I left Messeix, had been told about the
strange Englishman who was walking down the Dordogne and
immediately set off in pursuit – and people say the French are
offhand and difficult.

Monsieur de la Brosse was a charming man and we chatted
amicably all the way, although I found his habit of taking his hands
off the steering-wheel to emphasize a point somewhat alarming.
Quite soon we entered a forest and the road began to wind down the
side of the gorge to a small stone bridge that crossed the Dordogne. I
was looking forward to my first glimpse of the river since the dam at
La Bourboule, but when it did come into view I was disappointed to
see a gentle, purling stream rather than the rushing torrent I had
hoped to find.

Once across the bridge, the road climbed steeply through the trees to the top of the gorge and then continued along a narrow valley, hemmed in by densely wooded hills, to La Guingette, where we arrived just before midday.

Madame *la patronne*, who was built like the farmers' wives I had met at Messeix, was clearly taken aback when I entered the bar and asked for my room. I had told her I was walking and not to expect me for another three hours and, only twenty minutes later, here I was. She also seemed somewhat disconcerted when I asked if I could have lunch, but nevertheless said yes.

It was a very basic *auberge*: the bar was at one end (I had a beer right away) and at the other was a large dining room; in between was the kitchen which doubled as the family's living room. An open staircase led out of the dining-room to the bedrooms. Although my room was big it was almost filled by a huge double bed. In what space was left was a large *armoire* and a washbasin. The shower was in the family's bathroom at the end of the corridor.

The dining-room was really too large for the number of diners. One long table and six smaller ones were arranged in two rows down one side of the room, leaving a large open space on the other. Only five of the tables were occupied by eleven diners in all. On the back wall was an enormous photographic blow up of a mountain lake; the other walls were covered by wallpaper with a design of large brown flowers against a cream background. With its echoing wooden floor the dining room felt more like a school hall than a restaurant.

As soon as lunch started, I realised the reason for Madame's discomfort: she had catered for an exact number and there was little to spare. The first course was mixed *charcuterie* but by the time I was served there was only a piece of smoked ham and the tail of a spicy garlic sausage. This was followed by a stuffed tomato, after which the main course should have been fried chicken but there was none left so I got a tough escalope instead, with tinned *petits pois* and *pommes frites*. Cheese and *flan* completed the meal.

Later that afternoon I walked uphill to the village of Singles, thinking there might be a view down to the Dordogne. The road started opposite the *auberge* and wound its way up the flank of the hill, shaded by trees. It was quite steep but I was in no hurry so I walked slowly, trying to keep out of the sun. The village had one or two old houses with fish-scale roofs and a typical mountain church, built of undressed stone, otherwise it was unremarkable. The road continued beyond the last houses to end in an open field. There was no sign of the Dordogne which was somewhere below, hidden by trees, but when I turned round to start back I saw to my surprise the Puy de Sancy, sharply etched against a clear blue sky and lower down to the left the Banne d'Ordanche above La Bourboule.

I ate dinner alone, the main course consisting of chicken 'left over' from lunch-time. Afterwards I sat outside enjoying a last drink before I turned in. On the opposite side of the road a girl of about twelve was skipping. Soon an older girl of about fifteen took over and started to show off with tricky variations and seeing how many skips she could total without a break. Before long she was surrounded by an admiring crowd of neighbours. Then a girl in her early twenties, who had served me at lunch, had to have a go. Seeing this, Madame *la patronne* couldn't resist joining in. Amidst general applause she skipped briskly on surprisingly light feet, considering her build. A small black kitten, attracted by the noise, came to investigate and stayed to enjoy the fun. It was an engaging scene and a pleasantly relaxing end to the day.

There was a thunderstorm in the night but I slept well, even so. Breakfast the next morning was very good: chocolate, a hunk of fresh bread, a bowl of home-made *confiture aux myrtilles* and a large slab of butter. A nice change from those horrid little plastic pots of runny jam and miniscule squares of foil-wrapped butter that usually accompany *le petit déjeuner* in French hotels these days. The bill for my room, lunch, dinner and breakfast came to only 160 francs, worth it for the room alone.

When I left La Guingette at eight o'clock it was cloudy and humid. I walked down hill for half-a-mile until I reached a crossroads. To the left was the road to Bort-les-Orgues, over fifteen miles away. The right hand road led to the Pont d'Arpiat at the confluence of the Dordogne and its tributary the Burande. The Pont d'Arpiat marks the end of the narrowest part of the gorges and the start of the lake created by the huge dam at Bort-les-Orgues.

I now had several options: I could take the left-hand fork direct to Bort-les-Orgues, or go right to Pont d'Arpiat. If I chose the second course, I could either return to the crossroads and follow the Bort-les-Orgues road, or cross the bridge and continue down the west side of the lake. In the end, I decided to go down to Pont d'Arpiat and make up my mind when I got there.

It was a steep descent: on my right a sheer, tree-covered cliff towered over me; on the left another heavily-wooded slope fell away sharply. From somewhere far below came the sound of a fast-flowing torrent, completely hidden by trees. At first I thought it was the Dordogne but then I realised it was the Burande. Further down I caught an occasional glimpse of the tributary, tumbling down its rock-strewn gully.

The Pont d'Arpiat proved to be a very small dam and the lake behind it looked rather tame, an impression reinforced by the fishermen, sitting hunched over their lines in their green punts. On either side, wooded cliffs plunged straight down to the water and by their proximity blocked out any distant view up the gorge. Downstream, I could see a larger stretch of lake but here too a river-bend quickly hid the Dordogne from view. It was a sombre scene and the far shore line looked very wild. Before leaving the *auberge*, Madame had told me that there was a better chance of finding an hotel on the left bank of the Dordogne and, after my experience at Messeix, I was not in the mood to take a risk, so I returned to the crossroads.

It was now 9.30 a.m. and I had already walked two-and-a-half miles. A short easy descent brought me to the bottom of a little valley where I crossed the Burande, here out in the open and far from turbulent. Just the other side was a small holiday camp. Two girls were playing tennis, dressed in the latest Wimbledon fashions, with the shortest of pleated skirts, but their game was mere patball.

There now began what proved to be a very long, arduous ascent. Sweating profusely, I toiled slowly upwards, pausing frequently to regain my breath. Thick forest hid the view on either side and there was so little to see that I was forced to look more closely at the trees themselves. For the most part they were Scots pine and oaks, both huge in size, but accacia, silver birch, larch and many other varieties that I could not identify were mixed in with them. Higher up I came across a team of EDF–GDF workmen, wearing bright orange overalls and hard hats, overhauling the electricity cables that swept down a gap in the forest, carried on tall pylons. A little further on was a holiday camp in a clearing. Children of primary school age sat at long trestle tables applying themselves to holiday tasks.

An hour later I was still climbing but now I was high enough to be able to look back and see Singles on its hill and on up the valley towards Messeix which, of course, was too far away to identify. Further away still, I could just make out the dark line of forest that marked the course of the Dordogne in the Gorges d'Avèze.

Another ten minutes' steady climbing brought me to the village of Larodde where, to my great relief there was an hotel and a bar. I flopped down and slaked my thirst with a nice cool Kronenbourg.

After Larodde the road went downhill briefly and then started to climb again, while the forest closed in once more. At last, at 11.30, I emerged from the woods on to a plateau where there was an even more spectacular panorama, although it no longer possible to make out Singles, let alone Messeix. The Mont Dore range, however, remained hidden by clouds.

> Hark! Hark! the dogs do bark,
> The beggars are come to town.

I certainly felt like a beggar walking through Fourroux. As soon as I reached the outskirts a dog started barking at me and I was handed on, as it were, from dog to dog as I passed each house, throughout the hamlet. What was even more disconcerting was that no matter how loudly the dogs barked, the villagers paid not the slightest attention. It was as if, because I was on foot, I did not exist. I felt humiliated and it was a relief when I left Fourroux behind and its damned dogs. A shame really, because I had noticed some nice old houses on my way through.

At 11.45 I reached a crossroads where I turned right for Labessette; the left-hand fork would have brought me to the busy main road from La Bourboule to Bort-les-Orgues, which I wished to avoid.

The sign-post gave the distance to Bort as sixteen kilometres and I worked out that I had already walked over over ten miles in three-and-three-quarter hours, climbing over 800 feet in the process. Only ten miles to go . . .

I was crossing an upland plain with scruffy fields, some cows, the odd tree and patches of bracken: it was not good land. I was feeling hungry now and was glad when I saw a shady cart track leading off the road to the right. I wandered down it until I found a gap in the hedge that gave me a view of distant hills. Here I had my picnic, out of the glare of the sun.

By 12.30 I was on my way again and soon afterwards came to Labessette. I don't remember much about the village, probably because I was looking at a fine view of the Mont-Dore range, which had reappeared to my left, having been hidden by clouds all the morning.

Beyond Labessette there was yet another long incline but when at last I reached the top, the view that stretched before me was quite different. I was looking at Le Cézallier, a high plateau lying at an altitude of 3937 feet between the Mont-Dore range to the north and the Monts du Cantal further south. This gently undulating landscape owes its profile to the flows of molten lava which spread evenly over the existing primary rocks in the tertiary era, leaving a layer of basalt without the jagged summits found at Mont-Dore or even the cones and craters of the Cantal. The highest point is the Signal de Luguet (5088 feet), which I thought I could just identify someway to the south-east.

Soon afterwards I reached Journiac, the first village I had come to with its name ending in *ac*. This termination is characteristic of the Langue d'Oc, the southern tongue which developed from Latin in the early middle ages and differentiated the peoples of the south from the northern French. I was surprised to find it here for it usually occurs further south. The *département* of the Dordogne, for example, is full of them.

At Journiac I had a brief glimpse of the lake before I began a punishing descent. The slope was one in twelve and the weight of my pack pushed me along faster than I wanted to go while my feet were driven forward painfully into the toes of my boots. At the bottom of the descent I crossed the Panouille, a tributary of the Dordogne enclosed in its own narrow tree-lined gorge. On the far side I was faced by a stiff climb up the southern cliff. By now I was very weary and needed frequent rests as I toiled slowly upwards. The road was narrow and winding with a low stone wall on the left where there was a sheer drop to the river below. At about every fifty yards there was an opening in the wall where I was able to stop without risk of being hit by a car. I reached the top at last, after which the going was easier and quite soon I came to the village of Lanobre. Here I stopped for a drink at a very smart *Logis*. I was so thirsty that I ordered a beer and a lemonade and mixed them to make myself a shandy. Afterwards I asked *le patron* if he had a room but unfortunately the hotel was *complet*. There was no help for it, I would have to walk another three miles to Bort-les-Orgues.

I was now back on the main road which here looked typically French, running straight across the plateau bordered by large plane trees. Those last few miles seemed endless but eventually I reached the outskirts of Bort. A long, depressing road led to the centre. On one side was a large, evil-smelling tannery and on the other a disused goods yard with dry grass growing between the rusty rails. I felt very fed-up, especially when I saw the drab Hôtel de la Gare, it looked like being a grim night. Tired as I was, I continued down this mean street until I came to the Hôtel Central. This looked altogether more promising: it had white window boxes with begonias in them and recommendations from the French Tourist Board and others. A few steps further on was a bridge across the Dordogne. From here I could see the back of the Hôtel Central and that it had a large terrace overlooking the river. This was good enough for me: I straightaway went and asked for a room. I was lucky; there was one on the river side, above the terrace. It had no shower but I was given a key which gave me exclusive use of one in a *cabinet*, outside in the corridor. Inside the *cabinet* there was a step up into the shower itself. Having stripped off, I mounted the step and promptly cracked my head on the curtain rail, otherwise all was well.

The window of my room looked straight across the Dordogne (which I could not actually see because the roof of the terrace hid it from view) to the old town. Just opposite was a narrow market-place, shaded by brutally pollarded plane trees. To the left a narrow street wound up to the church whose great, grey square tower and tall spire looms over the old town's steep slate roofs. Behind the church, at the top of a sheer, tree-covered cliff, I could see the '*orgues*', that strange rock formation which is supposed to resemble a set of organ pipes and which gives the town its name.

The *orgues* consists of columns of phonolite, or clinkstone, formed by jets of molten lava, cooling very quickly on contact with the air. The cliffs are over three hundred feet high and a mile long, so the original eruption must have been spectacular indeed.

I ate dinner on the terrace, from which I had a good view of the Dordogne flowing swiftly over the black stony river bed. It was a real river now and there were treacherous-looking back-eddies under the bridge. My dinner was very different from the one I had eaten last night at the auberge: melon; *terrine de brochet* with a warm, buttery sauce; *poulet au riz* and two good, local cheeses *bleu d'auvergne* and *chèvre*. For wine I chose a half-bottle of St-Pourçain, a fresh, dry *rosé*. After that I felt a lot better.

I woke up at 6 a.m. with a slight headache. Low clouds concealed the *orgues* but across the river there was great activity as the market traders set up their stalls with their brightly-coloured canopies. After breakfast I crossed the bridge to look at the market, which by now was in full swing. Down by the riverside were the clothes stalls, and what a strange mixture: frumpy, flowered frocks that no self-respecting English woman would be seen dead in, alongside trendy boiler suits for younger women; a stall covered with every kind of headgear from woollen bobble hats to *chasseurs'* leather caps with peaks and side flaps; jogging oufits for tiny tots and camouflage flack-jackets. One stall sold nothing but socks, another haberdashery, buttons, cotton reels, zips, needles and scissors. Nearby an unmanned stall was covered with slices of oranges, apples, cucumber, tomatoes and carrots – all apparently the product of some indispensable kitchen gadget. The demonstrator had no doubt nipped off for a quick cognac. Down by the riverside another stall had a fetching display of day-glow pink, viridian and electric blue teddy-bears.

Blaring pop-music and strobe lighting drew me unwillingly towards the fairground carousels and dodgems sandwiched betwen the clothing stalls, but I was disappointed to see that most of the kids riding the merry-go-round sat in rockets, space ships, helicopter gunships, tanks and police cars with flashing blue lights on their roofs. True there were a few old-fashioned horses amongst them but only one had a rider.

Sadly, I turned away and made for the church. The narrow street leading up to it had been closed to traffic and this too was full of stalls. There were live chickens and rabbits in cages, enormous cured hams, trestle-tables covered with spicy smoked sausages and pots of dark, rich honey. I weaved my way past these tempting offerings until I reached the covered market at the top of the town, where they were selling meat, fruit and vegetables. The church was close by but when I got there it was locked. I was on my way downhill when I met the *curé* hurrying up. Although still a young man, in his late twenties, he looked harassed and bowed. He seemed to think I was someone important and not only let me into the church but turned on the lights to show me its treasure – a fifteenth century polychrome statue of Saint Anne. It is a strange piece: the body is well modelled but the head is out of all proportion, huge with large, staring eyes like those of Saint Baudime at St-Nectaire, and shoulder length hair. Saint Anne holds in her left hand a diminutive Virgin Mary who in turn clasps a tiny naked Jesus who has his hands on a bible held in Saint Anne's right hand. Very odd.

As so often, the east end is the most interesting part of the church. The romanesque chancel has a tunnel vault, supported by columns with carved foliage capitals, and walls of undressed stone. The rest of the interior is unremarkable gothic and there are some crude modern stained glass windows. Outside the chief feature is the sturdy tower which, unusually, is built over the chancel, not the crossing. When I looked at the exterior of the apse, I thought I could see that there had once been machicolation, at roof level, under the eaves. Taken with the size of the tower, this suggested that the church was once fortified, which seemed only too likely in these remote regions.

I now decided to walk to the Barrage de Bort, the great dam,

which, after the 'orgues' is Bort's most famous sight, but soon lost my
way and found myself back at the market. My toe was hurting badly
so I thought I would take a taxi. I found the taxi alright but no sign of
the driver: he was obviously in one of the bars having a quick drink,
but which one? At the end of the bridge was a *gendarme* directing
traffic, with the usual frenzied whistles and a conspicuous lack of
success. After a while he gave up the unequal struggle and I was able
to ask him where I could find the taxi man. He went straight into a
nearby bar and hauled him out.

It took less time to reach the dam than it had to find the driver. The
barrage was certainly impressive. A wide road runs across the top, on
the west side of which is the lake. On the other side is a drop of nearly
four hundred feet to the bed of the Dordogne and a bird's eye view
over the town. The dam stretches across the gorge in a great concave
curve 433 yards wide, and descends in a series of giant steps to the
valley below, interrupted at mid point by an enormous concave
buttress. It is a magnificent piece of engineering.

Between Bort-les-Orgues and Argentat, a distance of some
seventy five miles, the Dordogne drops over nine hundred feet. The
Barrage de Bort is the first and most important of four great dams
built to harness the energy generated by this rapid fall. The first was
built at Marèges, between 1932 and 1935, then came l'Aigle (1940–
1945). The Barrage de Bort was begun in 1942 and took three years to
complete, during which time there were many set-backs, including
an avalanche. Altogether twenty-five workmen perished in the
course of its construction. The last of the big four to be completed
was Chastang (1945–1952) but a smaller dam, Le Sablier, was built
just above Argentat, between 1951 and 1958 and there are many more
on the Diège, the Maronne and other tributaries of the Dordogne.

This elaborate system of dams is responsible for five per cent of
France's production of hydroelectric power, amounting to 2.5 million kilowatts annually. Had I so wished, I could have visited the *halle
d'information*, at the north end of the dam, and watched a film on the
construction of the whole network; instead I walked to the opposite
end, where I knew I would find a pleasure boat that made trips up the
lake to the beautiful Château de Val. Unfortunately, I was too early:
the first trip was not until eleven o'clock and it was still only ten.

Reluctantly, I decided to walk the three miles to Lanobre; from there it was another half mile to the lake shore and the château.

Progress was very slow because of my blistered toe but luckily I managed to hitch a lift and the friendly French driver took me not just to Lanobre but all the way to the château's car park. At first a screen of trees hid the view but suddenly I emerged into the open and saw the castle immediately below me, its many towers, with their 'pepper pot' roofs reflected in the still waters of the lake.

The Château du Val stands on a rocky islet, entirely surrounded by water except for a narrow causeway on its eastern side. But it was not always so: originally, the castle was built on a steep escarpment, some way from the banks of the Dordogne. It was not until 1948, after the construction of the dam, that the waters rose to their present level, drowning several villages in the process but leaving the château with the lake lapping at its foot. I stood for a moment, admiring this fairy-tale view, then I noticed that there was a pleasure boat about to leave the causeway for a trip up the Gorges of the Dordogne and I hurried down to join it.

As soon as I had clambered on board, the gang-plank was pulled up and the boat set sail. I was impressed by the size and comfort of the craft. It must have been eighty feet long and nearly a hundred passengers sat in well-padded seats under a clear perspex roof. I was amused, too, by the skipper who steered the boat standing with his back to the wheel, talking non-stop to his captive audience. Mind you, there seemed little for him to worry about: I saw only two other craft on the lake, a small sailing boat and an outboard, and the waters are deep.

To start with we circled the château while the passengers, including myself, snapped it from all angles, then we set off northwards. At this point the lake was over half-a-mile wide, but gradually the steep, tree-covered cliffs closed in as we entered the gorges. Here and there, on the eastern heights, I could see clearings where cattle grazed, but along the western shore the forest wall was unbroken. After a while the unchanging backdrop of trees became monotonous. A buzzard flapped lazily down and perched picturesquely on a dead branch, sticking out of the water, otherwise there was nothing to see until we reached Trappe, a tiny romanesque chapel, built on a rocky promontory jutting out on the western shore. Yesterday, at Pont d'Arpiat, I had been tempted by the thought of visiting this twelfth-century priory to choose the route down the west side of the lake. Now, seeing the chapel shrouded in scaffolding and clearly in the process of restoration, I was glad I had not succumbed.

Soon after Trappe, and about a mile below Pont d'Arpiat, the gorge grew narrower still and the boat turned round. On the return journey the skipper pointed out the ruins of the Château de Thynières on another rocky headland on the eastern shore, but so little remains of the castle that it is indistinguishable from the surrounding undergrowth. It was midday when we arrived back at the château – time for lunch. I drank a beer in a nearby bar-restaurant but was put off eating there by the high prices; instead I decided to walk back to the Beau Rivage at Lanobre, where I had mixed my shandy the day before. Here I enjoyed a very good meal for only sixty francs, with the main course *coq au vin*.

After lunch I returned to the lake and joined a guided tour of the Château du Val. It is a tall, compact building, flanked by five large round towers and a sixth, slimmer one on the south-east angle, all capped by pointed, 'pepper pot' roofs. The two towers on the landward side are built of dark basalt with slate roofs, the rest of the castle of a lighter stone and both the main building and the remaining four towers have red-tiled roofs.

The entrance is through the remnants of the original fifteenth-century gateway, of which only the bottom six feet or so remain standing. Once inside, I found myself in a small courtyard. On my left was a rather plain fifteenth-century chapel and beyond it a flight of steep steps, leading up to the castle's main block. To the right, a low wall, all that remained of the original curtain wall, stretched in a shallow D round the edge of the escarpment to rejoin the castle block at its far end. A number of visitors were sitting on the wall, admiring the view over the lake while they waited, like myself, for the tour to begin or looking at a pretty brick dove-cote built on the base of a demolished thirteenth-century tower.

Crossing the courtyard, I came to the part of the castle furthest away from the entrance. I was looking at the sole vestige of the earliest castle built on the site, a blocked-up arch, high up in the wall, that was the entrance to the eleventh century keep, originally approached by a movable wooden staircase. This primitive fortress was transformed in the thirteenth century by the Seigneurs de Thynières who extended the keep to the south east, more than doubling its original size, and replaced the wooden stairway by a barbican. They also built a high curtain wall to protect the more vulnerable northwestern flank.

In 1440 the castle was acquired by Guillaume IV d'Estaing who, reflecting the period of greater security that followed the ending of the Hundred Years War, set about making the castle less of a fortress. He demolished the barbican, replacing it by the present more convenient staircase, and lightened the interior by introducing large, mullion and transome windows. He was also responsible for the tiled 'pepper pot' roofs that add so much to the château's romantic appearance.

A bell sounded and it was time to join the guided tour. Returning to the entry staircase, I climbed the thirty-seven steps up to a fine gothic doorway, surmounted by the coat of arms of the Estaings, three fleurs de lys, sculpted in stone.

The interior of Val, as so often in France, was a disappointment. The château was compulsorily purchased by *Électricité de France* in 1946 when the last owner, Mademoiselle Leontine d'Arcy, left, taking most of the fittings and furniture with her. Subsequently, Val was sold by EDF to the town of Bort-les-Orgues for a nominal sum. The town has spent a great deal of money restoring the exterior of the castle but most of the rooms remain either empty or furnished with a few indifferent pieces. We assembled first of all in the *salon*, a large gloomy apartment that suffered a heavy-handed restoration in the then fashionable 'renaissance' style in the 1860s. I usually enjoy these forays into historical romanticism but I found the decoration at Val cheap and vulgar.

The room is dominated by a hideous ornamental fireplace. On either side of the hearth, supporting the lintel, are gilded caryatids, dressed in flowing robes, wearing grecian helmets and armed with spears. Above the mantelpiece is a triumph, a composition of roman breastplates and weapons, surmounted by a helmet, all in gilt against a deep-blue background, adorned with gold fleurs de lys. The right to incorporate the fleurs de lys in their coat of arms was granted to the Estaing family after Pierre d'Estaing saved the life of the French king, Philippe Augustus, in the battle of Bouvins in 1214 AD. Philip Augustus, alone and surrounded, had been unhorsed by a Flemish pikeman who was in the act of despatching him when Pierre d'Estaing rode up at the head of a band of knights, killed the king's assailant and helped him to remount. The chimney-piece at Val was built over two hundred years after the last member of the Estaing family quit the château forever, so the incorporation of the fleurs de lys in the design of the overmantle was clearly intended to bring glory by association to its nouveau riche owner Monsieur Jules Souchard.

Apart from the fireplace, the only other item in the room worth a second glance was a fine Aubusson tapestry. Next door, in the dining-room, was another egregious chimney-piece. Once again the lintel was supported by caryatids, this time young women wearing green tops over gold skirts, bay leaves in their hair and bemused expressions. Above them was a bust of Marcus Aurelius, representing wisdom, flanked by corpulent putti bearing garlands – a totally bogus composition and badly executed to boot.

The remaining rooms were virtually empty except for one that contained an exhibition of local paintings, most of them worthless daubs. Eventually we climbed in single file up a winding staircase to the sentry walk under the eaves. We shuffled along a narrow corridor, occasionally peering out through an embrasure at the sun-speckled lake below like prisoners in the Bastille. Much as I like castles, I have to admit that the sight of a speed boat, setting out from the causeway below, with two topless girls preening themselves on deck, filled me with envy and I was glad when the tour came to an end.

That evening, after dinner, I telephoned Sybil and we spoke for a long time. I was feeling depressed, probably a reaction to my exhausting journey from La Guingette, and was undecided what my next move should be. After Bort-les-Orgues the Dordogne disappears once more into deep gorges, swinging westwards for ten miles or so before turning southwards, after its junction with the Diège, to emerge into the plain over sixty miles further on at Argentat. In between is a stretch of rugged country with few villages and fewer hotels.

After my experience at Messeix, I was reluctant to go wandering off into the wilderness without being sure of somewhere to rest my head at night. There were hotels at Champignac and Neuvic, two nearby villages, but it was now the height of the French holiday season and when I telephoned them both were *complet*. Yet even if I had been successful in booking a room, it is doubtful if I could have actually got there. Neuvic is twenty-five miles from Bort and in between there is difficult mountain country with deep ravines. After my trek from La Guingette I knew this distance was close to my limit, even were I fully fit, with my badly blistered toe it was out of the question. Champignac is nearer and I might have got there but afterwards it was not clear where I could go next.

All this I discussed with Sybil at great length, ending up by saying I thought I should abandon my trip for the time being, and return when the season was over. Sybil, who is very determined, did not think this was a good idea (I think she was enjoying not having me around for a while!) and in the end we agreed that I should investigate the possibility of taking a train to somewhere further down the Dordogne where the going would be easier and there were more hotels.

CHAPTER 3

THE FLIGHT
TO VAYRAC

Next morning, I went to the station and discovered that there was a train at 13.50 which would take me to Vayrac, near Souillac, changing at Aurillac in the Cantal. I bought a ticket costing eighty-six francs, went back to the hotel and checked out. The bill came to 616 francs, which for two nights, two dinners, two breakfasts and use of the telephone seemed good value. Afterwards I went to see a doctor who painted my blister with that bright red antiseptic that has adorned the limbs of generations of French children and gave me a prescription. I spent the rest of the morning shopping and writing postcards.

The train was a little local diesel with only one coach. There were two passengers, myself and a girl in her twenties, who sat in the smokers' section. We set off on time and chugged slowly up to the plateau. I was not sorry to see the last of Bort. It is a small, dour town hemmed in by dark cliffs whose constant presence I had found very oppressive, so it was a relief to turn my back on the *orgues* and look instead at the strange moon landscape of Le Cézallier.

I peered out of the left hand window trying to identify some of the peaks and thought I could see the Signal de Luguet and, further away to the south, the Puy Violent (5223 feet) and the Puy Mory (5863 feet) in the Cantal. For a while the view was hidden by trees but then we emerged into the open and crossed a viaduct. Far below was the dry, stony bed of a mountain stream, the Mars, which later joins the Sumène, a tributary of the Dordogne.

We went on climbing and at about 2.30, came out of the woods on to a

plain dotted with small farms. We were on the outskirts of the market
town of Mauriac and I saw some nice old stone buildings with fish scale
roofs. From the station itself I could see handsome eighteenth and
nineteenth-century houses, again with traditional roofs. The inside of
the train, when we stopped, was uncomfortably warm. The glare from
the white gravel platform outside hurt the eyes and a bed of dark red
roses wilted in the intense heat.

After Mauriac, the countryside was mainly pasture land, although I
saw a few small fields of maize. Red and white cows stood sheltering
from the sun beneath the oak trees or lay down under the hedges but
soon the landscape became hillier as we approached the Cantal. At 2.45
we stopped at Salins, where a family with two children got on. The man
was thin, about thirty and had a rather arresting face that reminded me
of the young Jean-Louis Barrault. His wife, however, did not look a bit
like Arletty, rather more like Penelope Keith. He was wearing a black
T-shirt with RENAISSANCE on it; for a moment I thought of Kenneth
Branagh's theatre company but then I remembered that there is a pop
group of the same name. Oddly, considering the heat, they all wore
boots. His were of leather and buckled on like flying boots, the rest wore
brightly coloured rubber yachting boots.

On we went past an old stone farmhouse, where two boys stood by a
tractor staring at the train, and into hilly country with a great many
tunnels and viaducts. Grunting and wheezing, the little train edged its
way ever more slowly up the steep gradiant, while I scuttled from side to
side of the carriage, hoping for a view. Infuriatingly, there was mostly
nothing to see but an impenetrable screen of trees.

Half-an-hour later we arrived at Loupiac-St-Christophe, a tiny
station with only one platform. The station building was really a small
house with a ticket office on the ground floor and living quarters above
with shuttered windows. On the opposite side of the line was a grassy
bank and then open country. At one end of the platform was a trellis arch
with wild roses straggling over it; there was a bed of asters, a coiled
hosepipe, a wooden bench that had seen better days and two metal
trollies and that was all. No-one got on or off.

After Loupiac-St-Christophe the terrain altered dramatically. We
had entered the Gorges de la Maronne, another of the Dordogne's
many tributaries. but there were tantalisingly few opportunities to

admire the scenery as once again the train entered a series of tunnels and deep cuttings. Occasionally, a steep, tree-covered cliff came into sight and once I glimpsed a wooded ravine with a small stone house perched on a rocky outcrop, then we plunged back into a tunnel. But at last I did get a fine view of a sweep of valley, far below, with the river, looking very shallow and stony, winding through it. On either side, the banks were a vivid green, a sure sign of marshland. Another cutting blocked the view but this time when we emerged it was on to a viaduct crossing a broad stretch of water. Looking at the map I saw that this was the confluence of the rivers Maronne, the Bertrande and L'Eize.

The line now followed the valley of the L'Eize upstream. At first the river was wide with large, suspicious-looking green patches on either side, but gradually it narrowed and turned into a mountain torrent. The forest closed in and once again there was nothing to be seen but trees. At 3.10 we stopped at St Illide, a mountain halt entirely surrounded by steep wooded slopes, and shortly afterwards the train at last reached the top of its long climb and we came out of the trees onto a plateau. It was scrubland, stony and poor, the tip of a church spire poked above a distant hillside and then we were back into the trees once more, but this time we were going downhill. The train rattled down a steep incline and through a long cutting to Viescamp-Jalles, a much larger station with pollarded trees on the platform. Here RENAISSANCE man and family got off. The train continued its downward track but the woods were thinning out to be replaced by pasture land with farms and occasional houses. At Ytrac, our next stop, there was a sizeable housing estate: small white houses with first floor terraces, each with their white tables and lounging chairs, red pantile roofs and neat gardens filled with bright flowers – they looked exactly like a child's drawing of a house. Soon afterwards it became clear that we were approaching the outskirts of of a large town, factories, hypermarkets, goods waggons and a multiplicity of lines: Aurillac.

The station was quite a grand affair with several platforms covered by a wide roof, supported by cast-iron columns. Tourist coaches waited in a large car park and outside the station buffet stood a man wearing a jacket and carrying an executive briefcase. We were back in civilization.

The train for Vayrac, another small diesel, was already standing at the platform with passengers on board, many of them back-packers like myself but all considerably younger. The inside of the carriage was stiflingly hot so I waited on the platform until the last moment before taking my seat.

We set off at 4.05 p.m., travelling back up the track to Viescamp-sous-Jalles where the line divided. At first there was nothing but trees, trees, trees, a cutting, a tunnel, then trees again; finally we went through a tunnel and when we came out of the far end, there on the left was a large lake and a dam, the Barrage de St. Etienne-Cantales. We crossed the lake and soon after came to Laroquebrou. At once it was clear that we were in different country, here were creamy-brown-coloured stone houses with red roman-tiled roofs. I saw a half-timbered dwelling with yellow clay infilling and on a hill, overlooking the town, was a small château built of the same cream-brown stone, with squat towers capped by brown-tiled pointed roofs. These buildings were quite different from the dark stone mountain dwellings I had grown accustomed to and a sign that the lowlands were not far off.

After Laroquebrou the track followed the left bank of the Cère, one of the Dordogne's most beautiful tributaries. Long fronds of white-flowered water weed swayed in the swift-running stream. A lone fisher-man, wearing green waders, stood waist-high in the water, waving a languid rod over the green surface of the river. The track ran along a narrow ledge with high, tree-covered cliffs to the left and the Cère a hundred feet below on the right, tumbling rapidly over a rocky, boulder-strewn bed. There were frequent tunnels and cuttings but all of them very short and every time we emerged there was another spectacular view of the turbulant river below. It was easily the most exciting train journey I have ever made and one that would appeal to that inveterate railway traveller, Paul Theroux.

At five o'clock we reached Laval de Cère which, after the beauty of the gorges, came as a sad shock: rusty goods waggons, an unsightly timber-yard and small, shabby houses straggling up the wooded hillside. After Laval the scenery changed: the river became wider, placid and slow-moving under a fringe of trees and there were people in pedalos. Soon the banks were wide enough to accommodate large campsites and there were cars parked in the shade of trees at the river's edge. The valley grew broader still and now there were small farms with fields of maize, orchards and meadows. I saw a little stone house with a wavy red-tiled roof and logs stacked outside, then there were white villas and small red-roofed villages.

At Biers-Bretenoux, a much larger, busy-looking station, most of the back-packers left the train. The next stop was Vayrac: I had arrived.

No one else got off and the station was deserted. Outside an empty country road with one small house in it and no sign of life. My heart sank – where was I to spend the night? I limped slowly to the end of the road and looking to the right saw a small cluster of houses which I took to be Vayrac. Five minutes more brought me to a crossroads; on the opposite corner was a café-bar with HÔTEL written above the window. I went in, ordered a beer and asked for a room for the night. To my relief there was one free. A small girl took me to my room. It was in an annexe, a bleak, concrete and breeze-block building, completely devoid of any decoration. The room was impersonal with pale green distempered walls and a window that looked out onto a well with a blank wall opposite, but I was so pleased to be settled for the night that I accepted it without demur.

I showered and changed and then went and sat down at a pavement table outside the bar. Vayrac is on the D703, a busy little road running east west between Souillac and Bretenoux. The bar was on the corner of the lights-controlled crossroads and was not an ideal place to sip an aperitif. Sitting there I noticed that every other car seemed to have a GB registration; in the mountains I had seen none.

Dinner was as lacking in imagination as my room: I had expected something rather special now that I was in the rich lower valley of the Dordogne, but nothing could mar my pleasure at having escaped from Bort-les-Orgues. Afterwards I spent a futile hour trying to ring Sybil but, after repeatedly being told that I had dialled the wrong number, that lines to London were engaged or that the number didn't exist, I gave up in a fury and went to bed.

After another abortive attempt to contact Sybil, I left Vayrac at 9.30 the next day. I was making for Beaulieu-sur-Dordogne, up river from Vayrac, on my way to Argentat where the Dordogne emerges from the gorges. Here I intended to resume my interrupted journey down the

Dordogne.I had imagined that there would be a local bus to Beaulieu, but no such luck. I went back to the station thinking that I might take a train back to Bretenoux but there was none until six in the evening: there was no help for it, I would have to walk.

Beaulieu lies north-east of Vayrac and I had worked out from the map that instead of going south-eastwards down the D703 to Bretenoux and then northwards up the D940 to Beaulieu, two sides of a triangle, I could cut a corner by taking a cross-country road via Queyssac-les-Vignes, a distance of about nine miles, although this meant climbing a thousand foot hill on the way. Ordinarily I could have managed this easily enough but my little toe was hurting so much that progress was painfully slow.

After two miles I reached the village of Betaille where I turned left up the road to Queyssac. The centre of Betaille had some old stone houses, one of them with an attached tower or *pigeonnier*. These pigeon-towers are a feature of south-west France and can take many forms, some of them very attractive. The simplest ones are straightforward stone towers, square or round, capped by pointed tiled roofs with openings for the pigeons to fly in and out. Further south, where stone is scarce, the *pigeonniers* are often half-timbered and stand on mushroom-headed stone stilts. The pigeons that covered the roof were originally kept not as a supplementary food supply but for the sake of their droppings. In areas where there were few cattle the guano was a valuable source of nitrates. So strong was the fertilizer that it could not be spread on the ground until the rain was starting to fall, otherwise the stalks and surface roots would have been burned by the concentrated nitrates. Until the revolution the pigeon-tower and its guano belonged exclusively to the local lord who thus controlled the sale of this commodity. Today the pigeon droppings are no longer used but there is still a certain cachet in possessing a pigeon-tower, although now it is just as likely to contain a smart tiled bathroom as pigeons.

The climb up to Queyssac was very gradual and easy enough if it hadn't been for my toe. After half an hour I stopped and looked back. Below me I could see the wooded valley of the Dordogne, although the river itself was hidden from view, and beyond a dark, grim cliff wall that marked the northern limit of the Causse de Gramat. Much of the Quercy consists of a stony, undulating plain covered with scrubby oak trees, blackthorn and juniper: this is the *causse*, a limestone plateau laid down about 200 million years ago in the second geological era when this part of south-west France was covered by the sea. Limestone is porous so that water sinks straight through it to from underground rivers and streams that sometimes find their way to the surface many miles away. Some of these underground systems are accessible from the surface and have become tourist attractions. One of the most famous is the Gouffre de Padirac, situated near Rocamadour, on the Causse de Gramat, in the direction I was now looking. The *causse* continues north of the river in the Causse de Martel which lay to my right, west of Vayrac but my route was taking me away from the *causses*, towards the *châtaigneraie*, the vast chestnut forests that cover the foothills of the *massif central*.

By now it was eleven o'clock and the temperature was already in the eighties. Feeling hot and tired I stopped at a small house and asked for a drink of water. A nice old boy, who came originally from Sedan in the Ardennes, gave me a glass laced with *syrop de citron vert*. He also suggested that I could shorten my route if I by-passed Queyssac, advice which I was inclined to take because I had already visited the village some years ago when Sybil and I were researching for our book *Food and Wine of South West France*.

We had heard that a very rare wine called *vin de paille* was made there and we wanted to find out if it were true. Despite its name, there are very few vines to be seen at Queyssac-les-Vignes, the area having never fully recovered from the phylloxera blight that devastated the vineyards of the southwest during the 1870s, and it took us some time to find anyone who knew where the *vin de paille* was made. At last, after several false starts, we tracked down Monsieur Soursac. Even now our troubles were not over for Monsieur Soursac spoke a dialect so thick that we had great difficulty understanding him. He explained that a number of local farmers made the wine but on a very small scale and purely for their own use. The name derives not as we had supposed from the colour of the wine but from the fact that at one time the grapes were spread out on straw to dry. *Vin de paille* is made from a variety of local grapes and according to Monsieur Soursac it does not matter very much which are used – this after all is not an *appellation contrôlée* wine. They are picked late, from towards the end of September up until the end of October. Instead of the wine being made right away, the grapes are spread out to dry, but nowadays shallow fruit trays are used rather than straw. The grapes remain in the trays until they are quite dry before they are pressed. In practice this means the New Year, sometimes as late as February. By then the sugar content is very high and the fermentation takes a long time, perhaps as much as six months. The wine is matured in the cask for two years before it is drunk. *Vin de paille* is a strong, sweet red wine that reminds one distantly of port, although it is not fortified of course. In most years it reaches a strength of fifteen degrees but a really good vintage can be as high as twenty degrees. We were lucky enough to be able to buy a bottle from Monsieur Soursac's small stock. Drunk like port at the end of a meal we found it very good. *Vin de paille* also goes very well with the delicious orange-fleshed charentais melons.

I reached the crossroads just outside Queyssac at about 11.30 thirty. The sign post said it was twelve kilometres to Beaulieu-sur-Dordogne, approximately seven-and-a-half miles, which at my present rate of progress meant another four hours. I was debating whether to go into Queyssac in the hope of finding somewhere to eat, when rescue came in the shape of a farmer's wife who stopped her car and asked if I would like a lift. As I was on my way *up* the Dordogne I had no scruples about accepting her offer. When I saw the steep winding descent, through a thick chestnut forest, that I would have had to negotiate I was doubly grateful to this kind lady for her timely offer.

We arrived in Beaulieu at midday and at once I saw a comfortable-looking hotel called Le Turenne which looked as though it had once been a small *gentilhommière*. They had a room which was reached by climbing a winding stone staircase inside a round tower up to a wide, carpeted landing on the first floor. The room was spacious with a view over roman-tiled roofs to the backs of some half-timbered houses. To the right was a crumbling stone wall and to the left the curve of another tower. Inside there was a patterned wallpaper of pale blue flowers against a cream background. There were two beds with chintz beds-preads and a pink tiled bathroom – a greater contrast to my room at Vayrac could hardly be imagined.

Refreshed after a shower, I walked into the town looking for some-where to eat. The hotel is situated on the corner of the main square which occupies a triangle formed by the junction of the D940 running north south from Bretenoux to Argentat and the D41 from Puybrun to the south-west. The constant roar of traffic on both sides of the square was unsupportable and I quickly turned my back on it and set off down one of the narrow lanes leading to the old town.

Beaulieu owes its name to the Benedictines who founded the Abbey of Saint Pierre here *circa* 850 AD on the right bank of the Dordogne where the river flows smoothly, between wooded hills, round a wide bend. Such was the beauty of the site that they called it *bellus locus*, later corrupted in the *langue d'oc* to Belloc which changed in the *langue d'oil* to Beaulieu.

The present abbey building dates from the twelfth century. It lies on one of the medieval pilgrimage routes to Santiago de Compostela and the constant procession of pilgrims, combined with the growing wealth and power of the abbey itself must have led to the rapid development of the town to service their needs, not all of which were of a purely religious nature.

The pattern of streets and the size of the buildings surrounding Saint Pierre cannot have changed much since medieval times: the small houses press up close to the abbey, making it difficult to get far enough back to take in the whole building, although there is a small market place just outside the south porch. The surrounding houses were very different from those I had become accustomed to seeing in the mountains. Many of them were half-timbered with red-brown timbers and yellow clay infilling. These often had first floor wooden balconies made bright with terracotta pots of petunias, begonias and the ubiquitous geranium.

Round the corner from the abbey I found a cheap restaurant, the equivalent of a workman's *caff* in England, but how different! The inside was scruffy but clean. I sat down at a table covered with an oilcloth and a paper tablecloth. Only three other tables were occupied, at one sat another tourist, a young woman who left soon after I arrived, at another were seven jolly *ouvriers*, enjoying themselves hugely and drinking their way through bottle after bottle of red plonk. The only other diner, an old man, sat by himself steadily chomping his way through course after course without raising his eyes from his plate.

After a short siesta I went shopping for some *espadrilles* which I hoped would be easier on my blistered toe. I ended up with a pair of flip-flops, those minimal sandals with a thong between the second and big toes and a single band across the foot. They looked horrible, the band being rainbow coloured, but for the first time for days I was able to forget the blister and with nothing to rub against it and exposed to the air it improved rapidly.

Satisfactorily shod at last, I made a quick circuit of the abbey (I had already decided to come back next morning for a closer look) and then made my way through the back streets of the old town to the river. Wandering down a lane, I passed under a little wooden bridge uniting two houses. Trailing geraniums in pots lining the balustrade made scarlet splashes against the clear blue sky. The lane lead me to the Chapelle des Pénitents, a small, twelfth century church standing at the edge of the river.

Down by the riverside it was easy to see how Beaulieu had earned its name: the wide, curving, stream flowed smoothly over a weir and disappeared from sight behind a small island; on both banks tree-lined walks offered shady promenades. Close by the Chapelle des Pénitents is a footbridge leading across the weir to the opposite bank. From the middle of the bridge is a splendid view taking in the chapel and a stretch of the right bank, shaded by chestnut trees, which makes an ideal picnic spot.

On the left bank I found a large, permanent campsite, hidden amongst the trees. As I was to discover, there are many such sites along the Dordogne between Argentat and Bergerac. They are extremely well organized with water and electricity laid on, daily rubbish collections and sometimes even television cables. All of them have small bars selling beer and soft drinks but some of the larger ones have on-site restaurants. The French certainly take their holidays seriously: come the *quatorze*, the 14th of July, there is a mass exodus from the cities to the country and the seaside. For two months until the *rentrée*, when the schools go back, the whole family goes *en vacances* together, although the *pater familias* may go back to work after a month, joining his family at weekends.

Predictably, a highly lucrative industry has grown up exploiting this annual collective fantasy. The supermarkets fill with holiday gear; cooking stoves, elaborate tents, wind-surf boards, cold boxes, garden furniture but above all the latest fashionable leisure wear. It is vital, if you are French, not to be seen in last year's gear and so a whole new holiday wardrobe is acquired each time the holiday season comes round.

This year knee-length surfing shorts were all the rage, garishly coloured in abstract combinations of lemon yellow, orange and electric blue.

Recrossing the footbridge I saw a flotilla of canoeists making for the bank· where there was a portage to the next stretch of river below the weir. This gave me an idea: perhaps I could hire a canoe and paddle down the river. I remembered hearing that there were hire companies who would take your luggage on ahead by road, which would make a nice change fom back-packing. I determined to look into the possibilities.

That evening I enjoyed one of the best meals of my whole trip. Dinner was in the courtyard in front of the hotel with a view, through low pointed arches, of the main square, mercifully far enough away for traffic noise not to impinge; behind me the hotel, its cream walls dripping with ivy, a round stone tower at one end, dark brown shutters framing the tall windows. White chippings covered the floor of the courtyard and tubs of blue hydrangeas were placed strategically between the tables.

Charmed by the setting I sat down with a tingle of pleasurable anticipation. While waiting for my first course I studied my fellow diners: on one side sat a very old man, extremely thin, with finely chiselled features that reminded me of the aged Cocteau, although his hooded eyes were more reminiscent of Somerset Maugham. A beautiful young man (his catemite, I wondered) danced attendance on him and there was a little scene when his bottle of Cahors was tasted, condemned and sent back. Opposite them was an English couple in their thirties. They were planning the next day's journey and the man was giving his wife hell because she couldn't find the relevent Michelin map. She spent most of the dinner scrabbling in their car, parked just outside, while he grew more and more irritated.

The first course was *feuilleté aux cèpes à la sauce morilles*, a puff pastry envelope which literally melted in the mouth, releasing the rich flavour of the *cèpe* mushrooms with a hint of truffle.

This was followed by *cuisse de Canard braisé au Cahors*. Duck and goose, in one form or another, turn up frequently on menus in this part of France. My duck's leg was a confit, a speciality of the region. Before the days of canning and freezers, ducks' thighs and wings were preserved in large stone pots sealed with their own fat. The *confit* can be served fried, grilled or cold. Mine was served braised in Cahors, the dark red wine from the Quercy, the old name of the modern *département* of the Lot, whose northern border is just south of Beaulieu. Seeing that Cahors had been used in the sauce, I ordered half a bottle with my meal. It will surprise my friends to learn that this was the first red wine I had drunk since starting my trip. The weather was too hot for heavy wines and as there are few good whites to be found in the mountains I usually opted for the local St-Pourçain rosé. which I found pleasant enough. But now I was near a recognised wine area, I thought I would treat myself to something a little more interesting, at least this once.

Dinner continued with *cabecou en salade*. *Cabecou* is another local speciality, little round goats' cheeses served toasted on a bed of mixed salad. The dessert was *assiette aux noix*, another exquisite puff pastry concoction in the shape of a crescent containing a delicious mixture of walnut and apple purée, served with *crème anglaise* and two vanilla icecreams.

It was twilight by the time I had finished this feast. Well content, I sauntered down to the river and found a bridge across to a small island, just down river from the Chapelle des Pénitents. It was full of campers, most of them sitting at long trestle tables under the trees. Like me they had just finished dinner and were lingering over their *digestifs* in the gathering dusk. On the far side of the island the Dordogne was swirling past at high speed yet, towards the middle of the river I could dimly make out the figures of two solitary fishermen, up to their waists in the flood.

When I returned to the hotel the wretched English woman was still searching for the Michelin map, so I gave her mine. It was pushed under the door of my room ten minutes later.

I had been saving up my visit to the abbey and after a good night's sleep I felt the moment had arrived. The original church was built in the middle of the ninth century and was founded by Archbishop Raoul of Bourges, son of the Count of Quercy, but most of the present building dates from the twelfth century. The plan is one common to a number of great churches of this date found on the pilgrimage route to the great shrine of Santiago de Compostela, in northern Spain: a short four-bay nave, with side aisles, is followed by a transept and then a choir with a semi-circular ambulatory, off which project three chapels. This characteristic arrangement of the east end seems to have been designed to cope with the huge numbers of pilgrims who wished to visit these churches *en route* to Santiago to venerate the holy relics that all of them contained. The pilgrims were really the first tourists and they brought not only great wealth to the churches and towns on the *chemin de Saint Jacques* but all the attendant problems of crowd control. The semi-circular ambulatory and radiating chapels allowed the pilgrims to enter the ambulatory on one side, to process round behind the high altar, thus ensuring that they did not interrupt the monks at their devotions in the choir, to goggle at the relics in the chapels and leave the ambulatory in an orderly fashion on the far side. St-Pierre de Beaulieu still has its medieval treasures, the most famous of which is a beautiful twelfth century silver statue of the Virgin Mary.

The glory of Beaulieu is not the silver virgin but the magnificent sculpture of the tympanum in the south porch. Stylistically, this belongs to a school of eleventh-century sculpture peculiar to a number of great churches of south-west France, the most famous being the Last Judgement at Moissac, which is thought to have originated at the cathedral of St-Sernin, Toulouse and is often referred to as the Toulouse school.

At Beaulieu the theme of the sculpture is Christ's victory at the Second Coming. The semi-circular tympanum is dominated by the colossal figure of Christ, seated on his throne, his arms outspread in a gesture that at once seems to embrace all mankind and to recall the crucifixion. To reinforce this message two angels display the sign of the cross, off centre, just to the right of Christ's head. This is no Jesus, meek and mild, but a conquering hero who has triumphed over the forces of evil and now asserts his dominion over heaven and earth. Beneath Christ's outstretched arms two angels sound the last trumpet. Above his head two more angels bear his crown and a pair of nails, symbol of the passion. To the left and right of Christ sit the apostles and the elect, conversing animatedly. At a lower level are some small figures wearing phrygian caps whose exact significance has been the subject of great scholarly debate; one possible explanation is that they represent Jews and pagans who are not excluded from Christ's universal salvation. On the same level are small figures climbing out of their tombs, summoned by the angels' trumpets.

Christ wears a long flowing robe ending in a hem with rippling folds, one of the signatures of the Toulouse style. He is bearded and his hair is parted in the middle. The stylised treatment of the hair, the locks being represented by a series of inscribed lines, is also typical of this school of sculpture.

Below the tympanum is a broad lintel, divided into two horizontal bands, covered with lively carvings of monstrous beasts, amongst them a many headed dragon, a griffin and a serpent with a man's head. They seem to represent the horrors awaiting the unjust in hell and, indeed, some of the beasts are crunching the limbs of unfortunate sinners in their jaws. I always enjoy these fantastic beasts. It is as if, liberated from the constraints of depicting conventional Christian iconography, the sculptor delighted in wild flights of fancy and carved with an exuberance that is often missing from the more traditional scenes.

The marvellous creativity and compositional skill of the master of Beaulieu is beautifully demonstrated by the carving of the central pillar, supporting the lintel. On each of its three exposed sides there is a caryatid: on the west and south faces they are young men, their hands raised above their heads, pressing against the lintel. Their bent heads, hunched shoulders and narrow, elongated bodies, compressed between thin, undulating columns, give a vivid impression of the enormous burden they carry.

The most interesting of the column figures is on the east face. Here the sculptor has depicted the figure of an old man with a thick forked beard. Unlike his younger counterparts his arms are at his side and he carries the weight of the lintel on his shoulders. Whereas the other caryatids seem to be struggling against their fate, the old man has an expression of wearied resignation and immense sadness, which is very moving.

The remaining sculpture in the porch is less engaging: on the side piers, below the tympanum are the much eroded figures of Saint Peter and Saint Paul. On the east wall of the porch, contained within twin arches, are two scenes showing the temptation of Christ. In the right-hand scene Christ is seen rejecting the temptation of a peculiarly repulsive devil to throw himself off a high romanesque tower. Christ's controposto pose is another stylistic mannerism frequently found in this

Toulouse school of sculpture. In the left hand scene two skeletal devils offer Christ the whole world if he will worship Satan.

On the opposite wall is Daniel in the lions' den and a very badly eroded scene alleged to show Habakuk, carried by an angel, taking food to Daniel. Above the angel, the holy city of Jerusalem is represented by three arches, the centre one containing a staring face, surmounted by three bell towers.

By the time I had finished looking at the south porch, it was midday; it was also getting very hot, so I bought myself some *jambon de pays*, tomatoes and fruit and ambled down to the riverside. Near the Chapelle des Pénitents, I found a shady spot under some chestnut trees and sat there happily eating my picnic and watching the wagtails flicking to and fro over the surface of the stream.

Back at the abbey I went first to the west end but found it ruined by an ugly fourteenth-century tower built at the south-west corner and masking much of the right-hand side of the façade. The crossing tower was also a disappointment: it consists of of a squat, square base, surmounted by a single storey octagonal stage, covered by a pointed, tiled roof, and is much too small for the size of the building.

I was re-assured when I reached the east end and found once more the satisfying combination of curves created by the apse and its radiating chapels. Inside, too, it was the east end that immediately caught my eye: I could see, framing the choir, the curved arcade of the ambulatory and above the semi-dome of the apse, illuminated by four large windows through which light poured down on to the altar.

The beauty of the sculpture of the south porch had whetted my appetite for the carved capitals of the arcade and choir, but disappointingly, most of them had dull geometrical designs and those that were decorated with fabulous beasts were indifferently executed. But I was recompensed by the exciting discovery of two archaic pieces of sculpture that must have belonged to the original building and been re-used when the abbey was rebuilt.

They are carved on single slabs of stone, roughly blocked into the shape of a flattened triangle, and must originally have been the lintels of narrow doorways in the earlier building.

One of them, embedded in the east wall of the south transept depicts the crudely carved figure of a man holding a club in his right hand and the halter of a large, snarling beast in his left. A similar beast is devouring what looks like a dog on his right. These monstrous animals have been identified as lions but I think they could just as well be bears. In the Middle Ages bears were common in the nearby mountains and taming them for bear-baiting or dancing was one way of earning a living in those hard times. This practice continued until the early years of the twentieth century in the Pyrenees and less than a hundred years ago, dancing bears from the Ariège could be seen in the streets of English towns.

The second lintel is in the north wall of the last bay of the nave before the crossing and shows Daniel sitting between two lions. Crude they may be but these carvings have a certain rude vigour and, of couse, they are amongst the earliest romanesque sculpture to be found in France.

By now I has seen enough; I left the abbey and made my way back to the hotel, stopping on my way at the *Syndicat d'Initiative*, where I discovered that there was a bus to Argentat following day at the early hour of 6.45 a.m.

I was up *de bonne heure* the next morning and reached the Place de Champs de Mars in good time to catch the bus, but at 6.45 there was no sign of it. The timetable at the *Syndicat d'Initiative* showed that there was another bus at 7.30 a.m., so I decided to have a cup of tea and come back, but at the appointed hour still no bus. I had now been joined by a young Dutch couple who were hoping to make a day trip to Argentat. Together we waited until 8 a.m. but when nothing came I went into the nearest hotel and asked if they knew what had happened to the bus. Monsieur *le patron* looked at the timetable and said the time had been changed to 8.30 a.m., so I decided to have breakfast at the hotel and chose a table by the window from which I could survey the square, but at 8.30 a.m. no bus came.

Back in the Place de Champs de Mars I noticed a mini-bus with a notice in the windscreen saying Beaulieu-Argentat. It had a telephone number on the side and when at 9 a.m. neither bus nor driver had appeared I asked the Dutch couple to guard my rucksack and went round the corner to telephone the bus company.

The 'phone was answered by a lady. I explained our dilemma and she confirmed that the bus was running and said that I must have missed it. I countered that this was impossible, I had been in the square the whole time and if there had been a bus I would have seen it. She said the bus must certainly be there by now and that I should go back to the square.

I went back to the Place de Champs de Mars. No bus.

Furious, I telephoned again and went on the attack. Summoning up all my reserves, I told her in my fractured French that it was up to her to do something. She was extremely offhand:

Qu'est ce que vous voulez que je fasse?

Je ne sais pas, Madame, mais c'est à vous . . . . c'est votre problème. Vous avez affiché l'horaire, et il vous faut faire quelque chose.

I went back to the Place de Champs de Mars. We waited for another half-an-hour and then the Dutch girl, who also spoke a little French, went off to telephone. She soon returned saying that a driver was on his way.

At 9.50 a.m. a young man arrived by car and made for the mini-bus. We rushed over to him, thinking that we were on our way at last but he explained that he had to go to Bretenoux first but he promised faithfully to return at one o'clock and take us to Argentat. At this the Dutch couple groaned and gave up. I continued talking to the driver, trying to find out what had happened to the scheduled service. I could not understand his local accent very well but as far as I could gather he was not the regular driver. I think he was the son of the woman I had spoken to on the 'phone who was on holiday and had agreed to make the run to Argentat because there was no-one else. What had happened to the regular driver I could not discover. I felt I could trust this man and agreed to meet him in the Place de Champs de Mars at one o'clock. He offered to look after my rucksack for me and put it in the boot of his car. As he drove off I realised I had done a rather stupid thing and quickly took a note of his car number – just in case.

So I had three hours to kill.

I went back to the abbey and took up the offer of a free guided tour of the church. A nice young man showed me round: he was a biology student but interested in art and was acting as a guide in his holidays. We got on well and I was glad I had taken the tour because although he was unable to tell me much that was new about the church, he did show me the chapter house, which is not usually open to the public, and the treasure. I had a good look at the famous silver virgin. In many ways it is similar to Notre-Dame de Cornadore that I had seen at St-Nectaire.

The pose is almost identical: the virgin seated, holding the infant Jesus on her knees, but here, instead of large hands encircling the child, the virgin's right hand is cupped; originally she held a pearl between her thumb and first finger, symbol of her purity. But the chief difference between the two pieces of sculpture is that whereas Notre-Dame de Cornadore is made entirely of wood, the Beaulieu virgin is wood covered with beaten silver. The craftsmanship of the silver virgin is superb with great subtlety in the treatment of details like the folds of the virgin's wimple and cloak and the modelling of her features and those of the infant Jesus is very fine.

At one o'clock I was back in the Place de Champs de Mars, full of apprehension, but bang on time the driver appeared and to my surprise we set off for Argentat, not in the mini-bus but in his car, for which he charged the standard fare of twenty francs.

The road ran along the right bank of the Dordogne, with occasional tantalising views of the river, although most of the time it was hidden by trees. Small fields of maize alternated with meadows and at the river's edge there were many campsites, some of them very extensive indeed.

It took only twenty minutes to reach Argentat and we went straight to my hotel. After Le Turenne it was a bit of a come down. It struck me as a typical commercial travellers' hotel, everything worked but the stair-carpet was very worn, the varnish on the doors was blistered and in the room there was the inevitable faded, olive-green candlewick bedspread. The shabbiness was accentuated by the shards of a broken ashtray on the floor so having telephoned Monsieur *le patron* and asked him to get the mess cleared up I left my rucksack and went out to explore.

I quickly found my way to the bridge over the Dordogne and looked down at the famous view of the quay with its beautiful old houses. They are not very big, two storeys most of them, with the living quarters on the first floor; the ground floor, originally reserved for animals and stores, now occupied by cafés and bars or turned into garages; but what makes them so attractive are the first-floor wooden balconies and the steep roofs with their heavy brown tiles, rough-hewn from the local schist and quartz, called *lauzes*. These roofs, which are incredibly heavy, are held up by beautifully carpentered chestnut frames.

The cobbled quay was almost empty, except for a few tourists sitting at café tables or staring at the large wrought-iron sundial embedded in the hard and looking like a piece of modern sculpture. I couldn't help reflecting how different the scene would have looked a hundred years ago, the quay piled high with merchandise, the sound of waggon wheels rumbling over the cobbles and the shouts of the drivers mingling with the noise of boatbuilders' hammers and saws; children running in and out between the boats and woodstacks and women leaning on the balconies chatting and keeping an eye on the animated spectacle below.

The river, so tranquil now as it flowed gently under the bridge, would have been full of boats, for in those days, before the coming of the railways destroyed its way of life, Argentat was a thriving port, famous for the skill of its watermen. Twice a year they made the difficult journey downstream to Libourne, carrying cargoes of local cheese, fruit and honey, coal from a nearby mine and, from the great forests of the Corrèze, chestnut poles to stake out the vineyards of Bordeaux and oak staves for the coopers of the wine châteaux to make their barrels. The voyage was made by *gabare*, a large wooden craft, that looked like a huge punt or lighter, built on the quay at Argentat and at one or two smaller ports upstream. Up to sixty feet in length, thirteen feet wide and with a three-foot freeboard, the *gabare* was flat-bottomed with a wide rounded bow and a high counter stern on which stood the helmsman, clasping a huge steering oar the size of a small telegraph pole.

The Dordogne is not a deep river and this perilous jouney was only possible in the spring, after the snow in the mountains had melted, and following the first autumn rains. Once the river had risen it flowed very swifly and as there are many rapids between Argentat and Lalinde the voyage was extremely dangerous. The crew of the *gabare* relied on the speed of the current to propel their craft downstream and a great deal depended on the skill and experience of the helmsman. He was chosen for his unrivalled knowledge of the Dordogne and its hazards, based on the many previous voyages he had made and on a careful study of the river's most difficult passages when the waters were low. The unwieldy *gabare* responded only slowly to the helm, so it was up to the helmsman to anticipate the twists and turns of the river a long way ahead and set his course accordingly. Not an easy task in the blinding spray. To help him there were two men in the bows with long oars which were used to help pull the bow round; beyond them at the stem stood the *gaffeur*, a man with a long boathook which he used to try and fend off the boat's head from the rocks as they passed through the rapids. Sometimes the pole became stuck, tossing the *gaffeur* into the flood; the *gabare* could not stop and the wretched man was left to make his own way home. Often the *gabares* were dashed against the rocks and capsized or smashed to pieces. They usually travelled in convoys of up to ten craft and if one of them was wrecked the others would stop to recover the cargo, which, unlike the crew was not expendable. The whole voyage lasted six days, the *gabare* tying up each night at a different port on the way. Once the cargo had been discharged the *gabare* was broken up and the crew began the long trek home on foot.

At the height of this trade some three hundred vessels made this hazardous journey each year, now the only *gabares* to be seen are used to take tourists on pleasure cruises; they are driven by outboard motors and although the massive steering oar still extends over the stern its purpose is now purely decorative.

Behind the houses on the quay are larger dwellings with similar roofs, some of them having round towers with pepper pot roofs, stretching up the hillside and there are more of them on the opposite side of the river. Leaving the bridge, I went down to the quay and sat at one of the cafés drinking beer and admiring the view. The beer was rather strong and after a couple of pints I felt very sleepy and went back to the hotel for a siesta.

That evening, I was passing through the bar when I heard someone asking Monsieur *le patron* if he knew the test score. I had been listening to the cricket on the World Service so I was able to tell him. His name was Derek Arthur, he worked at a Nuclear Power Station and was looking forward to retirement. He was on holiday with a younger friend, Roger Perkins, and both of them were amateur lepidopterists and were looking for rare butterflies with the object of taking home eggs or live specimens for breeding. We had a drink together and I racked my brain to recall butterfly events in my life. I remembered a rare black-winged specimen Sybil and I had seen near Lescun in the Pyrenees that is only found in these mountains and another occasion when we were picnicking in the forest of the Landes and suddenly found ourselves surrounded by a swarm of newly-hatched dark orange butterflies. Roger and Arthur had been staying at Mauriac and had climbed the Puy de Sancy. They said that the Vallée de Chaudefour was good for butterflies but the best place, apparently, is Provence in the spring. Every so often, Roger, who was a very intense young man, would leap up to examine the walls of the courtyard where we were sitting or peer at the light bulbs in the wisteria that festooned them, looking for moths. He was still at it when I went to bed at half past eleven.

CHAPTER 4

BACKWARDS TO BEAULIEU

By ten o'clock the next morning I was on my way to the Barrage de Chastang, about seven miles north of Argentat. To begin with I followed a path along the left bank of the river with a good view of the quay opposite but soon this joined a small white road that continued alongside the Dordogne, although at first the river was mostly hidden by trees. After about ten minutes I reached the Barrage d'Argentat. The smallest and least impressive of the five dams of the Dordogne gorges, it is only 114 feet in height and 620 feet wide. Behind it there was a pretty lake, its placid surface, criss-crossed by the gaily coloured sails of wind surfers, reflecting the twin towers of the Château du Gibanel. Here I was lucky enough to hitch a lift from a holiday couple who turned out to come from St Sylvestre, not far from our house at Villeneuve-sur-Lot. Twenty minutes later I was at the dam.

The Barrage de Chastang is altogether a grander affair than the Barrage d'Argentat. Although not as big as the Barrage de Bort it produces more energy, 520 millions of kilowatts a year. Like Bort it is shaped like a shallow horseshoe with two vast chutes on the downstream face. Its height is 278 feet and it is 980 feet wide. A road runs across the top and I made my way to the middle of it. The lake behind seems small and quickly disappears from sight into the hills but looking downstream over the cliff-like face of the dam itself the view is much more exciting as the Dordogne plunges into a narrow gorge and is lost to sight behind the overlapping shoulders of the steep, tree-lined cliffs.

Now it was time to resume my walk down the Dordogne. The way down from the dam was steep and twisting; suddenly, at a turn in the

The Dordogne:

from the Puy de Sancy to Limeuil

Map 2

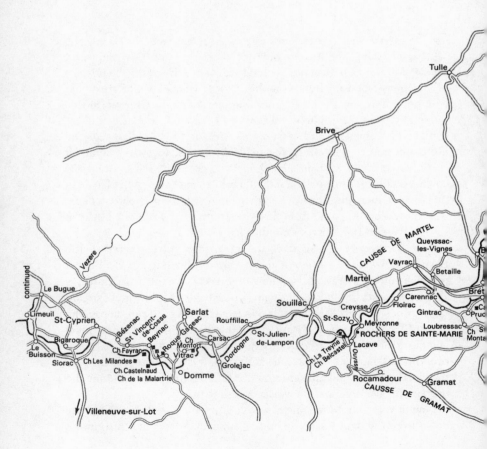

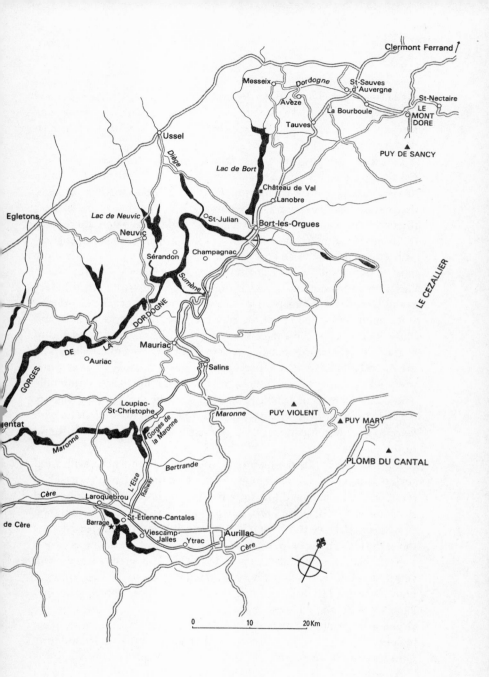

Clermont Ferrand

Messeix
Dordogne
St-Sauves
d'Auvergne
St-Nectaire
Avèze
La Bourboule
LE
MONT
DORE
Tauves
PUY DE SANCY
Ussel
Diège
Lac de Bort
Château de Val
Lanobre
Egletons
Lac de Neuvic
St-Julian
Bort-les-Orgues
Neuvic
Sérandon
Champagnac
LE CEZALLIER
Sumène
DORDOGNE
LA
Mauriac
DE
Auriac
Salins
GORGES
Loupiac-
St-Christophe
Maronne
PUY VIOLENT
PUY MARY
entat
Maronne
Gorges de
la Maronne
Bertrande
PLOMB DU CANTAL
L'Etze
Railway
Cère
Laroquebrou
St-Étienne-Cantales
de Cère
Barrage
Viescamp-
Jalles
Ytrac
Aurillac
Cère

0   10   20 Km

road I found myself confronted by the great cliff wall of the *barrage*. I was looking at the dam from a vantage point, about a third of the way down its face and viewed from here, it was even more impressive than when seen from above.

Down at the bottom of the *barrage* the road ran level with the Dordogne on its right and a steep, tree-covered slope on the left. It was a lovely morning and I was enjoying the walk. The sun was not yet high, there was a little breeze and I was carrying only my light day-pack. After fifteen minutes or so I reached a hamlet called Glény where there were the ruins of a romanesque church. All that remained was the chancel with a bell gable above and the semi-circular apse at the east end; of the nave nothing was to be seen but a few large stones. Nearby was a handsome, restored mill-house by the side of a little stream, a tributary of the Dordogne. Glény perhaps marks the point where the Dordogne stops being a mountain river for here there are wide, grassy banks and immediately below the village there was a broad reach with a stand of poplars on the opposite bank, a tree never found in the mountains. The high wooded hills were still there, of course, but the valley was growing wider all the time. I passed through another hamlet called Graffeuille where there was a small château on a hill. Despite the changing scenery the houses here, as in Glény, were still built of undressed stone with *lauze* roofs; there was no sign yet of the roman tiles universally found further south.

Beyond Graffeuille the Dordogne widened out into a lake with wind surfers and conoeists from a huge campsite on the far bank. It stretched for about half a mile and the noise from it was horrific, a cacophany of shrieking children, motor horns and barking dogs. I hurried on and soon came to the Barrage d'Argentat beyond which I could already see the the top of the church tower in Argentat itself. Just below the dam was Croisy a pretty hamlet with *lauze* roofs. The houses had small gardens with vegetable plots, surrounded by flowers: pinks, dahlias, roses and tiger lilies. It seemed a clear sign that the Dordogne was entering warmer climes. Quite soon I came back to the path that lead down to the riverside, opposite the quay. Here I found a bench and sat down to eat my picnic lunch. The time was 1.10 and I had taken two hours and forty minutes to walk seven miles.

After lunch I crossed the bridge and went down to the quay where I

86

hired a canoe, or rather a kayak, for next day, having previously established that the hire firm would take my pack on ahead of me by road to Le Turenne at Beaulieu. A trip by canoe would make a pleasant change from back-packing and it would be interesting to see what the river looked like from the middle. It would give my toe more time to heal. The kayak booked I retuned to my hotel for a well earned siesta.

Picture my feelings the next morning when I looked out of my window and saw that the sky was overcast. After the seemingly endless days of sun this summer, it was difficult to believe. At breakfast I asked Madame if she knew the forecast. She said it would be *pertubé* for the next three days, with perhaps some rain and cooler than of late, a summary that had a familiar ring to it. I consoled myself with the thought that at least I need not worry about getting sunstroke on the water.

By 8.30 a.m. I was at the riverside looking doubtfully at a slim, black, cigar-shaped, fibre-glass kayak. I handed over my rucksack to the hirer who in return gave me a small waterproof bag into which I put my picnic and oilskin jacket. Now came the moment I had been dreading. The kayak is a very unstable vessel until you are actually sitting in it and easily capsized in the act of getting aboard. I had, in fact, done some canoeing before but this was over thirty years ago and then it was a canvas double canoe with a much larger cockpit that was easier to get in and out of than the kayak, which is derived from the Eskimo, or should I say Inuit, canoe and has a very small central cockpit. Eyeing it I was dubious that I would fit in. Many years ago I used to row for my college, Birkbeck, and this has inevitably led to some thickening in the region of the hips, which combined with a certain lack of suppleness made me wary. However, I had paid my 100 francs hire fee and the moment had come. The boatman made life easier for me by letting me struggle into the cockpit on dry land, then he pushed the kayak, with me in it, into the water: the frail craft rocked violently and I held my breath, then it settled down. I was afloat.

Gently I glided by the quay, breaking the perfect reflection of the balconied houses with their *lauze* roofs, and drifted under the bridge. Gingerly I essayed my first strokes with the double paddle. I had chosen a kayak instead of a canadian canoe because it has a double paddle, that is to say a paddle with a blade at each end, whereas the canadian canoe is propelled by a single paddle which is used as a rudder as well. I had imagined that the double paddle, used now on one side and now on the other, would be easier to handle. Alas, I soon found that keeping the kayak on course was no easy matter: as soon as I stopped paddling the kayak spun rapidly to one side or the other and I found myself proceeding down the Dordogne backwards! I pride myself that I am a good waterman, otherwise I would never have embarked on this trip. I have tackled most kinds of craft in my time from sailing yachts to punts, so I was somewhat peeved that I couldn't control my kayak. I tried everything: first I paddled very fast. This certainly kept the kayak on course but it quickly exhausted me and as soon as I stopped the canoe spun round even faster than before rocking violently as it did so and putting the fear of God into me in case I capsized. Then I tried paddling very gently and this worked better, but was very slow. The best of all was to stop paddling altogether and to drift with the current but progress was even slower. Still I wasn't too worried, there was plenty of time and I felt sure I would get the hang of it eventually.

Downstream from the bridge was a long, beautiful stretch where the Dordogne ran straight for about a mile between low wooded hills. Tiny white flowers flecked the gently undulating waterweed and swallows dipped and fluttered over the surface of the smoothly-flowing stream. It was an idyllic scene and I felt very contented as I part drifted, part paddled, often in reverse, towards the first bend. As I approached closer I heard a low murmuring noise that sounded vaguely familiar and when I turned the corner I saw ahead, what my brain had just that moment identified: WHITE WATER!

It was a nasty shock. I had never expected to encounter rapids on this stretch of the Dordogne and was mentally quite unprepared to negotiate this one. As the kayak neared the angry-looking overfalls there was precious little time to assess the situation. The main thing was not to go though them backwards, so I stopped paddling and concentrated on steering a straight course. I aimed the bow at the centre of the river where there was no white water, although the surface was still covered with nasty little choppy wavelets. Suddenly I was in the middle of them and they were slapping the sides of the kayak and breaking over the bow;

but the canoe swept through as buoyant as a cork and in a moment I was in smooth water and could draw breath once more.

Somewhat shaken, I paddled warily on all senses alert for the next indications of a rapid. This time I saw it all too soon: huge boulders littered the banks and stretched into the river, framing the entrance to a gloomy gorge. Under the trees on the right I glimpsed a campsite, some of whose inmates were fishing precariously from the rocks. Poking out of the river were more rocks, each with a narrow necklace of foam at its throat. The only way through was a little to the right of middle where the stream swirled through a narrow channel, curving over a shallow ledge into an agitated pool. I didn't like what I saw but I had no choice so I made for the gap. As the kayak surged fowards, I had the horrible feeling that the rocks were rushing *towards* me and that the foaming waves at their base were teeth waiting to devour their prey. It was the reverse of the sensation one has in a stationary train when another passes that yours is the one that is moving. As it swept into the overfalls, black waves attacked the kayak from all angles, slapping against the sides, and one broke over the bows and dumped itself into the cockpit. I lost control and the canoe was knocked broadside to the stream; it rocked violently and for a moment I thought it was going to capsize. As it slipped over the ledge I glimpsed a look of horror in the eyes of one of the fishermen on the rocks, then I was in the pool below, still the right way up and drifting out of danger. I realised that I had been holding my breath and expelled it in a long relieved gasp.

I didn't know it at the time but the rapid I had just negotiated is called Le Malpas, a name which certainly does it justice. I found this out when I subsequently bought a canoeist's guide to the Dordogne which has maps of sections of the river and descriptions of the hazards. Le Malpas has a danger symbol against it and the following entry

'. . . difficultés techniques, en particulier contre-courants, remous tourbillonnants, violents par niveau d'eau moyen ou élevé . . . en cas de technique insuffisante le portage est recommendé.'

Le Malpas certainly increased my admiration for *les gabariers*. After all, the water level was low in this dry summer and the speed of the current was not great. Even so, Le Malpas had given me a fright.

What must it have looked like in the days before the dams were built and when the melting snows had changed the Dordogne into a raging torrent?

The kayak had taken in a lot of water and I was sitting in it, so I paddled over to a low pebble spit, projecting from the left-hand bank, and beached. With some difficulty I extricated myself from the cockpit using the paddle as a lever, hauling myself up on it and breaking a large piece off the edge of the blade in the process. The whole of my bottom half was soaking: I was wearing my Rohan trousers but in the waterproof bag I had a spare pair of shorts which I started to put on.

Unfortunately, it was ages since I had last worn them and in the interval my girth had thickened somewhat so that struggle as I might I could not get them past my hips. Cursing I gave up and donned my dripping Rohan bags again. I turned my attention to emptying the canoe. It proved quite difficult, the water slopped about inside and didnt want to come out and it made the craft very heavy. Eventually I succeeded, got back into the cockpit, pushed off with the broken paddle and set damply forth once more.

I was paddling through a deep gorge which shut out the sun and I was quite alone. Occasionally the bank was wide enough for a campsite: I passed a huge one with an outdoor restaurant big enough to seat a hundred, but most of the time I saw no one. Once a canadian canoe came up fast behind me, paddled rhythmically by two strong, determined young men; they quickly passed me and disappeared round the next bend, leaving me alone again.

Alerted by my experience at Le Malpas, my senses were a quiver to detect the next rapid – and there were plenty of them ahead. As soon as I saw the tell-tale signs of white turbulence and heard the accompanying sibilant murmur, I slowed down to reconnoitre, making sure I was not going backwards at the time. Approaching tentatively, I scanned the river, looking for a passage. It was not that easy for the kayak sits very low on the water and by the time I was close enough to get a clear view I was in imminent danger of being swept into the rapid. Often I had to paddle furiously as I backed away from the brink. The first things I looked for were thick patches of weed; it only grows in slow moving water and is a sure sign that the going there is easier. At the same time I took care to avoid the rafts of floating branches which could easily have capsized my canoe; underwater the branches collect a mesh of weeds and grasses which can be very dangerous to anyone struggling in the water. I also knew that the river flows much faster round the outside of the bend than the inside and of course there are sometimes counter-currents and backwaters where the stream is slack. All these factors had to be quickly assessed before choosing my course.

And so I negotiated rapid after rapid, none of them as difficult as Le Malpas, thank God. Once I came upon a long island. The Dordogne poured through a narrow channel full of white water on the left-hand side but on the right was a tree-covered backwater where there were no overfalls, although I had to be careful not get caught in the overhanging branches. By midday I was feeling tired and hungry so I started looking for somewhere to beach the kayak. It was then that I found myself facing another very difficult stretch of white water. I skirted the edge searching for an easy way through but could not find one; in the end I decided there was nothing for it but to have a go. I managed to avoid the worst of the overfalls but just when I thought I was safe the kayak spun round and started to go backwards down the river – not a nice feeling. Luckily I was swept into a back-eddy, turned the right way round and saw ahead of me another pebble bank. Thankfully I made for it and beached the canoe.

I was terribly tired and scarcely had the strength to drag myself out of the canoe but somehow I managed it and dragged the the canoe up the bank. I stood there shivering; my trousers were soaking and I felt very cold and miserable. Then I remembered that I had brought my lightweight waterproof with me so I took off my life-jacket and trousers and put the waterproof on. I soon felt warmer and after I had eaten some melon, *jambon de pays*, squashed peaches and chocolate and drunk some Volvic I felt even better.

After half-an-hour's rest I donned my trousers again and set off once more. Round the next bend things looked altogether better. The hillside was no longer covered with an unbroken screen of trees, there were watermeadows and high up to the left was a small château. But the river gods were not yet finished with me. Ahead was a beautiful reach with an island in the middle of it. Tall trees were reflected in the calm waters and the whole scene was idyllic. But as I got closer I heard the familiar roaring noise to which by then my ears were well attuned. The main channel was to the left but here there was a nasty obstacle in the shape of a concrete weir over which the river cascaded to surge through a narrow channel until it reached the further end of the island. I skirted the edge of the weir looking for an alternative route but the more I looked, the less I liked what I saw. Once I went too near the edge, the current caught me and I had to paddle fiercely to stop myself being swept over backwards.

The right-hand channel was very overgrown and it was impossible to guess what I might find if I went that way, although looking down the left-hand channel it appeared that there was white water at the far end of the island coming from the right. Still the weir was too dangerous to attempt, I would have to take a chance on the right-hand side of the island. I worked my way under the overhanging boughs. The river was very shallow here and in places I scraped the bottom. About a hundred yards further on there was a rapid but nothing serious. I slipped over a shallow ledge and, still under a pergola of interlaced boughs, was squirted down a narrow channel, whose waters danced with small harmless waves, until I reached the end of the island, where I shot out into a seething froth of white wavelets like a cork from a champagne bottle. Luckily this rapid was less dangerous than it looked and the kayak quickly spun into safe waters.

This was the last of my river adventures: ahead lay a serene stretch of the Dordogne leading up to Beaulieu and soon I could see on the right bank the Chapelle des Pénitents. I reached the landing stage alongside the chapel at four o'clock. After so many hours I could scarcely drag myself out of the cockpit. Somehow I managed to pull the kayak up the bank and hand over my gear to the boatman then, soaking wet, I squelched through the narrow streets of Beaulieu, past the abbey, to Le Turenne, where I presented myself damply at the reception desk. To her credit Madame Déglise showed not the slightest surprise at my disreputable appearance and confirmed with a smile that they had given me the same room as before. I asked whether my rucksack had arrived.

'*Quel sac, Monsieur?*'

I explained the arrangement I had made with the boatman at Argentat but to my dismay the pack had not been delivered. Madame was marvellous; she asked the name of the hire firm and luckily I had one of their leaflets, giving their telephone number, in my wallet. Madame said to leave it to her, she would deal with the matter and I went to my room.

I stripped and showered and hung up my clothes to dry; then, as I had nothing to change into, I had no option but to go to bed. I lay there thinking about life and wondering what I would do if my pack were lost forever. Then, after an anxious hour there came a knock at the door. At my call of *entrez*, a young man came into the room, staggering under the weight of my rucksack and dumped it on the floor. The news of relief of Mafeking was not received with more joy.

That evening I treated myself to another slap-up dinner:

> Gâteau de cèpes à la coriandre
> Emincé de canard aux deux fruits
> Fromage
> Assiette gourmande de quatre desserts.

The *gâteau de cèpes* was a kind of quiche and a little disappointing, since the flavour of *cèpes* was not very strong. The main course I liked very much, finely sliced duck's breast with *cassis* berries, slices of apple and sautée potatoes, but the highlight was the pudding. A raspberry tartlet, a slice of *tarte aux pommes* made with flaky pastry, a slice of chocolate mousse and one of coffee mousse made up the four desserts but as well as these there was a raspberry sorbet in the middle of the plate and a little choux pastry crescent containing *orange moulée*, the whole delicious concoction carefully finished off with a topping of *crème anglaise*.

It certainly made up for the day's travails.

CHAPTER 5

INTO THE CAUSSE

I was sad to book out of Le Turenne next morning. Everyone had been very kind to me, the food was excellent and altogether I had been very comfortable there. Indeed I had enjoyed all the time I had spent at Beaulieu and was sorry to be moving on. My next destination was Bretenoux, a mere five miles to the south. The road was dead straight, slightly undulating and shaded by plane trees. I soon noticed how much the country had changed since I left Argentat: I was walking through a wide valley with high wooded hills on my left and fields to the right with another line of hills two or three miles away in the distance. The Dordogne was hidden somewhere the other side of the hill on my left. The farmhouses here were built of grey/white limestone and had red, flat-tiled roofs, although these were still steeply pitched; but the main difference was the large fields of maize, of very good quality so far as I could judge, which was obviously an important cash crop here. There were some cattle but not in the same numbers that I had seen in the mountains.

After walking for about an hour, I came to a large marker stone: the top was painted yellow with D940 picked out in black on it. Below, a vertical line divided the face into two halves, on the right were the letters CZE, standing for Corrèze, and below the word TULLE; on the left I read LOT and below FIGEAC. Emphasising this change from one *département* to another, the line of plane trees bordering the road disappeared, leaving a shadeless vista stretching into the distance, all the way to Bretenoux.

Soon afterwards I came to Biars, an ugly railway halt with one long

97

road bisected by a level crossing. Here a queue of cars was held up waiting while a rusty goods train went clanking through. Biars is less than a mile from Bretenoux, which I reached twenty minutes later. I soon found my hotel at the beginning of the town, where the *route nationale* swings left and crosses the Cère, the same beautiful river I had last seen from the train on my way down from Aurillac. I was given a pleasant room overlooking the Cère and, as there was still an hour or so to go before lunch, I went to look round the town.

For a while I lingered on the bridge looking at the Cère. Up-river on the east side there were people swimming, or rather splashing about, the water level being very low in this hot dry summer. Beyond them was a wooded island, sheltering a small municipal campsite. Downriver was a grassy picnic site and some fishermen. Beyond the bridge, on either side of the *route nationale* was a short stretch of shops and cafes. I was wandering idly along, looking in shop windows, when I saw, down a street to the right, brightly-coloured umbrellas, trestle tables and a gaggle of people – a market.

I have never been able to resist French country markets with their cornucopias of local produce and the one at Bretenoux looked very inviting. I was not disappointed: boxes of glistening ruby-red straw-berries; ripe charentais melons, some cut open to reveal their sweet-smelling orange flesh; huge, mis-shapen tomatoes, tasting so different from the acid snooker balls we are accustomed to; every variety of lettuce, frizzy, round, oak leaf and, of course, *pissenlit* (dandelion) to add astringency to your *salade*, and everything picked freshly this morning.

The market at Bretenoux reflects the town's geographical position, close to the junction of the Cère and the Dordogne and on the frontier where the crystalline rock of the *massif central* meets the limestone country of the Lot; its prosperity has always been based on trade between the mountain people and the lowland farmers. So, alongside the mouthwatering fruit and fresh vegetables there were Laguiole and Cantal cheeses from the Aurillac region and dark, perfumed honey from the uplands. The temptation to buy something was irresistible and I chose some luscious white peaches. One of the disadavantages of travelling on foot is that there is a limit to what you can carry, otherwise I would not have been so restrained in my purchases.

By now it was midday and the stall-holders were beginning to pack up, so I went to lunch. When I retuned to the Place des Consuls an hour or so later all the stalls had gone and I was able to take a good look at the square and the surrounding buildings. Immediately I saw, what the market had obscured, that Bretenoux is a *bastide* town, another sign that I was in different country. *Bastides* were new towns and in the late twelfth and thirteenth-century a large number of them were built in south-west France. Most of them were constructed according to a common plan and are easily recognised by their distinctive grid pattern of streets and their central squares, surrounded by arcades, usually with heavy stone pointed arches. There is often a covered market in the square with a tiled roof, supported by wooden posts or stone piers and the town church is nearly always to be found at one corner of the main square.

Many *bastides* were royal towns, founded by the kings of England or France in partnership (*pareage*) with a local lord or prelate; others were created by great nobles like the Count of Quercy. The aim seems on the one hand to have been to establish local communities who would owe their allegiance to their founder and thus maintain his presence in the region: this was particularly important in disputed territories like the Quercy which, during the Hundred Years War, was constantly fought over by the English and the French. On the other hand, these new towns also encouraged trade which resulted in greater prosperity and increased revenue in the form of taxes for their founders.

Bretenoux was founded by a powerful local lord, Guérin de Castenau, in 1277 under the name of Villefranca de Orlanda.

The Place des Consuls has survived almost intact although most of the buildings seem to date from the fifteenth rather than the thirteenth century. Tucked into the north-west corner is the Hôtel de Ville, a modest building with two wings, covered by red tiled hipped roofs, not unlike a mansard roof although they are known locally as Périgordine roofs, presumably because they originate in Périgord, the old name for the Dordogne, just north of the Lot; they are certainly common there. Between the wings is a small *cour d'honneur*, entered by a classical renaissance gateway. At the back of the courtyard is a tall stone tower flanked on its south-west corner by a brick turret. It looked to me as though the tower dated from the fourteenth century and the wings and entrance gate were added later at the end of the sixteenth century.

Across the cobbled square on the south-west side are some attractive half timbered dwellings over arcades, although here there are stone piers rather than pointed arches. The middle house has a hipped Périgordine roof with two little dormer windows peeping out. On the east side are two old houses, over round stone arches and opposite them in the south-west corner of the square another pretty house with a first-floor wooden balcony.

In the middle of the Place des Consuls is a blocked-up well, surmounted by pots of geraniums and a wrought-iron cross and on the east side two brutally-pollarded plane trees with busy lizzies growing at their feet. On the west side a pointed stone arch leads out to the river bank just opposite the island campsite. At the back of the square was the familiar grid pattern of streets with some nice stone houses and little gardens full of flowers and beyond them, on the southern outskirts of the town, I discovered a short stretch of the original ramparts. I liked Bretenoux; true it was all on a very small scale but it had kept much of its original character and yet was still quite lively, no doubt due to the proximity of the *route nationale*.

That night I was kept awake by a rock band thumping away somewhere on the island. An indefatigable traveller would have got up and gone to investigate but I had discovered that I was only too 'fatigable', so I lay there seething until eventually I dropped off.

My reason for coming to Bretenoux was to visit one of the most famous castles in the region which I had long wished to see: the Château de Castelnau. So, after shopping for a picnic, I set off at 7.55 down a country road leading south-westwards from Bretenoux to the village of Prud-homat, about two miles away.

It was a beautiful morning, already sunny but with a slight freshness in the air as an old gentleman, watering his flowers, and I agreed. I was walking down the valley of the Cère, although the river soon vanished from sight behind some trees, with a high hill on my left and farmland to the right, bounded by more distant hills, probably on the far side of the Dordogne. Soon the château loomed into sight on the left-hand hill. It is built of red sandstone and completely dominates the landcape. Pierre Loti, the author of *Pecheur d'Islande*, who spent much of his childhood at Bretenoux, wrote of it:

A plus d'une lieue à la ronde, c'est le point marquant . . . la chose qu'on regarde malgré soi de partout; cette dentelure de pierres de couleur sanguine, émergeant d'un fouillis d'arbres, cette ruine posée encouronne sur un piédestal garni d'une belle verdure de châtaigniers et de chênes.

It sounds as though Loti is remembering the castle as it was before 1896 when an extensive programme of restoration was begun and when Castelnau must have looked much more romantic than it does today. Even so I was very impressed.

It took only half an hour to reach Prudhomat, where I found a steep road leading up to the château; fifteen minutes later I was at the castle gates. There was still a quarter of an hour to go before the first guided tour of the inside of the château, so I wandered round the outside on a wide, grassy terrace that was once a defensive ditch until it was filled in at the time of the revolution. The castle stands on a rocky spur commanding the river valleys of the Dordogne, the Bave and the Cère, on the borders of the Quercy, Périgord, the Auvergne and the Limousin, a position of immense strategic importance in the Middle Ages and one that offers wonderful views in all directions. To the south west is the serene valley of the Bave, an arcadian landscape of green pastures, slow-moving cattle, small farms, poplars and walnut trees. On the crest of the ridge, on the far side of the valley, stands the village of Loubressac, looking very like a hill village in Tuscany; further south, up the valley, the square towers of the Château of St-Laurent stand out sharply against the skyline. To the north, just below the walls, I could see another lush valley and the road along which I had walked that morning; beyond that a stretch of the Dordogne above Bretenoux and in the distance, just discernable above the trees, the tower of Beaulieu abbey. Far away to the north west the sun lit up a line of cliffs where the unseen Dordogne cut its way through the limestone plateau that starts just to the west of Bretenoux. I was admiring this magnificent panorama when I saw a French couple taking photographs of each other and asked the man if he would take one of me, which he did. We chatted amiably for a while, sharing our enthusiasm for what we were seeing until a bell rang announcing that the tour had begun.

The first mention of Castelnau is in a document dating from the eleventh century, but this early castle was taken and sacked by the English and no trace of it remains. Rebuilding began at the end of the twelfth century and the oldest surviving parts of the castle, the tall keep known as the Saracen's tower and the building next to it called *l'Auditoire*, belong to this period, although the great hall at the top of the *Auditoire*, with its graceful gothic windows, was added in the thirteenth century. It was here that the barons of Quercy held their council meetings. But most of what we see today dates from the fourteenth century when the size of the château was enormously increased and it assumed its present triangular shape. Massive round towers were built at the corners, reinforced by smaller, half-round towers placed at intervals along the intervening ramparts; outside a huge ditch was dug protected by a curtain wall. Originally there was a third outer wall, over a mile in circumference, at the foot of the castle, protecting a whole village. Only a few fragments of this wall survive along with a small church and one or two stone houses. At its apogee this huge fortress was defended by a garrison of no less than 1500 men and stabled a hundred horses.

The suzerains of this small army were the barons of Castelnau, the self-styled 'second barons of Christendom' and one of the most powerful families of the region. Inordinately proud, they claimed to owe allegiance direct to Count Raymond of Toulouse but when this same count made their neighbour, the Viscount of Turenne, their overlord they took up arms rather than submit to this humiliation. Eventually the king himself was drawn into the dispute and forced to arbitrate between the disputants. Louis VIII found in favour of the Viscount of Turenne and ruled that the Barons of Castelnau should make the annual offering of an egg to the Viscounts of Turenne, as a sign of homage. So, each year, with great solemnity, a cart drawn by four bullocks made the jouney from Castelnau to Turenne bearing a single new-laid egg.

The castle remained in the hands of the Castelnau family until the line became extinct in 1493. Subsequently, it passed to the family of Clermont Lodève who added two more buildings and an arcaded gallery to the main block. In the eighteenth century the castle fell into ruin and remained so until it was purchased by Monsieur Jean Moulierat, who had made a fortune singing at the Opéra Comique and now proceeded to spend it restoring Castelnau to its former glory. Just before he died in 1932 he willed the castle to the state.

The entrance to the château was across a stone bridge, replacing the drawbridge destroyed in the French revolution, and through a door in a tower flanked on the right by another huge round bastion that commands the approach. Inside, was a narrow triangular courtyard, a large part of which was filled with temporary seating erected for *son et lumière*, obscuring the view. Even so I could see that the living quarters on the north-east side were in ruins. The courtyard was dominated by the tall Saracen's tower in the south-east corner at the foot of which was the entrance to the south wing restored by Jean Moulierat. The interior came as an agreeable surprise: it is full of fine paintings and antiques collected by Monsieur Moulierat which by now must be worth millions. The cream of the collection is to be found in the vaulted chamber called the *Oratoire* where I saw a superb fifteenth-century Aragonese retable and an exquisite Siennese Madonna and Child, both of which the National Gallery would be proud to possess. There is also a fifteenth-century stained-glass window from the cathedral of Quimper in Brittany. Elsewhere there are tapestries by Aubusson, Louis XIV furniture and a gallery devoted to medieval sculpture, including capitals from the church of St-Croix, in the Entre-Deux-Mers, which was demolished in 1874. It is rare to find such treasures in a French château, most of them having been looted or destroyed in the Revolution.

I was strolling round the ramparts afterwards, marvelling again at the classic landscape when I bumped into the man who had taken my photo. He was full of enthusiasm for what he had seen, particularly the Limoges china, of which he was something of a connoisseur. I told him about my walk down the Dordogne and he asked me where I was going next. I told him I was undecided whether to walk to Loubressac and immediately he offered to take me there in his car; so off we went, with Madame insisting on moving into the back, despite my protests.

We descended into the valley of the Bave and began to climb the opposite hill. Half way up we stopped and got out to look back at Castelnau. The great red hulk brooded over the landcape like a monstrous spider waiting for its prey: it was an awesome sight. Further up to our right we could see Loubressac straggling along the top of the ridge, its château, puny by comparison with Castelnau, perched precariously at the edge of a sheer drop to the valley below. Loubressac reminded me of a Cotswold village. It was built of a similar honey-coloured stone and was full of flowers; every house had its collection of terracotta pots or black-painted cauldrons full of geraniums, busy lizzies or begonias and many had neat little gardens full of roses, marguerites and even hollyhocks. But it soon became obvious that this was no working village: all the houses were owned by elderly retired people or were *maisons secondaires*, and like all such places it is a little too pretty, too well ordered and too full of tourists like myself. We wandered up and down the narrow winding streets, admiring the admittedly beautiful stone houses with their brown tiled roofs, and then made for the eastern outskirts. Passing through a fortified gateway we saw before us another superb panorama of the Bave valley with châteaux of Castelnau and Montal and the towers of St-Laurent all in view.

By now it was getting hot so we made for a café. Over a beer my new friend told me that his name was André Chesne and that he was a guard on the SNCF. Somehow I couldn't imagine a guard on British Railways having the same interests. He told me he was near to retirement and said he couldn't wait for the day when he could devote more time to his study of Majolica and visiting châteaux. Afterwards these kind people drove me back to Bretenoux in good time for lunch.

I ate my picnic sitting under a willow tree just downstream from the bridge. Afterwards, I felt like a siesta but first I went to the *libraire* to buy a book. To my dismay I had already finished my hundred pages of Proust and now had nothing to read. It was too much to expect to find a book in English, other than a dictionary, in a small place like Bretenoux, so I was looking for something in French that was not too taxing. Eventually I bought a novel called *Ramuntcho* by Pierre Loti. There was quite a number of Loti's books in the shop, presumably because of his connection with the town.

I spent the rest of the afternoon in my room, sleeping, reading and listening to the World Service. I quite enjoyed *Ramuntcho*. It is a gripping smuggling yarn set in the mountains of the Pays Basque, with daring excursions across the Pyrenees, loaded with contraband, under the noses of the customs men. There is a rather sentimental love affair but the novel is redeemed by Loti's loving evocation of the mountains and the Basque way of life. What is more, it is a region that I knew slightly for it is set in the region of the pretty basque village of Sarre that Sybil and I had visited only the previous autumn.

It was another superb morning when I set off for Carennac, my next stop seven miles to the west on the left bank of the Dordogne. At first I followed the road to Castelnau and soon there was the great red mass of the château high up on its hill to my left. At Prudhomat I turned right, crossed a small stream and started down a small, white country road. Ahead I could see the hill that Loubressac stands on sweeping in a great curve round to my right. At this stage there was no sign of either the Cère or the Dordogne, although I knew that they were close at hand. I passed a market garden with a large area of strawberries under plastic and further on fields of maize on either hand.

Soon afterwards I had my first glimpse of the Dordogne, at least I assumed it must be the Dordogne for as far as I could see from my map I had already passed the confluence of the Cère and the Dordogne near Prudhomat. White shingle banks extended far into the river leaving only a narrow watercourse in the middle, through which flowed a sluggish stream: it was not a particularly exciting sight. I soon lost sight of the river once more but after passing through a hamlet called Granou, I came to a small bridge crossing the Bave, running strongly in a narrow, stony gully. By now the hill had closed in, so that there was a high cliff wall right ahead, apparently barring the way, but the other side of the bridge I came to a T-junction and turned right.

Despite the weight of my pack, I was enjoying myself, the weather was good, not yet too hot, like a perfect English summer's day and there was very little traffic on the road to worry about. To the left, the high tree-covered cliff continued; on my right the Bave wound its

way through peaceful meadows, sometimes close to the road, sometimes far away and hidden by woods. Where there was enough space
between the road and the river there were small fields of maize or
plantations of walnut trees and all the way along the road the verges
were full of wild flowers.

After I had been walking for about an hour, I reached the junction
of the Bave and the Dordogne. There was a large pebble bar across
the mouth of the Bave, leaving only a small exit channel but beyond it
the Dordogne was wide and fast flowing, although here too the the
river was full of stony banks. On the far side I could see more fields
and woods and far away in the distance a line of hills, the same hills I
had climbed so painfully a week ago on my way to Beaulieu.

At 10.30 I stopped at a hamlet called Gintrac for a beer. After
Gintrac the road was covered by a canopy of trees, masking the river
from view. When it did reappear it was flowing sluggishly through a
narrow channel and the opposite bank was thick with weeping
willows, their long fronds trailing in the muddy stream. I was a bit
surprised by this until I realised that I was looking at a large island,
l'Isle des Escouanes and that the main branch of the river was on the
far side.

Just after 11 a.m. I reached another crossroads. To the right a
bridge crossed the river to Vayrac, ahead the road led up a mercifully short incline to Carennac. I quickly found the Hôstellerie de
Fénelon, a nice old hotel where Sybil and I had stayed once before.
My room was very simple but had a lovely view out over an old tiled
roof and down to the Dordogne below, although here too I was
looking at a minor branch, bounded by the heavily wooded Isle de
Calypso. The island is named in honour of Fénelon (full name
François de Salignac de la Mothe-Fénelon 1651–1715) who was for a
while prior of Carennac and is supposed to have written his *Adventures de Télémaque* on the island. This story, ostensibly concerned
with the adventures of the son of Odysseus, was in fact a critique of
Louis XIV and earned its author banishment from court to
Cambrai, where he spent the rest of his days. Fénelon became prior
of Carennac in 1681 and has left a delightful description of his
reception by the townsfolk when he arrived by water to take up his
post:

'At Cavennac I find a great crowd awaiting me on the quay. Two boats full of the *élite* of the local *bourgeoisie* put out to meet me and, as they do so, I notice that, by an imaginative stratagem, the best trained of the local regiments was hidden away on that beautiful island that you know so well (Isle de Calypso). They advance in battle order and salute me with volleys of musket fire: the air is soon dark with gunpowder smoke and we are deafened by the noise of firing. As my mettlesome steed shows every inclination to toss me into the water I decide that caution is the better part of valour, and dismount. The noise of firing is augmented by a roll of drums as, accompanied by a fleet of small craft, I cross the lovely Dordogne. I am met on the quay by some venerable monks who sing my praises in a highly rhetorical style. I reply in similar vein, but with due modesty. The crowd parts to let me through and every eye scans my face, thinking to read there what lies in store for them. Slowly, with measured tread, so that everyone can have a good look at me, I make my way up to the castle, cheered on by innumerable well-wishers, and up goes the cry, "he will be our pride and joy".'

The dining room of the hotel had windows all down one side giving a pleasant view of a vegetable garden and beyond it the Isle de Calypso. It was just the kind of restaurant that Sybil and I like best of all: black-and-white floor tiles, white linen tablecloths, high-backed rush-bottom chairs, a stone fifteenth-century fireplace at one end, a large bar, faced with roman bricks at the other and a white ceiling with black beams above and, best of all, a satisfying four course lunch for fifty-eight francs.

I had come to Carennac to see another famous romanesque tympanum above the west doorway of the priory church, so after lunch I walked up the hill, passing a bust of Fénelon set in the wall of what remains of the priory on the way. The entrance to the priory, on the corner of the road, is at an angle to the church, which is inside the walls on the far side of a narrow courtyard. This meant that my first glimpse of the tympanum was a tantalising three-quarter view. Once through the arch I crossed the courtyard to the foot of the steps leading up to the porch that contained the sculpture.

When I first saw the tympanum some years ago I was very impressed, but coming to it fresh from Beaulieu I found it dis-appointing. The composition is rather rigid and lacks the dynamism to be found at Beaulieu and Moissac. The design is dominated by the figure of Christ enthroned in majesty contained within a mandorla. His right hand is raised in benediction while his left holds the book of life which rests on his knee. The carving of Christ's head is clumsy with thick lips and a bulbous nose and the modelling of the body has the stiff, hieratic quality of a Byzantine ivory. The mandorla sits within a rectangle with the signs of the evangelists in the corners, rendered with much greater freedom than the Christ figure. The eagle of Saint John with its outspread wings, looking as though it is about to take flight, is especially lively. The rest of the tympanum is divided into four by a horizontal bar which creates two box-like compartments below and two triangular ones above. In the boxes below sit eight apostles, four on either side of the mandorla. They converse amiably but seemingly without much awareness of their lord and master on his throne. Above, in the triangles, are the remaining apostles but the one on the far left, presumably Judas, has been smashed. The rest of this awkward space is filled by angels, their legs widespread as if bringing good news on the run. Their wings break out into the decorated frieze of the surrounding arch.

The lintel below the tympanum is decorated with a kind of elongated greek key design, containing lively renderings of a fish, a tortoise, a lion, a peacock, a dog and a duck, while the arch outside the tympanum has a deeply carved inhabited vine scroll.

The precision and geometrical rigidity of the sculpture suggests that the model for the tympanum was indeed an ivory carving or perhaps a piece from a jeweller's workshop, an idea reinforced by the holes punched into the rim of the mandorla, as if it were intended to be studded with jewels.

Inside the porch, the columns on either side of the inner doorway have capitals with very rudimentary carvings. Two of them bear inscriptions *Girbertus cementarius fecit istum portanum* (on the left); and *Benidicta sit anima eius* (on the right), which taken together read, 'Girbertus made this porch; blessed be his soul'.

Passing into the nave, I was struck by the huge size of the piers of the arcade for such a small church. Presumably this was because the narrow aisles were not thought sufficient to buttress the heavy tunnel vault. Looking more closely at them I saw that the capitals were decorated with more primitive carvings, too poorly executed to be interesting. A door on the right led into the cloister, alas very badly damaged during the Revolution. Only a few arches on the south side belong to the twelfth-century church and even here the original vaults have been replaced by gothic ones; the remaining three sides are fifteenth century but heavily restored. A staircase in the south-east corner leads to a roof level walk.

In a chapel on the north side of the cloister is a collection of medieval sculpture, including a beautiful fifteenth-century *mise au tombeau*. The body of Christ is shown stretched out on his tomb between Joseph of Aramathea and Nicodemus, who each hold one end of his winding sheet. Christ's hair and beard are rendered in a very stylised manner and the blood from the wound in his side is also formalised into a pattern. Nicodemus and Joseph of Aramathea are both realistically dressed in contemporary clothes, with some closely observed details. Nicodemus wears a kind of stocking cap and a purse at his waist; Joseph on the other hand looks altogether smarter in a peaked hat with a tassel and what looks like a mayor's chain of office round his shoulders.

Behind the tomb stands the grieving figure of Mary, her arms hanging down in a very sad gesture, as if she wished to touch the body of her Son, but she is restrained by a woman disciple on her left. On her right hand stands Saint John, looking with sorrow and resignation into the face of the dead Christ. At the far end of the tomb, next to Joseph of Aramathea, stands Mary Magdalene, her hair hanging down to her waist in long plaits, a hand raised to her eye to brush away a tear.

The group was probably carved by a local craftsman – there is one like it at Rodez apparently – but clearly shows the influence of the Flemish sculptors who worked at the court of the Duke of Burgundy, although the style here is less dramatic. In fact, despite a certain naïvety, the sculpture has a sad serenity that I found very moving.

Leaving the church, I wandered up the main road that runs along the edge of the escarpment on which Carennac is built, looking idly down at the Isle de Calypso. Suddenly an extraordinary cacophony shattered the peace; it was pop music played at full blast on a ghetto-blaster belonging to a young German tourist. Devastated I fled into the backstreets behind the priory. Like Loubressac, Carennac is a show village but for some reason I liked it better. Perhaps the church, with its famous tympanum, provides a centre of gravity that Loubressac lacks. Clearly it was a more important place and this is reflected in the buildings, many of which are larger than at Loubressac and architecturally more interesting. I enjoyed strolling round the winding streets admiring the honey-coloured stone houses with their brown-tiled roofs, wooden balconies and neat gardens. I discovered two late fifteenth- or early sixteenth-century houses with mullion and transome windows, outlined by pilasters and two more with pediments containing carved cockleshells, a symbol often found in renaissance art as well as being the pilgrim's badge on the route to Santiago de Compostela.

By the time I returned to the main road, the moron with the ghetto-blaster had disappeared and there was a small crowd peering down at a great shoal of brown fish in the river. One man, obviously a keen fisherman, said he thought they were bream. I scrambled down a little path to the river's edge but the fish had gone, so I walked a short way along the bank util the path petered out and then returned to the Hôstellerie Fénelon to await dinner.

When I opened the shutters next morning the sun was just rising over the treetops on the Isle de Calypso. The great orange globe seemed to fill the whole casement and hurt my eyes. Clearly it was going to be another hot day. After a good breakfast of hot chocolate and hot croissants, I left Hôstellerie Fénelon at 8.30 a.m., my destination Creysse, about ten miles to the west on the right bank of the Dordogne. For some way after Carennac the road was confined to a narrow ledge between a tree-covered cliff on the left and a branch of the Dordogne on the right. This stretch was full of islands and the inside channel was sometimes reduced to little more than a muddy ditch. It was another lovely morning, a strong smell of fresh mint rose from the verges and from high overhead came the screeching of magpies as I walked under a canopy of trees. After half-an-hour I came to the end of the first island and saw the Dordogne running in a narrow bed between two large white shingle banks. Little broken wavelets marked a shallow rapid which looked tame after those I had negotiated on my way to Beaulieu. Across the river I had my first view of the great grim cliffs of the Causse de Martel. They were to stay with me, seen and unseen, for the rest of the day. I had reached the point where the Dordogne cuts through the limestone plateau, creating the Causse de Martel to the north of the river and the Causse de Gramat to the south. Ahead I could see a high limestone bluff towering above the trees, an outrider of the Causse de Gramat, and soon I was walking in its shadow. The rock face was an unattractive dull-grey in colour with huge horizontal fractures. Scrubby oak trees grew on top of the cliff and out of some of the fissures, otherwise it was bare of vegetation. To my amazement I spotted high up the wooden walls of a cliff house. Presumably it was a cave dwelling with an entrance from the cliff top.

After walking for about an hour-and-a-half, I reached a crossroads. To the right was a suspension bridge across the Dordogne beyond which I could see the cliffs of the Causse de Martel, here a more attractive rust colour. Below the bridge the stretch of land between the cliffs and the river was wider and here for the first time I noticed signs of devastation: on all sides there were uprooted trees, their earth-clogged roofs pointing forlornly skywards, others had been snapped like matchsticks, leaving jagged stumps and many of those still standing had broken branches hanging down like gibbets. A whole walnut plantation had been wrecked, the smashed trees making it looking like the aftermath of a First World War battle. An old man was hard at work chopping up fallen branches; he told me that on 24 July, a tornado had swept up the valley of the Dordogne at a speed of over one hundred miles an hour, uprooting everything in its path, at least not quite everything, for mysteriously some trees in the path of the whirlwind had been spared, for no apparent reason. After a short climb I reached the village of Floirac. I had covered five miles in exactly two hours.

Floirac is a *causse* village, built of grey limestone and looks rather dour. A large, forbidding-looking fifteenth-century church overlooks the main square, dominated by a free-standing square tower which at first I thought was a belfry but turned out to be all that remained of a fourteenth-century castle. It was market day, although there were only a few stalls, set up in the shade of the church. Amongst them was one of those butcher's vans, with a side that lets down to make a counter. I joined a queue of gossiping ladies, all of whom seemed to have relatives staying with them.

There was a lot of point scoring going on, depending on the status of the visitors: sons and daughters counted much higher than in-laws and grand-children outscored everyone. Eventually my turn came and I bought some *jambon de pays* and *salade de célerave*. At another stall I bought some tomatoes and a sweet-smelling charentais melon.

After Floriac the country changed. The cliffs curved away inland and then swung back ahead of me. This was the Cirque de Monvalent, a natural amphitheatre over a mile in section with great black cliffs over a hundred feet high. Within the deep crescent created by the *cirque* there was enough space for some sizeable fields but here too the tornado had wreaked its havoc, ripping through several large walnut groves. It was a sickening sight.

Half-an-hour later, the cliffs on the far side of the *cirque* were right ahead of me, grey and grim with a great shoulder of scree at their base. Here the road carved to the right and began to climb. At one point I could just see the Dordogne far below and, beyond, the cliffs on the far side of the river, but most of the way trees hid the view. I took ten minutes to get to the top and then began a rather dreary downhill trek until I came to a main road running alongside the Dordogne. For the first time since I had left Bretenoux I was faced with a continuous stream of traffic but luckily there was not far to go before I reached another bridge, which this time I crossed.

Pacing out the distance as I went, I made the width of the Dordogne at this point 280 feet. In the middle of the bridge I stopped to have a good look at the river. Upstream the scene was very peaceful, with green, tree-covered slopes on either side; downstream there was a large shingle bank jutting out from the right hand bank, with several canoes drawn up on it, which forced the river to the left and over a small, tame-looking rapid. On the left bank there was a large, noisy campsite. Further down, the Dordogne disappeared from sight round a bend and the view ahead was blocked by a massive cliff wall.

I was sitting in a bar on the far side of the bridge, having a beer, when I noticed a track leading down to the Dordogne. It was 12.30 by now, so I followed the track down to the river bank and found a secluded spot at a point where a little path went down to a sunken punt. Here, in the shade of a tree, I sat down and demolished my picnic. Below me the peaceful scene was periodically disrupted by flotillas of noisy canoeists, but they soon passed and all was tranquil once more.

I was lying on my back, dozing after lunch, when I became aware of a great noise of twittering above my head. Looking up, I made out a family of fledgling swallows being fed by their parents. There were four young birds, their beaks permanently wide open to receive the tasty morsels brought by the parent birds who never seemed to rest, feeding their insatiable offspring on the wing and flying off immediately to search for more nourishing titbits. I could not but admire this example of selfless devotion to the ungrateful nestlings.

I was reluctant to leave but eventually I struggled into my pack and made for Creysse, now only a couple of miles away. The road led along the right bank of the Dordogne underneath the great cliffs I had glimpsed at intervals during the morning. The rock face came right to the edge of the narrow, winding road, making walking difficult and dangerous, for if a car came round a bend too fast there was nowhere for me to go. Once, the cliff overhung the road so far that it was like walking in a cave. The river was only just below the level of the road to my left and I could see holiday-makers from the campsite by the bridge splashing in the shallows: a continual procession of canoes swept past.

Now came a steep climb up a corniche road, the cliff still on my right and a waist-high stone wall on the river side. The road was only wide enough for one car with passing places cut in the rock face, making it very tricky to negotiate and I had to be extremely careful. Half way up I paused for breath. Below me, to the left, was a hundred foot drop to farmland, the Dordogne having disappeared for the moment somewhere to the south. In the foreground was a large well-tended peach orchard but further away more uprooted trees marked the passage of the tornado. Some miles away, on the far side of the Dordogne were the great black cliffs of the Causse de Gramat.

Another ten minutes brought me to the top of the rise and I began my descent into a pleasant fertile valley, athough here too the tornado had left its trail of destruction. Soon I saw ahead of me a cluster of red roofs and some larger stone buildings – Creysse.

I quickly found the Hôtel de l'Isle, where I already had a room, standing at the edge of a little stream that winds its way through the village. It was a small, comfortable *auberge*; my room had rose-patterned wallpaper, a flowered coverlet on the bed and a pink-tiled bathroom. The window looked out over a terrace, across the stream to a small church on a hill, which I thought might be worth a visit. But now it was time to rest. . . .

At five o'clock I got up and went for a look around. I liked what I saw: there were fewer tourists than at Loubressac or Carennac and some genuine villagers who worked the surrounding farmland, which in places came right up to the edge of the houses. I climbed up some steep cobbled steps to the church, a strange building with twin apses at the east end, a feature said to be unique. One of the apses is built of undressed stone and looks earlier than the other: they probably date from the eleventh and twelfth centuries respectively.

I went into the church through the south doorway and found myself in a nave with a flat wooden roof carried on beams. Beyond was a tunnel-vaulted chancel with a flat end-wall. The twin apses, with a single dividing wall in the middle, were to the right. In fact, as became clear when I looked outside, the chancel is an addition to the north side of the church and the altar is not orientated correctly.

Outside the church is a small dusty *place* and opposite a nonde-script *mairie*. On the west side of the *place* I had a good view of the Dordogne, here quite close, and on the far side woods and fields stretching to the distant cliffs. The other side overlooked the village roofs and the hotel. I walked round to the back of the church and saw some steps leading down, a gap and then a tall stone tower with a pointed roof, standing on another eminence about a hundred yards away.

Descending from the *place*, I took a path in the direction of the Dordogne, only to find that it led into a garden full of fallen trees, more victims of the tornado. A charming middle-aged lady was pruning her roses; she thought I had come to see the remains of the château which loomed above us, although I had not even realised that there was one to see. Immediately everything fell into place: of course, the church must at one time have been the castle chapel. Perhaps the twin apses were for some form of segregation: lord from retainers, men from women? When the church became part of the village, the two apses were no longer suitable for a large congregation and the new chancel was added. The *mairie* stands in what must have been the inner courtyard of the castle and hides the view of the remains of the château to the south, a square block, which rises above the rose lady's garden, and a second tower. Madame said that the base of the tower was twelfth century but that the rest had been destroyed during the Hundred Years War and rebuilt later.

Taking leave of Madame, I returned to the place and took a steep path on the west side down to the road at the bottom. From here I could clearly see the remains of a considerable wall stretching between the chapel and the château. It was now obvious that these apparently separate buildings, including the tower to the north of the church, were all part of the same system of fortifications, built on the rocky escarpment overlooking the village. It also meant that Creysse is a *castelnau*, that is to say an organic village that grew up round a fortified position or castle and was not planned like a *bastide*. *Castelnaus* are usually earlier in date than *bastides* and Creysse must date from at least the eleventh century, although hill sites like this were often favoured by the Celts for their settlements.

Continuing my tour of the village, I met a young couple from Paris busy restoring one of the houses. They gave me a graphic account of the fury of the tornado which had dislodged a great stone block, part of a hefty wall outside the house, and sent it crashing to the ground where it had broken into smithereens. Walking round I noticed many other signs of damage: one timbered barn was almost completely destroyed and many houses had lost tiles or slates.

On my way back to the hotel I passed a house with a garden backing onto the stream. Four women were sitting at a table, in the shade of a tree, shelling peas and gossiping. It was a charming scene, which incidentally reminded me it would soon be time for dinner.

The next day started badly: I was up and ready for breakfast by 7.30 a.m., but the hotel staff weren't and I had to wait until until eight o'clock before I was served: they are late risers in these parts. I finally got away at 8.55 on a muggy, overcast morning and I was not in a good mood. I was making for Souillac, ten miles away on the right bank of the Dordogne, although, because of the vagaries of the river, I should have to cross it twice to get there.

As soon as I reached the outskirts of Creysse, I saw more grim evidence of the damage caused by the whirlwind. On either side of the road were large walnut plantations. The one on the left was a pitiful sight: most of the trees were uprooted and those that still stood were cut off at half-mast leaving long jagged splinters stabbing at the sky. Amazingly, the grove on the right was untouched.

Crossing a stretch of open farmland, I saw ahead of me a large goose farm. The noise was deafening but as I passed by the birds turned their backs and scuttled to the far end of the compound. Not long afterwards, I saw the Dordogne, flowing peacefully between wooded banks: a heron standing on one leg at the river's edge took off on seeing me and flapped slowly away downstream.

Now the cliffs reappeared on my right and the road began to climb. Ten minutes later I reached the top, where I was confronted by a wall of grey cliffs, the Rochers de Ste-Marie, three miles away on the far side of the Dordogne. About the same distance away, to my right, were more cliffs, reddish in hue this time; below me the road fell away into another tranquil valley. As I began my descent the two lines of cliff converged to form another giant amphitheatre with myself like an ancient Greek thespian advancing on to the stage.

At the bottom of the hill a vivid daub of yellow proclaimed a field of sunflowers, beyond which I could see the grey tower of a small château: I had reached St Sozy.

The village is close to the river and a few minutes later I was crossing a suspension bridge to the left bank. Ahead, on a bluff overlooking the river, was the attractive village of Meyronne. I was tempted to explore but was put off by the steep climb and passed it by. At the next road junction I turned right along the road which follows the river under the Rochers de Ste-Marie. It was a gloomy scene: the great grey cliffs hard up to the road on the left, thick woods sloping down to the river on the right and a dense screen of leaves overhead, shutting out the light. After a while the Dordogne disappeared from sight, to be replaced by fields of stunted maize, alternating with derelict walnut plantations destroyed by the tornado. The sky grew dark and large, isolated raindrops began to splash on the road. I debated whether to put on my waterproof but decided against it: I could not face the struggle involved in shedding my pack. I knew I was not far from a well-known tourist spot, Lacave, where I hoped to find shelter before *le déluge*. Fortunately I reached the outskirts just as the downpour started and took refuge in a bar.

Lacave is famous for its caves which you go round in a little train, admiring stalactites and stalagmites. I had no intention of visiting them: I have detested such places ever since Sybil and I visited a cave in Majorca, some thirty years ago. We descended for miles into the bowels of the earth, surrounded by illuminated formations of of stalagmites and stalactites with fanciful names like Granada or New York. The fascination of the sights quickly palled to be replaced by excruciating boredom. At the bottom of the cave was a large lake which we had to cross to reach the exit. But first we were forced to sit in a natural amphitheatre at the lake's edge until enough tourists had assembled to make a respectable audience. Then, and only then, a boat appeared rowed by four oarsmen wearing striped jerseys and red neckerchiefs. In the sternsheets, lit by lanterns, sat four musicians in evening dress, playing a barcarole by Chopin (Chopin and George Sand had an affair in Majorca). Only when this water music was finished were we allowed to board a punt which took us across the lake to freedom. Never again!

By the time I had finished my beer the rain was over and I was on my way again. Lacave is ghastly: one hundred yards of pizza bars, restaurants and shops selling tourist tat lining the road under the cliffs. I was glad to get out of it.

Immediately after Lacave the road crosses the Ouysse, a tributary of the Dordogne which flows down from the Causse de Gramat. On the far side the road swung to the left to cicumvent a crag overhanging the Dordogne on top of which was perched a small white château – a spectacular sight. Looking at the map, I thought I could cut a corner by taking a narrow road up the cliff face, which was closed to traffic, *sauf riverains*. The track, for it was little more, was very steep but I managed it without much difficulty, considering the load I was carrying. I was obviously much fitter than when I had started at le Mont-Dore.

At the top, I saw on the other side of the road what looked like a log cabin, which, judging by the number of cars parked outside, I took to be a restaurant. Indeed it was and offered a set menu at only fifty-two francs. I accepted the offer with alacrity: I was hungry after the morning's slog.

Inside it was all very simple: wooden tables with paper tablecloths and a litre of red wine on each. But what a lunch: an excellent *terrine* with I swear some *foie gras* in it; grilled *confit* and *pommes frites*; *cabecou* (a local goat's cheese); a ripe peach AND as much wine as you could drink – all for a little over five pounds, a real bargain. I had made a resolution not to drink wine at lunch time when I was back-packing, but with a litre in front of me I could not resist a couple of glasses. Round about me others were not so restrained. If you wanted more wine when your litre was finished, there was a plastic barrel of the stuff in the middle of the restaurant with a tap from which you could refill your carafe – and many were availing themselves of this facility.

I left the restaurant well satisfied. A short way up the road I came to the entrance to Belcastel, the château I had seen from below at Lacave, and rang the bell. A smart middle-aged lady opened the gate and showed me round. Belcastel is pretty, rather than architecturally interesting: only a small part of the original medieval castle survives, the rest is seventeenth century or later, although there is a small, vaulted, fifteenth-century chapel with a fireplace that is worth a look. But what makes a visit to Belcastel so exciting is the superb views from its terraces, surely amongst the finest on the Dordogne.

The cliff that the château stands on is in the middle of one of the great horseshoe loops that are a feature of the river from here all the way to Lalinde. The crag juts out north-eastwards, giving a long vista back up river towards Creysse. I could clearly see the Dordogne flowing through its narrow valley, hemmed in by the bare cliffs of the *causse*, and on both banks the trail of wreckage left in the wake of the tornado.

Further round, I amused myself watching from my safe vantage point the antics of novice canoeists, negotiating a shallow rapid immediately below and sometimes being swept through backwards, just as had happened to me. Beyond the rapid, the Dordogne swung north and disappeared into a ravine, whose sheer cliffs fell sheer to the water, leaving no space for a road or even a footpath.

On the opposite side of the terrace, looking inland, I could see, close at hand, the great black cliffs above Lacave and below the river Ouysse, winding down from the causse through its narrow valley.

I lingered long, savouring the views, but at last it was time to move. After Belcastel, the road continued downhill across a rather dreary bit of heath to cross the Dordogne at La Treyne, where there is another famous château, right on the water's edge. I thought of visiting this, too, but the next conducted tour was not for half-an-hour and I wanted to get on, so I contented myself with taking a good look at it from the middle of the narrow suspension bridge that crosses the river close by. Apart from a square tower, dating from the fourteenth century, most of the chateau is seventeenth century and, like Belcastel, is picturesque rather than formidable. Reflected in the clear waters of the Dordogne, it is indeed a charming sight.

By now it was exceedingly hot and I was beginning to feel the effects of the wine I had drunk at lunch. Not that I was drunk, but wine is dehydrating and debilitating in that heat, which is why I had resolved not to drink it in the first place. I plodded on in a daze across a boring stretch of farmland contained in another horseshoe loop, or *cingle*, as they are known locally, created by the winding of the Dordogne. Gradually, I became aware of a bleak ashen-coloured cliff on my right, covered with scrubby oaks. I was once again trudging along at the foot of the barren cliff-face of the Causse de Martel, while the Dordogne, having completed its long curve to the south, was back on my left. The heat of the sun radiating from the bare limestone made me feel dizzy and I stopped for a while for a rest, but there was no shade and sitting in the full glare of the sun made me feel worse, so on I went, longing for Souillac, now less than a mile away.

I passed a stone bridge across the Dordogne and came at last to the long, busy road that runs through the centre of the town. It was 4.30. I soon found my hotel and retired to my room until 7.30, when I went down to dinner, only to be told that the dining-room was full and would I like to use their self-service cafeteria? No, I would not! I went out and found a restaurant just across the road where I had an unexciting but adequate meal for fifty-eight francs.

There is not a great deal to be said for Souillac: it is situated on an important river crossing on the main route from Brive to Cahors and is bigger than anywhere I had stayed since Bort-les-Orgues. The town is bisected by the RN 20, an extremely busy road at all times and getting from one side to the other is about as easy as crossing Piccadilly. Souillac is obviously used to transient tourists – no one in their right mind would want to stay there long – and the main road is lined with hotels, restaurants and bars, all giving the kind of efficient, impersonal service that you find wherever there is a regular passing trade. But down in the heart of what little remains of the old town, to the west of the main-road, is the romanesque abbey of Ste-Marie, which contains some remarkable sculpture, and that is what I had come to see.

Before I could visit the abbey, however, I had some chores to do. By now my pack was full of dirty washing, even though I tried to wash out my smalls each night in the bathroom, so I spent much of the next morning at the laundrette. On my way back to the hotel, I passed the offices of a firm called Copeyre who hired out canoes and, despite my alarming experiences on the stretch from Argentat to Beaulieu, I decided to have another go the following day. As before, the arrange-ment was that my pack would be taken on by road to my hotel at Grolejac, about twenty miles downstream.

After lunch I went to see the abbey. The first sight of the church, from the east end, was impressive: above five radiating chapels rose a high semi-circular apse with two rows of round-headed windows and a roof of roman tiles. Higher still was the easternmost of three shallow domes, covered by heavy *lauze* roofs like those at Argentat. Souillac is not the only domed romanesque church in the region: there are several other important examples, notably St-Front and St-Étienne at Perigueux in the Dordogne and the cathedral of Cahors in the Lot, although quite why this should be has never been satisfactorily explained.

The high walls of the transepts and nave looked rather austere,

THE PUY DE SANCY
IN THE FOREGROUND THE NEW-BORN DORDOGNE
(*Photo: Ciné Photo SULLY*)

Above
THE CHATEAU DE VAL
(Photo: Ciné Photo SULLY)

Left
ST-NECTAIRE
(Photo: French Government Tourist Office)

Above
THE CHAPELLE DES PENITANTS AT BEAULIEU
(*Photo: A. F. Kersting*)

Left
THE GORGES OF THE DORDOGNE AND THE
BARRAGE DE CHASTANG
(*Photo: Alain Perceval/Documentation Française*)

THE SOUTH PORCH OF THE ABBEY OF ST-PIERRE
BEAULIEU
(Photo: Zodiaque)

CASTELNAU DE BRETENOUX
(*Photo: French Government Tourist Office*)

THE CHATEAU DE LA TREYNE
(*Photo: A. F. Kersting*)

THE ABBEY OF STE-MARIE,
SOUILLAC
(*Photo: Douglas Dickens*)

Left
THE ROMANESQUE SCULPTURE OF ISAIAH IN THE ABBEY OF STE-MARIE,
SOUILLAC (*Photo: Zodiaque*)

Above
THE MAISON DE ETIENNE DE LA BOETIE, SARLAT
(*Photo: Douglas Dickens*)

THE CHATEAU DE MONFORT
(*Photo: Douglas Dickens*)

LA ROQUE-GAGEAC
(*Photo: Douglas Dickens*)

THE 13TH CENTURY PORTE DES TOURS, DOMME
(*Photo: French Government Tourist Office*)

MONTAIGNE'S TOWER
(*Photo: French Government Tourist Office*)

LIBOURNE

(Photo: French Government Tourist Office)

The Chateau de Vayres

Journey's End, Bec d'Ambes
(*Photo: Documentation Française*)

while the south porch, in the eleventh-century west tower felt more like the entrance to a castle than a church. The west tower is the earliest part of the abbey, the rest dating from the twelfth century.

Inside there is an impression of space and harmony. No gothic soaring of the spirit here as the eye travels higher and higher into the vaults: the flat cupolas scarcely interrupt the view eastwards to the altar, illuminated by shafts of light from the windows high up in the apse. But of course it was not primarily the church that I had come to see. On the the inside of the entrance to the nave are fragments from a great sculptural group which originally stood in the south porch, just like the one at Beaulieu, most of which was destroyed in the sixteenth-century Wars of Religion.

Above the door is a bas relief depicting scenes from the miracle of Theophilus. According to legend, Theophilus was the treasurer of a church in Silesia. For some reason (embezzlement?) he was dismissed from his post by a new bishop and made a pact with the devil as a result of which he was re-instated. Terrified by what he had done, Theophilus appealed to the Virgin Mary for help. Our Lady recovered the pact from the devil and Theophilus died in an odour of sanctity.

In the bas-relief Theophilus can be seen negotiating the pact with the devil (bottom left) and being dragged off to hell (bottom right). Above these figures, Theophilus is shown on his deathbed and higher up again an upside-down Mary, surrounded by angels, floats out of a cloud, pointing to the dying Theophilus below. To the right is Saint Peter, recognisable by his keys, and on the left Saint Benedict, holding a copy of the monastic rule of life. It cannot be said in all honesty that the quality of the work is very high but it is certainly worth a look.

To the right of the door is a column covered with the most extraordinary, sometimes bizarre sculpture. The left-hand side of the column shows the sacrifice of Isaac. At the foot, Abraham holds Isaac by his hair and lifts the knife, about to strike. Isaac's eyes are closed and he embraces his father. Abraham looks away into the distance, as if unable to bear what he is going to do. But, above his head, an angel, descending from a cloud, restrains Abraham's arm with one hand and presents him with a sacrificial lamb with the other.

The figures of Abraham and Isaac are very moving but the upside-down angel looks rather comic.

On the right-hand side are the figures of a man and woman embracing, repeated three times, thought by some to represent Adam and Eve after the fall, although this interpretation is by no means certain. But it is the front of the column that is the most fascinating: at first it looks completely chaotic but gradually a pattern emerges from the writhing forms. At the top a naked figure, contorted into the shape of a letter S has his head in the mouth of a strange lion-headed monster, while a fierce-looking bird-headed beast tears at the small of his back. Below, a peacock, a wild boar and a deer, all with their heads pointing downwards, are suffering much the same fate. What holds the composition together is the strong diagonal rhythm created by the four bird-headed beasts overlapping the bodies of the lion-headed monsters, their back feet resting on the lions' heads and their front claws on the rears of the monsters, higher up on the left. Their cruel beaks are turned back to the right, snapping at whatever victim is nearest. The meaning of this extraordinary work is obscure but there is no denying the skill of execution and the dramatic power of the nightmarish vision.

It is the figure of Isaiah, to the left of the column, that is the most beautiful and exciting piece of sculpture at Souillac. Isaiah's body is twisted into a kind of elongated S with his left leg advancing to the left and his head and torso bent back to the right. The impression of movement created by this pose is accentuated by the hem of his robe which curves upwards from his left ankle to reveal a trousered back leg. In his right hand Isaiah holds a scroll to which he points with his left hand, reminding the spectator of his prophesy of the coming of the Messiah. Over his shoulder Isaiah wears a cloak with a richly embroidered, floating hem. Inside the the cloak, his robed body is decorated with double incised lines, a stylistic device also found in the sculpture of the old man at Beaulieu and at St-Sernin, Toulouse, where it seems to have originated.

Round his neck Isaiah wears a richly embroidered collar, which perhaps represents a jewelled gorget. The prophet's hair is parted in the middle and drawn back in stylised locks, matched by his forked beard that is spread over his chest. His lips are slightly parted as if about to explain the words on the scroll and his eyes stare at you, commanding attention. The swing of Isaiah's body and the floating folds of his robe create a remarkable feeling of lightness and movement unique in the sculpture of the period. It is a splendid piece of work that makes one wonder how much was lost when the Huguenots set about destroying the original south porch.

CHAPTER 6

CHATEAUX COUNTRY

When I left the hotel next morning the desk clerk complimented me on my French. I replied, *Vous parlez très bien l'anglais*, a phrase that came straight out of my BBC text book when I was following their course *Répondez s'il vous plaît*, some years ago. I was amused that it had come in handy at last.

To find my kayak I had to walk through Quercyland, a children's amusement park down by the river, with a water chute, a blue pipe for crawling through, mini-golf, a dirt-track for racing powered bicycles and, inevitably, an enormous restaurant inside a gaily-striped marquee.

I found the *Bas de Canoë* and got myself fixed up with a kayak, paddle and life jacket but when I reminded the boatman of the arrangement for my rucksack to be transported to Grolejac he denied all knowledge of it. A heated argument ensued which was only resolved when the girl with whom I had made the arrangement the previous day arrived and confirmed that what I had said was true. However, she explained that Copeyre had no *Bas de Canoë* at Grolejac and that I would have to paddle a mile or two further down river to Vitrac, but she promised that my pack and I would be transported by road back to Grolejac.

So, with some misgivings, I set off. I had been paddling for about five minutes when I saw ahead of me an unexpected bridge; it was the one I had passed yesterday on the outskirts of Souillac: I was heading the wrong way. I turned round and started paddling downstream again.

It is very difficult to give a clear acount of a canoe trip: you are so busy manoeuvring the kayak or engrossed in scanning the river ahead for possible hazards that there is little time for anything else. Anyway, getting a notebook out of a safe pocket when you are sitting in a canoe is not all that easy and if you do succeed, the paper gets wet and your writing is indecipherable. To begin with I had the same problem as at Argentat of keeping the kayak on a straight course and for a while this took all my concentration, but gradually I became aware that a lot of water was slopping about inside the canoe and that my legs and bottom were soaking. Putting ashore on a pebble bank, I carefully emptied all the water out of the kayak and launched it again. In no time the inside of the canoe was just as wet as before. It was then I noticed that the bow seemed rather low in the water and that, whenever I tried to go a bit faster, a wave lapped over it and raced towards the cockpit. Looking carefully, I detected a small hole in the deck, near the stem. As soon as I paddled a bit harder, the bow dipped and water poured into the hole and slopped about inside. Luckily, I came quite soon to another *Bas de Canoë* belonging to Copeyre, so I beached the kayak and showed the boatman the hole: without a murmur he offered me another kayak and I resumed my voyage. I later found out that the hole in the bow was a drain hole to make it easier to empty water out of the canoe and it should have had a rubber cork in it!

The new kayak was shorter, floated higher on the water and remained dry throughout the rest of the voyage, but it was a pig to handle. I tried everything, paddling hard, paddling gently, leaning forwards, leaning backwards, but no matter what I did, as soon as I stopped paddling, the damned thing careered wildly to the left and spun round backwards. If I reacted quickly enough, I could stop the spin by jamming the paddle in hard on the right hand side and pushing it forward, so that it acted as a brake, but when I did this the kayak rocked violently and felt as if it were about to capsize, and in the end I gave up and let the brute have its way. Still, I felt a bit of a fool progressing backwards so much of the time.

The first part of the trip was unremarkable. There were some rapids but none very serious. The worst obstacle I had to negotiate was a new bridge that was being built: great lumps of concrete projected far into the river, leaving only a narrow gap in the middle through which the river sluiced. I had to work hard to steer the kayak into exactly the right position before I swept through. The river here was rather dull: the cliffs had been left behind for the moment and the Dordogne was meandering through a wide valley with large fields of maize on either side. Later on, the banks became wooded once more and there were campsites amongst the trees. I was amused as I paddled by some of the smaller sites, with only one or two tents, by the unselfconscious behaviour of the campers, dressing and undressing as if the passing canoeist didn't exist. In some of the more secluded spots there were naturists taking the sun but unfortunately they were all middle-aged men, looking more like Silenus than Apollo.

At 12.30 I stopped for lunch just upstream of a road bridge between the villages of St-Julien-de-Lampon and Roufillac, where there was a landing-place below a large campsite. After lunch I carried on, much as before, until I reached another bridge between Grolejac, on the south bank, and Carsac on the north. Downstream of the bridge the scenery changed dramatically: I was entering a great loop of the river with sheer limestone cliffs on the right and flat, wooded country on the left. Soon afterwards, high up on top of the cliff, I saw a spectacular castle, the Château de Monfort. I was in the *cingle* de Monfort, the start of one of the most beautiful stretches of the Dordogne – the ten miles between Monfort and Beynac.

Surprisingly, it was very shallow her and I was in constant danger of going aground. I was negotiating a rapid when to my alarm I felt the kayak scraping the bottom. Somehow I bumped along, feeling rather silly, into deeper water. Then I realised that all the other canoeists were having the same problem and I felt better. When I set off that morning, I had been on my own but now the river was full of canoes, mostly Canadian double-handers, and I was continually being passed, although this did have the advantage that I could use them to pilot me through the rapids.

Towards the end of the *cingle* the left bank was lined with campsites. By now, the river was very crowded with canoes and people swimming. It was still very shallow and I found it disconcerting that when the bathers stood up the water came only to their waists. This meant they were on the same level as myself in the kayak and in some places, where there was very little water, they towered above me: it was an odd feeling.

There were a great many shoals and islands in this stretch with sunbathers stretched out on the foreshore, amongst them some attractive topless girls. One, with a particularly fine figure so distracted me that I nearly went through a rapid backwards and had to take quick evasive action.

Nearing Vitrac, I fell in with a flotilla of canoes manned by muscular, bronzed, golden-haired German youths and caused havoc by spinning backwards into their midst, forcing them to paddle furiously to get out of my way. I felt very humiliated: here I was, the typical amateurish Englishman, making a fool of himself alongside these determined teutonic giants; but in truth it was four o'clock by now, I was very tired and finding it increasingly difficult to control my wayward craft. In the end we all swept down towards the bridge at Vitrac and for a moment it looked as though my kayak and one of the German canoes were going to collide with one of its stone buttresses but at the last minute we swept past and into Copeyre's *Bas de Canoë*, just the other side.

I was met by a rather surly boy of about twenty who helped me beach my canoe. When I asked him if my rucksack had arrrived, I was met with a blank stare, he knew nothing about it. The *Bas de Canoë* was located in a sandpit carved out of the river bank. Higher up on the road was a mini-bus waiting to take the German canoeists back to Souillac. The driver was more helpful than Surly Boy and went to ring the Copeyre office in Souillac. When he returned, he assured me that the rucksack was on its way. I was tired and wet but at least this time I had brought some spare clothes with me into which I now changed. Then I sat down to wait.

An hour later I was still waiting.

At six o'clock another young man arrived to take the empty canoes back to Souillac but he knew nothing about my rucksack. By now, I was getting very worried and made frequent anxious telephone calls to Copeyre. Each time I was told that the rucksack should arrive at any moment, but still nothing came.

Time passed exceedingly slowly. Surly Boy had shut up shop and was sitting in his car reading a motor magazine. I climbed up the bank to the road and turned right onto the bridge. To the right and below was the *Bas de Canoë* in its sandpit at the river's edge. Beyond was an island, at least it would have been an island in winter but the river was so low that a shingle bank at the upriver end prevented any water entering the inshore channel. Below the island, the Dordogne took a slow bend to the left. On the far bank was a row of poplars and behind them fields and distant hills. Looking upstream from the centre of the bridge I could see a big campsite on the far bank and further up river the cliffs of the *cingle* de

Monfort. There were no longer any canoes coming down river but there were still a lot of campers splashing in the shallows, although by now it was 7.30 p.m.

I returned to the north bank and turned right. Here there were three very smart hotels, their car parks full of expensive cars with GB plates. I had telephoned all three the previous day, trying to book a room, without success. It was now the height of the holiday season and all the hotels were full: it had taken me an hour, ringing round, before I had found a room at the Hôtel du Pont, Grolejac, and now it was so late I was afraid I should lose it. I telephoned the hotel and assured them that I was still coming and implored them not to let my room, then I returned to the sandpit.

Surly Boy, who had gone to sleep in the car, was now awake and even he was beginning to be concerned by the non-arrival of my pack. I persuaded him to ring Copeyre again but the reply was the same: the rucksack was on its way. We began to talk at last and I told him how difficult I had found steering the kayak. He explained that it was because the canoe was so short and said that the only answer was to paddle *facilement*. At last at 8.15 p.m. a van driven by the young man who had collected the empty canoes arrived with my rucksack and we set off for Grolejac. Almost immediately I realised we were going the wrong way, but the driver said the van needed some petrol. When we got to the filling-station it was closed so back we went to the sandpit. I was beginning to think I would never get away from this place and that perhaps this was my particular form of hell, but we transferred to Surly Boy's car and off we went again.

Surly Boy was anxious to get home and drove at speed along the winding corniche road at the top of the *cingle* de Monfort. I was fascinated to catch the odd glimpse of the river I had paddled down so recently and to see the landward side of the Château de Monfort, which looked formidable: a true castle compared with Belcastel and La Treyne. But the journey was hair-raising and I was very relieved when we finally reached the Hôtel du Pont at 8.45 p.m.

I was shown to a comfortable room with ice-blue walls and a very smart bathroom also in ice-blue and white tiles. Everything was very clean and the shower worked perfectly. By nine o'clock I was downstairs waiting for dinner. Here the atmosphere was more like that of a *Routier*.

There was a smoke-filled bar, full of local workmen and rustics and a large dining-room with a wooden floor, part of which was occupied by a billiard table. The food, however, was excellent: *omelette aux cèpes, confit de pigeon*, cheese and pudding.

As soon as I had finished dinner, I went to bed, worn out by the day's anxieties and exertions, only to be woken almost immediately by thunder and lightning. But the storm didn't last long, or if it did I slept through it.

It was still raining when I awoke next morning and did not clear up until ten o'clock. I was not too worried: my next destination was the beautiful medieval town of Sarlat, seven miles north of the river but a place not to be missed. I was feeling rather lethargic that morning and plodded along in a dream down a busy road, bordered most of the way by woods, but with occasional small clearings, planted with maize.

I reached the outskirts of Sarlat at midday and dropped into a bar for a beer. It turned out to be a real *Routier* and the tables were set for lunch, each with a bottle of wine on it. I asked for a table and was given one in a separate room, obviously reserved for posh clients, although the price of the meal, fifty francs, was the same.

First a big soup tureen arrived and was left on the table, a nourishing mixture of bread, beans, potatoes and carrots and very good. This was followed by *quiche lorraine*, then a thin steak and spaghetti. The steak was rare and the spaghetti served *al dente*, both just to my taste. A fairly ordinary cheese board, again left on the table, was succeeded by an horrific dessert with alternate layers of *crème anglaise* and chocolate sponge. Marvellous value at the price.

Restored, I walked on into Sarlat. As I neared the centre of the town the road became more and more congested with traffic, the pavements were full of people and the hubbub increased to a point where I began to wonder what I was doing here. Once I reached the old town things improved. Most of it was pedestrianised and the atmosphere was calmer, although here too I was taken aback by the size of the crowds.

I made straight for the *Syndicat d'Initiative* where, to my relief, they managed to find me a room. Old Sarlat has survived almost intact, within the circuit of the original walls, except for a straight road, driven ruthlessly through the centre, from north to south, dividing it into two. Most of the important buildings that I had come to see lie to the east of this road; my hotel was to the west of it, the wrong side of the tracks.

The hotel was extraordinary. It was part of the former *Couvent de Récollets*, a nunnery in a narrow twisting street with old stone dwellings down its whole length. The door to the hotel was so obscure that I missed it at first. Once inside, a short flight of stone steps led up to a small courtyard. Ahead and to the right was the family's living quarters and in front of an open door sat a young woman shelling peas; my room was on the left. Inside were two big windows, set within heavy stone arches, one with a view of the courtyard, the other looking out into a blank well. The bed was on the right, inside another blocked up arch. Opposite the bed was a large armoire with a washbasin in an alcove on one side and a loo on the other. It was certainly the strangest room I had yet stayed in but I rather liked it.

Once settled in, I made my way to the Place de la Liberté, Sarlat's main square, where the Hôtel de Ville is to be found and where the market is held. Today, there was no market and the square was crammed full of café tables with a narrow corridor between, through which ambled an endless procession of tourists, nearly all of them British. I sat down and ordered tea.

It was an ideal place to get my first feel of Sarlat. There are no great monuments here but then the whole town is a work of art: few other towns of comparable size can boast such a wealth of medieval and renaissance houses, all built in the same beautiful soft sandstone in a range of tones from off-white to ochre, although most are the colour of double-cream or Normandy butter. And then there are the roofs, all shapes and sizes, with a mixture of red tiles, brown slates and grey lauze, giving a rich variety of textures.

Opposite where I was sitting I could see a very high class wine merchant, the *Distillerie du Périgord* and outside it an *alambic ambulant*, one of those ancient itinerant stills, looking like a Heath Robinson steam engine, that used to tour the vineyards in the autumn, converting the lees from the vintage into volcanic *eau de vie*. Above the *Distillerie du Périgord* was a terrace restaurant and behind that the curving right wing of the sixteenth-century Hôtel de Maleville, whose main façade was to the left of the shop. It is a four-storey building with a round arch on the ground floor and mullion and transome windows above. The high gabled roof is covered with *lauze* tiles. Over the renaissance doorway were roundels bearing the portraits of Henry IV and Marie de Medici. To the left of the Hôtel de Maleville was a half-timbered house with a corner turret.

Looking to the right I could see the massive belfry and fine *lauze* roof of the deconsecrated church of Ste-Marie, which was badly damaged in the revolution. Further right again, up a slight incline, was a sixteenth-century house with an octagonal tower in butter-coloured stone and beyond it, where a road led out of the square, I could just see a medley of different-shaped, tiled roofs.

I was enjoying this architectural feast when a strange figure loped into the square. He was a tall, thin man of about thirty. His body, burned almost black by the sun, had an unpleasant leathery look, his head was completely bald and he wore nothing but a pair of faded navy blue boxing shorts and frogman's flippers on his feet. A guitar was slung over his shoulder and in one hand he carried a small collapsible stool. Having found himself some space near the stationary *alambic ambulant* he sat down on the stool and began to play the guitar, beating time with the flippers. Astonishingly he was very good. One of the pieces he played was Rodrigo's *Concierto de Aranjuez*, which I would not have thought was all that easy, but his technique was excellent. I could not understand why he ruined the effect by making such a noise with the flippers and was inclined to tell him so, but on reflection I decided this might be unwise and let it go.

Fortified by tea and music, I felt the moment had arrived to look at the rest of Sarlat. I started my exploration in the Place de Peyron, in front of the cathedral of St-Sacerdos, appropriately because the town grew up round a Benedictine abbey founded here in the ninth century which received the relics of Saint Sacerdos, a bisop of Limoges, from Charle-magne himself. Nothing remains of the original abbey and very little of the twelfth-century church that replaced it. Only the first two stages of the belfry are twelfth century, the upper storey having been added in the seventeenth century. The rest of the church was demolished in 1504 and rebuilt slowly over the next two centuries. The result is a gloomy, uninspiring building and I did not linger there.

In the same square is Sarlat's most famous house *La Maison de La*

Boétie. It is a narrow four-storey building with a steep, gabled roof, covered with *lauze* tiles. So far all the elements are gothic but the decoration is resolutely renaissance. The ground floor has a round headed arch, flanked by corinthian columns; on each of the next three floors are mullion and transome windows, framed by pilasters supporting architraves. The pilasters are adorned with roundels and lozenges, devices that would never have been tolerated in renaissance Italy. The proportions, too, are quite unclassical and the top architrave breaks out into the gable end. But these architectural solecisms don't matter a damn. The French architects of the period took what they wanted from Italy and created their own national style, and very attractive it is too.

Étienne de La Boétie has the dubious honour of being best known for this house and for the fact that he was a close friend of the essayist Montaigne. La Boétie was born in this house in 1530. During a short, brilliant career he became a member of the Bordeaux Parliament, translated the classics and wrote poetry. He also wrote a famous treatise on liberty *Discours sur la servitude volontaire* or *Contr'un*, which had a great influence on Jean Jacques Rousseau. His death at the early age of thirty-three inspired Montaigne's essay on friendship with the famous tribute:

> *Si on me presse de dire pourquoie je l'aimais, je sens que cela ne se peut exprimer qu'en repondant: parce que c'etait lui, parce que c'etait moi . . .*

To the right of the cathedral is the ancient bishop's palace, now a theatre, gothic below with mullion and transome windows but with a delightful loggia at the top, added by the Italian bishop Nicolo Goddi. Behind the bishop's palace, reached from the south transept of the cathedral, is the Chapelle des Pénitents Bleus, all that remains of the twelfth-century abbey. From here I climbed a path leading up to an eminence behind the cathedral on which stood a strange, stone tower with a tall conical roof. This is the so-called *Lanterne des Morts*. It was built in the twelfth century but, despite its name, nobody knows what for, although theories abound. One suggestion is that it was to commemorate a miracle performed by Saint Bernard when he visited the town in 1147, another is that it was used as a funeral chapel. The most likely explanation is that it was indeed a *lanterne des morts* but the problem is that although the upper chamber has four narrow windows it is inaccessible and it is difficult to see how the lantern or lanterns could have been lit. It remains an enigma. Alongside the tower is a small public garden from which there is a good view of the east end of the cathedral.

Leaving the tower I followed the narrow rue d'Albusse to the Presidial, a sixteenth-century law court established by Henry II in 1552. The façade has two large, open arches, one above the other, above which is a roman-tiled roof surmounted by an octagonal *lanterne* with a strange bell-shaped, slate roof whose overlapping edge is supported at intervals by wooden props. On my way down the narrow rue de la Salamandre, I passed the Hôtel de Grezel, the fifteenth-century home of a local magistrate, with a beautiful flamboyant gothic doorway, decorated with the carving of a salamander. Back in the Place de la Liberté, I crossed to the far side of the square where the rue des Consuls begins. Here are some of the finest houses in Sarlat, beginning with the Hôtel de Gisson, which I had noticed while I was having my tea. On the opposite corner was the Hôtel de Vassal with two wings at right angles to each other and a corner turret, but best of all was the Hôtel de Plamon, a beautiful building begun in the fourteenth century by an influential family of drapers – the Selves de Plamon – and enlarged and embellished over the centuries. The ground floor is fourteenth century and has two large gothic arches. On the first floor are three gothic windows with bar tracery and on the floor above fifteenth-century mullion and transome windows. The door was open so I went in to find myself in a large open courtyard with a magnificent seventeenth-century walnut staircase winding round above me. Outside again, the Hôtel de Plamont continued round the corner where a stone balcony overhung the street, supported by a bracket carved in the shape of a scallop shell.

Close by, I noticed a restaurant called the Jardin des Consuls which claimed to have a fifteenth-century courtyard and I made a mental note to return that evening. I had now reached the rue de la Republique which I crossed to enter the western half of the old town. It was much quieter here. There were no magnificent mansions or churches to see but, although they are smaller, the houses are built of the same beautiful stone and the *quartier* is mercifully free of tourists, so that I couldn't help thinking, as I strolled down the narrow rue Jean-Jacques Rousseau, that it was easier to imagine what Sarlat was really like in the middle ages in these winding lanes than in the more prosperous eastern half with its smart shops and restaurants.

At the bottom of the rue Jean-Jacques Rousseau I came across a stretch of the old town walls and one of the original gateways. I passed through and was immediately confronted by the twentieth century; traffic roared past on the wide boulevard that rings the town and the pavement was awash with tourists. I turned tail and scuttled back into the protective peace of the medieval town.

Les Jardins des Consuls lived up to expectations; it had a large, stone flagged courtyard divided into two by an arcade of round headed arches supported by fat stone pillars. The courtyard was open to the sky, except on the left-hand side where a second row of arches led into a vaulted aisle within which was a row of tables, at one of which I sat. From here I had a good view of the rest of the courtyard. There was a large open, stone fireplace in one of the wall and this convinced me that the space occupied by the restaurant had once been two rooms that had lost their ceiling as had the room above. Probably there had been a fire that had destroyed all but the shell. It made a lovely setting and I enjoyed myself between courses admiring the variations in the colour of the stone walls and pillars from a grey-white to a rich ochre.

I was walking down the rue Jean Jaques Rousseau on my way back to my hotel when I met Madame *la patronne* looking for a lost kitten. I joined her in the search but eventually as it grew darker we had to give up. I was on the telephone to Sybil in my room when I heard a scratching at the window and there was the kitten. I let it in and went on talking to Sybil while the kitten climbed all over me and ended up sitting on my head, after which I delivered it to its vastly relieved owner.

To reach my next goal, La Roque-Gageac, I had to retrace my steps down the the D704 as far as the village of Carsac where I would pick up the east west road that runs along the right bank of the Dordogne. I had no desire to plod down this rather boring road again, so I decided to try hitch-hiking and was lucky enough to get a lift almost straight away.

Just outside Carsac I stopped to look at a delightful little church in a grass oasis on the right of the road, surrounded by lime trees. The apse is romanesque with carved corbel ends and, like the nave, has a *lauze* roof. Inside, the nave and aisles have fifteenth-century vaults with keystones bearing portraits of local worthies. There is a dome over the crossing and two small gothic chapels either side of the choir. The entrance to the romanesque apse has paired columns with well-carved foliage capitals but in the apse itself there are more primitive capitals with indistinct animals savaging each other. To complete this assortment of periods and styles there are austere carvings of the stations of the cross round the walls by a modern sculptor called Zack, which I am afraid I found rather boring.

Beyond the church the road began to climb. At first there was nothing to see but a great black cliff, covered with scrubby holm oak, on the right and the tops of trees on the left but after a quarter of an hour's steady ascent I caught sight of the river below and then, a few paces further on a superb view of the Château de Monfort, all towers and pinnacles, crouched on the edge of a crag, straight ahead. I was standing at the apex of a huge horseshoe bend, the *cingle* de Monfort. Across the river, in the jaws of the horseshoe, was a huge walnut plantation, stretching back a mile or more. In the foreground, by the river bank, was a large flock of geese whose harsh cries I could hear even at this distance. Behind the walnut grove stretched a low line of hills; back up river, to my left the Dordogne was full of shingle banks, through which a flotilla of yellow canoes was threading its way; to the right, beyond the château, a line of cliffs curved away to the south to close the view. This surely is the archetypal Dordogne scene.

The closer I got to the château the less I could see. Monfort is surrounded on the landward side by a high red wall that hides any view of the building behind and unfortunately the castle is not open to the public.

I made a circuit of the wall and found on the western side a path down the cliff. From here I had an extraordinary view of the château poised precariously on the edge of a cliff so full of caves that it looked like a gigantic gruyère cheese. I had the uncomfortable feeling that the cliff face might crumble at any moment carrying the château and me with it into the river. But then I reflected it had survived for nearly eight hundred years and was likely to last a bit longer.

Nothing remains of the original twelfth-century castle which was taken and demolished in 1214 by the odious Simon de Monfort, leader of the only crusade against fellow Christians, the Albigensian heretical sect that was well established in this part of France. The castle was soon rebuilt and because of its strategic position on the frontier between the French and English, suffered repeated attacks during the Hundred Years War, changing hands frequently and being dismantled three times, only to be rebuilt again. The present château, the fifth on the site is heavily restored. The oldest buildings date from the fifteenth and sixteenth centuries but the west wing, containing the keep, was rebuilt as late as 1839.

Monfort is only two miles from Vitrac, where I had waited so long for my pack and such is the baleful effect of this name that on leaving the castle I took a wrong turning. Instead of cutting across the neck of the next horseshoe loop in the river, I followed a minor road down into the bend and, when I discovered my mistake, out again, adding a mile or more to my journey. On the outskirts of Vitrac a shackle holding one of the straps of my rucksack broke and running repairs were needed; then one of my bootlaces came undone and I had to stop again. I reached Vitrac at 11.05. Unbelievably, although I did not find out until much later, my watch stopped at this very moment. I don't believe in magic but it did seem as if Vitrac's evil *genius loci* had cast a spell on me.

As I passed the sandpit Surly Boy gave me a wave but I hastened on. I had no desire to linger in that benighted spot. After Vitrac, the road was flat and uninteresting until I reached a turning on the left leading across the river to Domme, a medieval village built on the edge of a high cliff overlooking the Dordogne and one of the river's most famous sites. My way, however, lay straight ahead across the base of another great bend in the river. Gradually the low hills on my right turned into butter-coloured cliffs that swung across my path, blocking the view. As I got nearer I could see the roofs of the houses of La Roque-Gageac but it was not until I was on the outskirts that I could see the whole village, rising in tiers up the cliff face and separated from the river by a narrow road.

La Roque-Gageac is built on a narrow triangle of land between the river and the cliff. At the east end, the one by which I had arrived, it is wide enough for three levels of houses, built in terraces one above the other; at the west end there is room for only one row, at street level. Looking from east to west the view is closed by the nineteenth-century Château de Malartrie, beautifully sited just where the river curves away to the left.

I found my hotel, La Belle Étoile, easily enough. It was half way along the river road and consisted of two buildings with high pitched, tiled roofs, linked by a vine covered terrace. On my way up to my room I passed a gloomy salon with a grandfather clock, some uncomfortable looking reproduction chairs and a stag's head on the wall. It did not look like a room that anyone ever used. As I climbed the staircase to the second floor I was disconcerted to see, through an internal window, the stag's head again, its mournful eyes on a level with my own. My room was comfortable with oak beams, a brown tiled bathroom and a splendid view up river towards Domme, which I intended to visit the following day.

After a satisfactory lunch and a siesta I went for a walk. I climbed up the little street immediately behind the hotel to the manoir de Tarde, a modest stone building with two unequal wings joined by a round tower with a pepper pot roof. The right half is tall and narrow, like a Scottish baronial castle, with a high, narrow gable. An arch leads through to the other half which is like a small house. Close to, the manoir looks delapidated and neglected but seen from a distance it certainly adds to the general appearance of the village.

Beyond the *manoir*, the road was overhung with a canopy of exotic plants and flowers: palm trees, orange trees, fig trees, oleanders and, unbelievably, bougainvillaea. It seems that the south facing cliff radiates such heat that a micro-climate is created that supports these tender plants. They made a brave show.

At the end of the road was a small rustic church with a heavy *lauze* roof. From here there was a good view over the village, a huddle of houses against the cliff face with a medley of brown tile and lauze roofs in all kinds of shapes and sizes. Beyond lay the Dordogne, glinting in the afternoon sun. A *gabare* with a white awning chugged slowly upstream, engraving a broad steely arrow in the surface of the river as it went.

The term 'organic' village might have been invented to describe La Roque-Gageac which truly seems to grow out of the rock face, so it comes as a shock to learn that the Germans totally destroyed it in 1944, following an attack by the *maquis*, and it was rebuilt, exactly as before, after the war.

A light mist was rising from the river when I left the hotel next morning. I was on my way to Domme, where I intended to spend most of the day, but first I had to buy my picnic. That done I hitched a lift back to the crossroads and started down the road to the bridge across the Dordogne. Seen from the river's edge the seven hundred foot high cliff on which Domme stands looks daunting indeed, so it is not surprising that in the twelfth century there was a castle here. It was captured and destroyed in 1214 by Simon de Monfort and virtually nothing of this early building survives. In 1281 Philip the Bold founded a *bastide*, further along the edge of the cliff from the remains of the château, and this has lasted almost intact until the present day.

Because of the restrictions of the site, Domme is trapezoidal in plan rather than rectangular but it has the usual grid plan of streets and the familiar town square with its market hall. Inland, where Domme overlooks a quiet valley and the slope is less dramatic, the town was defended by ramparts and a long stretch of these original walls still stand.

I crossed the bridge (182 yards wide here) and started slowly up the long road that winds its way up to the Porte del Bos, one of the surviving medieval gates at the rear of the town. Once through the gate I saw ahead a steep street of stone houses with wooden balconies, bright with flowers. Five minutes brought me to the town square and the market hall, an attractive building with a steep *lauze* roof and a projecting wooden balcony, supported by round stone piers. Inside the hall is the entrance to a complex of caves used as a place of refuge by the villagers in times of trouble. On the far side of the square is the church and behind it an open space leading to the *Barre*, as this part of the cliff is called.

The view from the *belvédère de la Barre*, that projects from the cliff edge, is probably the most famous on the whole river. I found it especially interesting because I could trace practically the whole of my route from Monfort to La Roque-Gageac. Looking north-east, to my right, I could just see the tops of the towers of Monfort, peeping above the trees; a little further to the left of the castle was the cliff above the *Bas de Canoë* (out of sight) at Vitrac. What was a revelation to me was that there was a village at the top of the cliff with what looked like a fine church – and I had missed it. Beyond Vitrac the Dordogne came into view for the first time, flowing evenly between rows of poplars. Just to the right of Domme itself the river began a great curve, passing below the cliff I was standing on before swinging northwards again towards a line of grey, tree-covered cliffs, where it disappeared from sight. Further on again I could see the ochre cliffs of La Roque-Gageac and the tower of the Château de la Malartrie. The cliff continued leftwards and in a gap, even further away, I saw the faint outline of the chateau de Beynac, whither I was bound the next day.

Immediately opposite Domme, contained within the bend, were cultivated fields, mostly maize, and a few walnut plantations. When I first came to Domme, over twenty years ago, the land was split up into small plots with many different kinds of crops. In those days polyculture was still widely practised in Périgord and the farmer had ducks, geese and cattle as well as the crops he rotated and his walnut trees. Sadly, monoculture has now taken over and the landscape is the poorer for it. I was certainly growing very weary of the ubiquitous maize.

Leaving the *belvédère de la Barre*, I went for a cliff top walk, through a small public garden, past a restored windmill, until I could go no further. At the extreme western end of the ridge were the vestigial remains of the castle destroyed by Simon de Monfort but it was fenced off and I could not get near enough to see anything but a pile of stones.

Retracing my steps I found a place at the edge of the cliff where I ate my picnic, untroubled by the hordes of tourists that roved the village behind me and with a magnificent panorama before me.

Sitting there, gazing down the cliff face I remembered one of the most extraordinary episodes in Domme's history. Philip the Bold claimed when Domme was built that no enemy would ever succeed in breaching its defences. How wrong he was: the town changed hands frequently during the Hundred Years War but it was in 1558, during the Wars of Religion, that the most spectacular assault took place. At that time Domme was a catholic stronghold and was being besieged by the Hugenots under the command of one of their most famous captains – Geoffroi de Vivans. After making a reconnaissance of the defences, de Vivans decided on a surprise attack. Choosing a moonless night, he lead thirty picked men up the sheer face of the *Barre*. As he anticipated, the cliff top was undefended, the townsfolk of Domme never suspecting that danger could come from that quarter. Quickly de Vivans and his men made their way to the place and there created such a racket that the whole town was in a turmoil. Taking advantage of the confusion, the attackers ran to the town gates and opened them to the rest of their troops – Domme had fallen. Looking at the precipitous *Barre*, I found it difficult to credit this famous exploit.

I was keen to see what remained of the town walls so I made my way back to the Porte del Bos, where the *promenade des ramparts* begins. Domme's defences were supposed to have been demolished by order of Henry IV but although their height was reduced, enough of the original walls survives to give a good idea of what they must have looked like in the Middle Ages. The Porte del Bos has a single pointed arch with grooves for a portcullis which was lowered from a now ruined upper storey. I climbed a short flight of steps up to the sentry walk on top of the walls and followed the *promenade* eastwards, looking outwards, down into a quiet valley and inwards at the brown roofs of Domme.

At the next gate, the Porte de la Combe, I had to descend to the road again and walk inside the next stretch of wall to the Porte des Tours, the best preserved of the thirteenth-century gateways with a pointed archway, flanked on either side by a sturdy round tower. From 1307 to 1318 the Porte des Tours served as a prison for a number of Knights Templar, whose order had been suppressed by order of the king. They left behind them some remarkable religious graffiti but the Porte des Tours is not open to the public and special permission is needed to see them. It is from outside this gateway that you get the best view of the ramparts.

Leaving the Porte des Tours I wandered off into the nearby streets. Few tourists penetrate this *quartier* of Domme, preferring to stay in the vicinity of the *belvedère de la Barre*, and yet there are many beautiful old houses, with gardens full of flowers, which make a stroll round the back streets a joy.

It was after two o'clock when I left Domme and without exerting myself, reached Roque Gageac in just over an hour.

My journey to Beynac next day was easy enough. It is only two-and-a-half miles from La Roque-Gageac and, of course, I could have gone further but Beynac possesses one of the finest castles on the Dordogne and I wanted time to look at it properly. What is more there is another splendid fortress at Castelnaud, about a mile away on the other side of the river which I was anxious to see, so it seemed logical to make Beynac my base.

The sun was lighting up the cliff ahead as I left La Roque-Gageac; not a ripple disturbed the river and the houses and trees lining the bank were perfectly reflected in the clear water. But soon the river disappeared from view as the road cut across the base of a big bend and the inevitable fields of maize, interspersed with walnut groves, appeared. I was beginning to feel rather bored when I saw ahead the château at Beynac, looking exactly as a feudal castle should, its massive walls and powerful keep towering over the cluster of village houses that straggled up the cliff face. Almost immediately the castle disappeared again only to reappear on my left as I arrived at a crossroads. A signpost pointed to the castle and the legend on it read Castelnaud – I had been looking at the wrong castle.

I walked on and in a moment the true Château de Beynac appeared dead ahead. Its profile was quite different from Castelnaud, the castle being strung out along the top of the cliff as if it were an outcrop of the rockface itself, rather than rising to a culminating point. The village of Beynac lies at the base of the cliff with only a narrow road between it and the river. Almost the first building I came to was the Hôtel Bonnet, made famous by Freda White whose classic book *Three Rivers of France*, published as long ago as 1952, first opened so many British eyes including my own, to the beauty of the Dordogne. Sadly the Bonnet is no longer the comfortable *auberge* that Freda White liked so much but a smart country hotel and commensurately expensive, so I had booked a room in the Hôtel du Château, a modest establishment at the far end of the village. It was still only 10.30 when I arrived and my room was not yet ready, so I dumped my rucksack and set off to see the château.

Immediately behind the hotel a steep cobbled road led up the cliff face to the top. It was hard going and every so often I stopped for a breather and to look back over the roofs to the river below. Near the top a high wall appeared on my right, the outer defences of the castle. It was not the first time I had visited the chateau but up to now I had found it confusing and disappointing, so before the conducted tour started I looked for a guide in one of the kiosks outside the main gate. All I could find was a postcard with an aerial view of the castle, from which I established that Beynac has a D plan, the cliff edge forming the upright and the curtain wall the curved back. Inside the wall, the castle is divided into two courtyards roughly even in size. The one to the west, which must once have been full of workshops that serviced the castle and the retainers' living quarters, is now empty; that on the east contains the thirteenth-century keep, the fifteenth-century hall, the chapel and the stables. This rather simple plan is the kind commonly found in eleventh and twelfth-century castles before the crusades radically changed military thinking on their design.

The original castle was besieged and taken in 1189 by Richard Cœur de Lion who left it under the command of the notorious English captain Mercadier. This scoundrel behaved like a robber baron, using the castle as his base to ravage the surrounding countryside. Scarcely had the region recovered from Mercadier's depredations than another scourge in the shape of Simon de Monfort appeared. He took Beynac in 1215 and dismantled most of it. The castle was soon rebuilt and the massive square keep probably belongs to this period, although it may have survived de Monfort's demolitions. After the defeat of the French at Poitiers, Beynac became, by the terms of the Treaty of Bretigny (1256), an English castle but was retaken in 1368 and remained French from then on.

The entrance to the castle leads straight into the eastern courtyard, which at this point is reduced to a narrow space between the curtain wall and the keep, so that you feel hemmed in and disorientated. The remedy is to walk to the far end of the courtyard where there is an extensive view over the Dordogne. Immediately below, on the far side of the river, is the Château of Fayrac, a fairy-tale castle built in the sixteenth century, an era when defence was no longer the first consideration and the machicolation that projects from the tops of the towers is purely ornamental.

To the left the Dordogne curves southwards and I looked down a a long straight reach, at the end of which I could see Castelnaud, high up on the left bank. To the right the Dordogne flowed on westwards through a fertile valley, its tree-lined banks flanked by a patchwork of fields.

Reluctantly, I abandoned contemplation of the view to follow the tour party into the keep. Like so many French châteaux, the interior of Beynac is bare and rather cheerless. The most impressive room is the vast, tunnel-vaulted *salle des États* whose stone floor is made up of wedge-shaped cobbles called *pises*, peculiar to the Périgord. The sole decoration of the hall was four faded pennants representing the four baronies of Périgord – Beynac, Biron, Mareuil and Bourdeilles – which only served to accentuate its bleakness. On one side is a small oratory, containing a fifteenth-century fresco depicting the Last Supper.

We passed through a seemingly endless series of empty rooms and I soon lost track of where I was, but I do remember climbing a magnificent newel staircase made entirely of oak. At last we came out on top of the keep and I found myself looking at an even finer panorama of the Dordogne, flowing westwards through a serene valley. From here I could clearly see the chapel at the east end of the courtyard and beyond it the bare outer courtyard. This was effectively the end of the tour, for the sixteenth-century wing, adjoining the keep, is not open to the public.

During the Hundred Years War the French castle of Beynac and the English castle of Castelnaud glowered at each other from opposite sides of the river. Their rivalry was intense and there were frequent sorties and skirmishes, all inconclusive. I had always wanted to see the English castle, so it was with a feeling of pleasurable anticipation that I set out next morning. Near the Bonnet I found a footpath leading to the river which, on enquiry, I found led along the river bank all the way to Castelnaud.

The path was shaded by trees and on my left was a big campsite. A little further on there was a small, sandy beach with canoes drawn up on it. Later in the day it would be covered with swimmers and sunbathers but now, at ten o'clock, it was too early and the campers were still finishing breakfast. The path continued under a railway bridge, past a large field of maize and then through the middle of an enormous caravan site. It was all highly organised with spaces for over eighty caravans, all neatly lined up betweeen lines of poplars, with standpipes and cabins with communal bathrooms and toilets at regular intervals. I crossed a meadow and saw for the first time Castelnaud, high up on its cliff to the right. Soon I was crossing the bridge with a splendid view of the castle, its massive walls rising sheer from the cliff edge and behind them the great square keep with its brown-tiled, pointed roof. As I got nearer, Castelnaud loomed over the road, a great dominating presence, brooding over the village below. A stiff climb up a stony, winding path and I had arrived at the barbican at the entrance to the castle.

It is not known when Castelnaud was originally built: the first documentary evidence dates from 1214 when Simon de Monfort beseiged the castle and captured it. Unusually for him, he did not dismantle the defences but reinforced them and installed a garrison before moving on to further conquests. In 1368 the castle passed by marriage into the hands of the Caumont family, who owed their allegiance to the Plantagenets and for the next seventy years it was an English stronghold.

The original castle was built right on the edge of a rocky outcrop, overlooking the Dordogne, and although its defences were strong, it was not very big. After the Hundred Years War it was considerably enlarged. An outer courtyard was added in the fifteenth century and in the sixteenth a great solid round tower, designed to house artillery, was built at the east end. During the Wars of Religion, Castelnaud was a Huguenot stronghold and successfully withstood attacks by the Catholic forces but after the Revolution the castle fell into disrepair and was quarried for building materials. Despite its ruined condition it was used by the French Resistance during the Second World War. On 24 June 1944 they seized the bridge below the castle but two days later the Germans returned and launched a fierce artillery bombardment on Castelnaud with mortars and machine guns. Fortunately the damage to the castle was only superficial and they failed to dislodge the *maquis*.

Restoration work on Castelnaud began in 1969, not a moment too soon, for photographs taken at the time show that it was in a ruinous state, the tops of the towers crumbling and the rest so covered with ivy that it was reduced to an indistinguishable mass. Today the ivy has all been cleared away, the towers have had their machicolation restored and the keep now has a pointed tiled roof. It could be argued that the restoration has gone too far and that the roof is an uneccessary embellishment. I have mixed feelings on the subject: close to, you can see only too clearly that a great deal of the stonework is new, yet you only have to look at the photographs to realise that this work was essential and that without it Castelnaud could never have been opened to the public. What is more, I am convinced that no scheme of restoration has been carried out at Castelnaud without good evidence based on thorough research and that the actual work has been carefully and thoughtfully executed.

It is a vexed question how far restoration of old buildings should be taken. Viollet-le Duc, who restored so many churches and châteaux in France at the end of the nineteenth century, has been heavily criticised for adding details for which there was no evidence in existing plans or engravings; yet if he had not undertaken the work, many of these buildings would be total ruins today. What is more, these very additions tell us something about the attitudes of Viollet-le-Duc and his contempories to the Middle Ages.

My favourite Viollet-le-Duc restoration is Pierrefonds, north east of Paris, near the Château de Compiègne. All that was left of the original castle were the foundations, so Viollet- le-Duc was able to give free rein to his imagination, backed enthusiastically by the Emperor, Napoleon III, who supplied him with unlimited funds from the public purse. Pierrefonds should be regarded therefore not as a genuine castle but as a medieval fantasy, as unreal as any film set by Cecil B. de Mille but fascinating as a representation of the nineteenth-century romantic view of the Middle Ages and the architectural equivalent of Tennyson's *Idylls of the King*.

The entrance to Castelnaud, as at Beynac, is on the inland side of the castle and is guarded by a thirteenth-century barbican which was reinforced in the fifteenth century by an angle tower on the north-east corner, designed to resist artillery bombardment. Unlike Beynac, there is no guided tour to the castle but a great deal of helpful information is provided. At the beginning I was given a well-printed leaflet showing the route to be followed during my visit and in one of the first rooms a video programme shows with the aid of computer graphics how the castle changed over the centuries.

The first stop was the artillery tower where there were models of fifteenth-century guns with dummy gunners about to fire them. A series of rooms followed furnished with suits of armour, collections of weapons, reproductions of colour plates from medieval manuscripts showing siege warfare and an excellent model of Castelnaud under siege. There were also reconstructions of siege engines and an extraordinary sixteenth-century gun called an *orgue*, designed by Leonardo da Vinci, but never actually used, with twelve barrels two feet long loaded with stone cannon balls, each barrel firing in turn – in fact a kind of ancient Gattling gun. It was in one of these rooms that I saw a series of photographs, taken in 1966, showing the delapidation of the castle before restoration began.

The view from the battlements is very fine: to the right I could see, through a telescope, the cliffs above La Roque-Gageac and below the tower of the Château de la Malartrie. Swinging further round to the left, the cliffs petered out to be replaced by low hills, curving in a shallow crescent round to Beynac where the cliffs began again. Directly opposite was a flat landscape of fields and poplar trees contained within the U of the bend. The river emerged from the trees on the right, passed below the castle walls and swung left up towards Beynac. Directly at the end of the reach was the Château of Beynac, watchful on its cliff.

My visit to Castelnaud at an end, I followed the river footpath back towards Beynac until I found a suitable spot for a picnic, where I spent most of the rest of the afternoon, very pleasantly.

After dinner that evening I climbed up the street behind the hotel and sat on a bench looking out over the *lauze* roofs of the houses to the Dordogne below. From this distance the river looked quite still, the poplars lining the banks reflecting perfectly in the clear water. To the west, above a line of wooded hills, the sky was pearl pink, shading upwards to a soft grey-blue with a faint tinge of yellow. Higher still a pale moon and the first faint evening star began to show against a pale blue backcloth. As I watched, the hills became a silhouette and a band of streaky crimson clouds appeared on the skyline. The moon and stars became sharply etched against a deepening blue. Below the Dordogne had changed to an inky black. It began to grow cold; the time had come to return to the hotel.

CHAPTER 7

A BRUSH WITH LE TROISIEME AGE

After the excitements of the last few days my journey to Siorac was something of an anticlimax. Once I had left the shadow of the cliff a gentle slope led down to a flat plain with fields of maize on either side of a long straight road with low hills in the distance. After half an hour I reached the village of St-Vincent-de-Cosse. To the left, across the Dordogne, I could see, amongst the trees, Les Milandes, the attractive château built by Francois de Caumont, lord of Castelnaud, whose wife found the old castle on the steep cliff uncongenial. It is better known today as the home of Josephine Baker, the famous cabaret artiste, and her family of adopted children of all nationalities and races. I would have liked to have visited the château but it meant too great a detour, so I plodded on. I was not enjoying myself: there was a lot of traffic on the road and the verge was narrow so that I was continually having to take evasive action. Another half hour brought me to the village of Bezanac, where I met the Dordogne again, flowing swiftly round a wide bend. The road was particularly narrow and difficult here and I was not surprised to see the *Conseil Géneral de la Dordogne* had voted a million francs for road improvements which had already started to the right of the old road.

There now followed another boring stretch alongside the railway line from Sarlat to Bergerac. It was a great relief when at last I turned off and struck down a country road to the riverside. Here I picked up the *Grande Randonneé 64*, one of a network of public footpaths found all over France, marked with red and white flashes. I had spotted it marked on my map and thought it would make a pleasant walk, free of traffic. In fact

GR 64 proved to be a disappointment. Instead of the footpath I expected, I found a minor road with houses at intervals along it. One had a large garden, planted with pampas grass, trees and shrubs and protected by an hibiscus hedge. From time to time a car or van passed me and once I was overtaken by a band of friendly joggers: it all felt a bit suburban. Nor was the Dordogne particularly exciting here. The opposite shore was thick with alder and willow and the river itself was the colour of pea soup. At the end of the GR 64 was a crossroads. To the right I saw the great hulk of the fortified church of Saint Cyprien, rising above the roofs of the town of the same name; but my way lay to the left, across a stone bridge to the far bank of the Dordogne. Here a quiet pastoral valley led south. Its grass slopes were sere and yellow and there was a dried-up stream in the bottom: there had been no rain here for three months. I turned right and climbed a track to the top of a small hill. From here I could see, to the north, Saint Cyprien on its hill; to the south range after range of wooded hills stretched southwards to Villeneuve-sur-Lot, only forty miles away. I was not far from home.

I reached Siorac at 12.30 only to find that my hotel was a mile further on. I was very hot and thirsty by now, so when I saw a café offering a *menu rapide* I decided to stop for lunch and find my hotel later.

La Petite Reine, as my hotel was called, was rather different from what I had been used to. It was a modern, purpose-built complex with a large restaurant at one end and the rooms at the other, separated by a terrace with an open-air swimming pool. My room was comfortable enough, although rather impersonal but it had a pleasant view, looking over a field with cows.

I was sitting on the terrace, quietly reading, when a stream of elderly, smartly-dressed ladies appeared, went to their rooms and reappeared wearing swim-suits to commandeer the pool. I quickly deduced that this was a *troisième âge* outing, a phenomenon that Sybil and I first encountered at Coutances in Normandy.

Le troisième âge is the French euphemism for old age pensioner and in France, senior citizens, as the English euphemism has it, are highly organised with a very full social calendar. Sybil and I arrived at our hotel in Coutances, after motoring all day, to find a charabanc load of *le troisième âge* already in possession. When we went down to dinner we were relegated to a side room; next door the dining-room reverberated with rude songs and ribald laughter. Every so often one of the young waiters retreated to our table to escape the attentions of the more forward of the *troisième âge* ladies who kept pinching his bottom. Long after we had gone to bed the corridors echoed with whispers and giggles as the *troisième âge* scuttled up and down, overcome with mirth at finding male underwear mixed up with their nighties or convulsed to see their friends struggling to get into an apple-pie beds. It was a long time before the uproar subsided and we were able to get to sleep.

The ladies at La Petite Reine were more refined than those at Coutances but their takeover of the hotel was as complete and I was soon driven from the poolside. There were no schenanigans that I know of that night but I had a brief encounter with them at *le petit déjeuner* the next morning. Breakfast at La Petite Reine was copious and good with a large variety of cereals, stewed fruits, different kinds of bread and toast, great slabs of butter, jam, marmalade and honey, but it was self-service. On my way round with my tray, I saw that there were eggs on offer and nearby a cauldron of simmering water. I popped an egg into the pot and sat down to eat my cereal. Soon afterwards *le troisiéme âge* arrived and started to pile their plates high. One of the ladies discovered my egg and called loudly, '*A qui est cet oeuf – la?*' I replied equally loudly '*C'est a moi!*' and was met with a stunned silence. The idea of a man boiling his own egg was evidently a novel one and they looked at me with a new respect. No one followed suit. The egg was very good.

Siorac is not far from the Dordogne and soon I was crossing the river again. I had decided to take a minor road on the right bank to Limeuil, my destination that day, rather than the D25 which runs along the left bank from Siorac to Le Buisson and is full of traffic. After the bridge there was a short stretch of busy road before I turned left and found myself entering a narrow valley with farmland and low hills on my right and more fields stretching down to a line of poplars about half-a-mile away that marked the course of the Dordogne. On the far side of the unseen river were more hills, wooded for the most part but with the tree line broken here and there by fields and small farmhouses.

For once maize was not the only crop and I recognised the large green leaves of the tobacco plant, which is widely grown in the vicinity of Bergerac. A tractor was taking a load of tobacco to a large black barn at the side of the road for drying. I had never seen the inside of a *sechoir* so I asked the farmer if I could have a look. The leaves are hung in bunches from the roof beams and take about two months to dry. I asked the farmer what kind of harvest it had been and received the inevitable reply, '*moyenne*'. It had been too dry, the plants had needed constant watering and there had been some terrible storms.

Beyond the *sechoir* the farmland on the right was replaced by a grey, scrub-covered cliff. Hard up against the rock face was a hamlet called Bigaroque. It had a romanesque church with a bell-gable and some good houses with *lauze* roofs. Here the road began to climb and became a corniche, overlooking the Dordogne, which had reappeared on the left. On the opposite bank I could see a large campsite and beyond it the railway junction of Le Buisson.

I reached a crossroads where the main road from Le Buisson to Le Bugue came in from the left. Here I turned right and headed north. It was a busy road, full of bends round which a stream of cars hurtled at speed, so that I had to proceed with great caution. The cliff to my right soon retreated to be replaced by vast fields of maize. Luckily this didn't last long and after about a mile I turned left on to another quiet country road. It was not long before I could see the roofs of Limeuil itself, poking above the trees at the top of a cliff: it looked interesting.

The road and the river came together and I looked for somewhere to have my picnic. The Dordogne was only six feet or so below me so I slithered down the bank and sat on the edge of a stony beach, close to a shallow rapid. Downstream was a fine stone bridge with four round-headed arches and beyond it a small *plage* with a bar in front of which were one or two tables covered by brightly-coloured, striped umbrellas.

I finished my picnic and walked on to find that there are two bridges, the one I had already seen, crossing the Dordogne, and another at right angles across its tributary, the Vézère. Together they are known as the Pont-Coudre, the elbow bridge. I crossed the bridge over the Vézère and took a path down to the plage. Here, close to the river's edge was a gothic gateway leading into Limeuil. I passed through the arch and started to climb up a steep winding street lined with beautiful old houses. I was looking for my hotel, Hostellerie des Terasses de

Beauregard but I couldn't see it anywhere. Once I actually went into the back door of a small *auberge* and wandered round the corridors until I realised I was in the wrong place and beat a hasty retreat. Limeuil is built on a steep hill and gradually, weighed down by my heavy pack, I worked my way up to the Place du Château, where there was another hotel with a tempting open-air restaurant, past the romanesque church and finally right through the village to another medieval gate on the far side. There was still no sign of my hotel.

Reluctantly I shrugged off my pack and took out my hotel guide, from which I learned that the Hostellerie des Terasses de Beauregard was outside Limeuil on the road to Trémolat. Back I went, down the narrow streets of this very attractive village, to the *plage*, sat down at a café table and ordered a beer.

It was a pleasant spot. To my left was the Vézère, flowing under its bridge into the Dordogne and creating a wide back-eddy as it did so. It was this, no doubt, that was responsible for the sandy spit that made the *plage*. Opposite was the other half of the Pont de Coudre across the Dordogne and beyond it the upstream reach stretching back to the unseen Le Buisson. To the right the united streams of the Vézère and the Dordogne flowed on and round another big bend out of sight. Although it was the height of the holiday season it was very quiet.The only other people on the *plage* was a young man assiduously oiling the back of his nubile, topless girlfriend. A family of mallards floated by, the ducklings paddling desperately to keep up with their parents. Just downstream was another shallow rapid and I watched with mixed feelings, remembering my own efforts in the kayak, as the flotilla of ducks swept through, even the smallest of them quite unruffled, reassembled in a back-eddy and continued on their way.

I sat there, recovering from my exertions in Limeil, for about half-an-hour and then set off again to find my hotel. A steep winding road brought me to the cliff top and a mile further on I found the Hostellerie des Terasses de Beauregard. It is a modern building with a long, vine-covered terrace, separated from the cliff edge by the road. At first it seemed shut up but eventually I found a little girl who fetched the *patron*. The room was large with a separate bathroom but the main feature was the superb view from the window. The hotel stands at the top of the first of three great horseshoe bends, starting at Le Buisson and finishing just below Mauzac, a distance of nine miles by river, but only five as the crow flies. Three hundred feet below was a patchwork of rectangular fields set at different angles and varying in colour from the bright green of tobacco to the plain chocolate of ploughed fields. The sun glinted on serried rows of strawberry tunnels and there were one or two small walnut groves, but as usual the dusty yellow of maize predominated and they were harvesting part of the crop as I watched. To my left the Dordogne was hidden from sight by the cliff edge as far as Limeuil, where I could just see the Pont de Coudre and beyond it the little white road I had followed after turning off the main road from Le Buisson. To the right the river was still hidden, except for a short stretch below a white limestone bluff called Les Roques Blanches, where it swung south, then it disappeared again, although I could follow its course from the line of cliffs and low hills until they merged with another range of hills, running east west immediately in front of me but about two miles away to the south.

The sense of well-being inculcated by the beauty of my surroundings was quickly dissipated in the dining room that evening. The first course was cold mushroom quiche in a tomato coulis, completely lacking in flavour. This was succeeded by an equally tasteless rabbit dish. I summoned the *patron* and informed him that the rabbit '*n'est pas chaud et n'a pas de goût*'. He was taken aback but agreed to replace the offending dish with a *confit de canard*. This, when it came, was hardly an improvement, both dishes having obviously been pre-cooked and warmed up in a microwave oven, a detestable gadget that has done more to ruin the flavour of good food than anything since the invention of tomato ketchup. However, I had made my stand and didn't feel like pushing my luck. It was, by the way, the first time I had ever sent back a dish in France – a melancholy landmark. The explanation is, I think, that the hotel's splendid position meant that they didn't have to make an effort to attract custom. I have frequently found that the quality of a restaurant's cuisine is in inverse ratio to the attractiveness of its setting and this was never more true than at the Hostellerie des Terasses de Beauregard.

When I went to bed that night I found that I had left the light on and the window open and my pillow, sheets and white bedside table were covered with bugs. I swept them off as best I could and turned in. I was awakened at 2 a.m. by the whine of a mosquito. There was a huge aerosol insect spray in the room, so this was clearly not an isolated problem. Without so much as thought of the depleted ozone layer or the damage I was doing to the local ecology I let the mosquito and bugs have it and went back to bed. After that there was no more trouble.

The sun was lighting up Les Roques Blanches and a slight mist hung over the river when I left next morning for Badefols. The road continued westwards along the cliff top, giving more admirable views, but after about ten minutes the way was interrupted by a narrow valley, which forced the road to turn inland. Another ten minutes brought me to a crossroads, where I turned left. Almost at once I saw a red and white flash on a tree to the left of the road, indicating the start of a GR64 footpath. I knew from my study of the map that the path was a short cut that would save me a long detour by road, so I struck off along it. A narrow track led upwards through a wood. It was overgrown with brambles and clearly had not been used for a long time. In one place I had to negotiate a fallen tree, but the red and white marks were still clearly discernible and kept me from losing my way. After twenty minutes I came out into the open with a dried up pasture on my left and the woods continuing on the right. At the end of the field was a lane where I turned right watched by three mournful cows. Because of the drought they were already being fed winter fodder – no wonder they looked sad.

The lane led back to the road but after a hundred yards the GR64 flash pointed to the right. A cart track led through some scruffy woodland, full of stunted oaks, typical of the *causse*. Every so often I came to a small clearing planted with maize, presumably intended for the farmer's own animals, the fields were too tiny for cash crops. It was poor land and I saw no-one but once a buzzard flew up immediately in front of me, flapped slowly away and settled on a nearby branch, staring at me reproachfully. Eventually the track came out of the woods and I dropped down through some fields to a valley road that led to Trémolat. It had taken exactly an hour to cover two and a half miles, slow going but at least I had not had any traffic to worry about.

Trémolat is famous as the place that Chabrol chose as the setting for his macabre film *Le Boucher*; it also has a remarkable twelfth-century church that completely dominates the village. The walls of the nave are very high with only four narrow windows and no aisles and the east end is flat, so that approaching from this direction you see a great rectangular, block that looks more like a prison than a church. Even more forbidding is the massive belfry at the west end, whose grim cliff-like face is spoiled by the insertion of a baroque entrance and the addition of a silly classical bell gable at the top. Inside, the aisleless nave has four domes and there is a medieval fresco depicting the entry into Jerusalem in the choir.

Leaving the church I took a narrow road that led northwards out of the village up to the top of the cliff, where I knew there was yet another of the Dordogne's most famous views, the *cingle* de Trémolat. At first there were houses on either side of the road but as the incline grew steeper these were left behind to be replaced by stunted oaks. At the top I turned left along a white stony track that glared in the sun. It was very hot. At first I could not see the Dordogne, although there was a wide prospect inland of rolling *causse* country, but as I got higher the river appeared on my left, swinging round a great cliff-lined bend. It took another forty-five minutes to reach the water tower, from the base of which I could see the whole horseshoe bend stretched out before me.

It was certainly a marvellous sight, not that dissimilar to the one I had seen from the window of my room at the Hostellerie des Terasses de Beauregard, the main difference being the view down the long, straight reach on the east side of the *cingle*, where rowing and sailing regattas are held in the summer.

It had been a long climb up to the water tower and I was feeling tired and hungry, so I retraced my steps to Trémolat where I found a bar offering *cassoulet* and a *pichet de vin* for fifty-five francs. By one o'clock I was on my way again. My first stop was the Chapelle St Hilaire on the outskirts of the village, a tiny church containing some horrific stained glass. The pièce de résistance is a window in which a pair of yellow, disembodied, supplicating hands reach up to an orange and scarlet heart, set against a sapphire-blue background.

A short walk brought me to a bridge over the Dordogne. The river was over two hundred yards wide here, allowing ample room for rowing eights to race abreast. From the middle of the bridge I had a good view of

the sombre grey cliffs to the north, swinging leftwards before disappearing behind a line of trees. On the far side of the bridge, the road
turned right, following the bend of the river until it reached the hamlet
of Larives where it turned south. On either side were some irregularly
shaped fields of maize, with here and there a tiny vineyard. Seen from
the water tower they made an attractive pattern but here at eye-level the
landscape with its serried ranks of sun-bleached corn and rows of vines
looked dull and featureless. Hot and bored I plodded on for an hour
until I reached a crossroads where I turned right on to a corniche road
with a grey, limestone cliff on my left and the Dordogne on the right.
Another twenty minutes brought me to my hotel at Badefols.

At first there seemed to be no one about. I found my way to the dining
room, where a young girl was clearing the tables. She assured me that
Madame would be back *tout de suite*, so I ordered a beer and sat down in
a courtyard behind the hotel to wait. Madame duly arrived and showed
me to my room, which was small but comfortable, and with some relief I
took off my boots and stretched out for a much needed rest.

Later I went out to look at Badefols. According to my guidebook there
were the ruins of a feudal castle on the cliff behind the hotel. During the
Middle Ages this was the stronghold of predatory local lords who
exacted tolls from the crews of river craft before allowing them to
proceed down river. The castle was dismantled in the fifteenth century,
restored in the sixteenth century and finally demolished during the
revolution. I climbed a short path up the cliff-face but there was nothing
to see at the end of it but a pile of stones, all that remained of the château.
At the foot of the cliff was a small romanesque chapel but it was too
heavily restored to be of interest. The rest of Badefols consisted of a few
houses, two more small hotels and a large *mairie*. There was nothing
here to detain me so I wandered down to the river bank. Here there was
a large campsite with its own swimming pool, restaurant and bar, where
I spent the rest of the afternoon.

It took me a long time to find anyone to give me breakfast next morning,
the reason being that none of the staff actually slept on the premises:
they all went home once dinner was served and did not reappear until

8.30 next morning. What would happen if someone were taken ill in the night or there were a fire I am not sure.

It was another fine morning and I could see two miles down river all the way to the bridge at Lalinde. The high, thickly wooded cliff continued on my left but across the river the country was more open with a low line of distant hills. What surprised me was that there were some vicious reefs here, great flat slabs, stretching across the river like stepping stones. Because of the dry summer they were easy to see but when the river rises they must be as great a hazard as the jagged rocks in the stretch below Argentat. It was because of these rapids that a canal was built in 1840 between Mauzac, on the right bank of the river, opposite Badefols, to Tuilières, ten miles to the west. Mauzac is situated at the end of the *cingle* de Trémolat, where the Dordogne, after cutting its way through the *causse* emerges at last into the lowlands. Above Mauzac the terrain made construction of a canal impossible. Before the canal de Lalinde was built, river craft were forced either to unload and take their cargoes overland or to hire a local pilot.

A mile further downstream I came to Pontours where there was an island and some fierce rapids. As I contemplated the over-falls a quartet of swans taxied down river and flew off in formation. Twenty minutes more brought me to Lalinde. Crossing the bridge my eye was caught by an iridescent flash; I was just in time to glimpse a kingfisher before it disappeared into the trees. Downstream the river was full of reefs and looked dangerous. This was the Saut de Gratusse, a famous rapid and one of the chief reasons for the constructions of the canal.

Lalinde is a *bastide*, built in the thirteenth century on the site of the gallo-roman town of Diolindum, and has the familiar grid pattern and central square. The river front is attractive with some fine old houses and a stretch of the original ramparts. Apart from the church, none of the buildings in Lalinde is more than three storeys high and seen from the opposite side of the river the town has the low profile typical of many riverside towns on the lower Dordogne.

The canal runs through Lalinde and I decided to walk alongside it for a while. It was pleasant, ambling along in the shade of the plane trees that line the banks, alone except for the occasional fisherman, but after a couple of miles I reached the village of Couze, where I crossed the Dordogne again. I could have continued to the end of the canal but this

would have meant walking the rest of the way to Bergerac, my destination that day, on a busy main road and I hoped the left bank would be
quieter. I also imagined I would see more of the Dordogne, but in this I
was mistaken: I was not to see the river again for another two hours. A
high wooded bluff on the opposite bank marked its course clearly
enough but this was never closer than two hundred yards and often it
was more than half-a-mile away.

There was a large paper mill at Couze, down river from the bridge,
which rather spoiled the view. On the far side, the road ran at the foot of
a cliff for a short way but after that there was a noticeable change in the
landscape to the south. The cliff gave way to a low range of hills that
gradually grew more distant as the valley widened. I trudged along a
glaring white road that ran dead straight towards a vanishing point that
continually retreated before me. On either side a seemingly endless sea
of maize stretched towards a hazy horizon, wavering in the heat. There
were no trees to give me shade and the only sound was a gentle
susurration of the parched corn stalks.

In all this time I passed through one tiny hamlet that did not even have
a bar where I could get a drink; otherwise it was all fields with nothing
but the occasional farmhouse to break the monotony. By midday I was
desparately tired and hungry but it was another half hour before I
reached Mouleydier on the right bank of the Dordogne and staggered
into the Auberge St Christophe. Blessed be Saint Christophe, the
patron saint of travellers and thrice blessed be the *patronne* of this
friendly, old fashioned inn. This large, motherly lady at once recognised
my need and quickly brought me an ice-cold beer. After a quick wash I
sat down to a simple but good lunch: a tureen of thick vegetable soup,
left on the table; an hors d'oeuvre of sliced tomatoes and hard-boiled
egg; a leg of chicken with spinach; a cheese board with a decent *chèvre*
and a piece of *Saint Nectaire* and a *pichet de rosé*. All this for forty-six
francs – a wonderful bargain and a life-saver.

The last stretch from Mouleydier to Bergerac was along the main
road. The traffic was frightful. Bergerac is a much bigger town than any
I had visited so far, with a population of over 24,000, as was evident from
the number of cars and heavy lorries on the road. It was not the moment
for sight-seeing but I did notice, after I passed through the village of
Creysse, five miles from Bergerac, that the wooded heights on the right

bank had given way to gently sloping hills, covered with vines, the first vineyards of any size that I had seen.

As I approached the outskirts of Bergerac the road became a dual carriage-way and the country disappeared to be replaced by factories, hypermarkets and petrol stations. One of the buildings I passed was the *Centre de formation et de perfectionnement des planteurs de tabac,* which looks after the interests of the local tobacco growers, the Bergeraçois being the most important tobacco growing region in the whole of France. It was 3.45 by the time I reached the Hotel du Commerce, in the centre of Bergerac. I had walked over sixteen miles in a heat of eighty degrees Farenheit, and it felt like it.

CHAPTER 8

THE PEN
AND
THE SWORD

After the previous day's trek I was in need of a rest so, after a very necessary visit to the nearest laundrette, I spent the morning sight-seeing. Sybil and I had passed through Bergerac many a time on our way to and from our home near Villeneuve-sur-Lot and had occasionally stopped to do some shopping, so I already had a superficial impression of a busy, commercial centre where we were liable to be caught in a traffic jam but it was not a place I had ever wished to visit. On closer inspection I realised that the town had more to offer than I had thought.

The centre, near the nineteenth-century cathedral of Notre-Dame, is the rue de la Résistance, a busy shopping street, lined with large department stores, a big, well-stocked bookshop, some tempting but expensive patisseries and a smart *salon de thé*. The old quarter, all that remains of the medieval town, stretches southwards from the rue de la Résistance to the river. There are no important buildings to see but the area has been pedestrianised and the old, half-timbered houses sensitively restored, so strolling round the narrow streets and dropping into the occasional bar was pleasant enough.

The oldest building is the church of St-Jacques which, as its name suggests, was founded in the eleventh century to look after the needs of pilgrims on the route to Santiago de Compostela. Unfortunately, the church is very heavily restored and nothing of its original character survives. A thriving town soon grew up round the church and as trade developed, Bergerac became an important entrepôt between Bordeaux and the interior. Throughout the Middle Ages, the wine trade played an

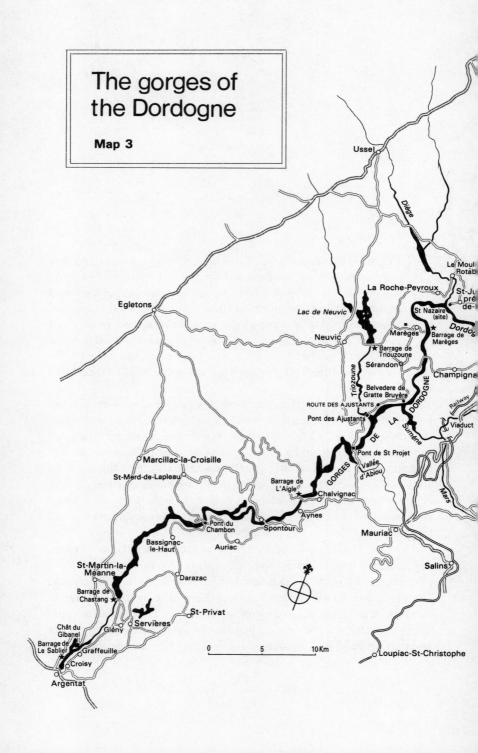

The gorges of
the Dordogne

Map 3

Ussel

Diège

Le Moul
Rotab

La Roche-Peyroux

St-Ju
pré
de-

Egletons

Lac de Neuvic

St Nazaire
(site)

Neuvic

Marèges

Barrage de
Marèges

Dordog

★ Barrage de
Triouzoune

Sérandon

Champigna

Triouzoune

Belvedere de
Gratte Bruyère

DE LA DORDOGNE

ROUTE DES AJUSTANTS

Sumène

Railway

Pont des Ajustants

Viaduct

Pont de St Projet

Marcillac-la-Croisille

GORGES

Vallée
d'Abiou

Mars

St-Merd-de-Lapleau

Barrage de
L'Aigle

Chalvignac

Aynes

Mauriac

Pont du
Chambon

Spontour

Salins

Bassignac-
le-Haut

Auriac

St-Martin-la-
Méanne

Darazac

St-Privat

Barrage de
Chastang

★

Servières

Chât du
Gibanel

Glény

Barrage de
Le Sablier

★

Graffeuille

Croisy

Argentat

Loupiac-St-Christophe

0   5   10 Km

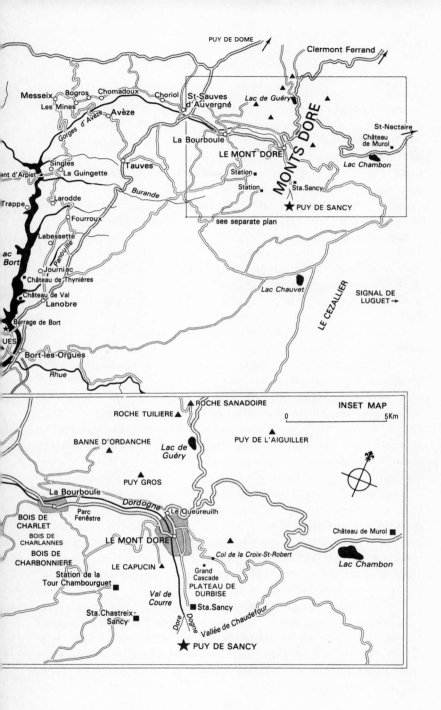

PUY DE DOME

Clermont Ferrand

Messeix   Bogros   Chomadoux   Choriol   St-Sauves
Les Mines   d'Avergné
         Gorges d'Avèze   Avèze   Lac de Guéry
                                                                          St-Nectaire
                                   La Bourboule   Château
                                                                          de Murol
                                        LE MONT DORE
Singles   Lac Chambon
nt d'Arpiet   La Guingette   Tauves   Station
                              Burande   Station   Sta.Sancy
Trappe   Larodde
                                                   ★ PUY DE SANCY
             Fourroux   see separate plan
         Labessette
                  Panouille
ac   Journiac   Lac Chauvet
Bort   Château de Thynières   SIGNAL DE
        Château de Val   LE CEZALLIER   LUGUET →
          Lanobre
   Barrage de Bort
UES
      Bort-les-Orgues
          Rhue

MONTS DORE

▲ ROCHE SANADOIRE

ROCHE TUILIERE ▲   INSET MAP

BANNE D'ORDANCHE   PUY DE L'AIGUILLER   0   5 Km
                     Lac de
                     Guéry
          ▲
              PUY GROS
   La Bourboule   Dordogne
                                Le Queureuilh
BOIS DE   Parc
CHARLET   Fenêstre
BOIS DE
CHARLANNES   Château de Murol ■
BOIS DE   LE MONT DORE
CHARBONNIERE   ▲
            LE CAPUCIN ▲   Col de la Croix-St-Robert   Lac Chambon
   Station de la
   Tour Chambourguet ■   Grand
                            Cascade
              Val de   PLATEAU DE
              Courre   DURBISE
   Sta.Chastreix-   ■ Sta.Sancy
   Sancy   Dore Dogne Vallée de Chaudefour
                   ★ PUY DE SANCY

increasingly significant role in the local economy. The wine was shipped down river to Bordeaux for onward transmission to England and Holland. This brought the Bergeraçois into conflict with the Bordelais who used custom duties and other protectionist devices to favour the local wines of Graves and Entre-Deux Mers. Nevertheless the town continued to prosper, despite being taken and sacked by the Earl of Derby in 1345, during the Hundred Years War.

In the sixteenth century Bergerac became famous as a protestant stronghold and earned the name of the Geneva of France but the town continued to prosper, even during the Wars of Religion, reaching its apogee at the end of the sixteenth century. It is said that when Louis XIII visited the town in 1621 the fountains flowed with wine. This happy state of affairs was brought to an end by the revocation of the Edict of Nantes in 1685, when many of the townsfolk fled abroad rather than renege on their faith.

A long period of recession followed and the fortunes of the town did not revive until 1820 when a port was built on the north bank just below the Couvent de Récollets. Here, river craft from Souillac unloaded cargoes of vine stakes and barrel staves for the wine trade and re-loaded with salt for the return journey. The building of the railways in the second half of the nineteenth century killed this river trade and Bergerac entered another long period of depression that lasted until the end of the Second World War. But now Bergerac is flourishing again; its market is one of the biggest in the region; the wine trade has revived and it is the commercial capital of the tobacco trade for the whole of France.

A narrow street south of the Eglise de St-Jacques brought me to the Place de Cayla, where there is a statue of Cyrano de Bergerac. The decision of the worthies of Bergerac to erect a memorial to this legendary swordsman, poet and wit, whose love life was ruined by the size of his nose, is a tribute to the power of the pen; for the myth of Cyrano was the creation of one man, Edmond Rostand, whose play *Cyrano de Bergerac* was first performed in Paris in 1897.

Rostand's play was loosely based on the life of Savien de Cyrano (1619–1655), whose family came from Bergerac near Paris. Like Rostand, Savien de Cyrano was a playwright whose most famous work was *l'Histoire comique des États et Empires de la Lune*, a kind of seventeenth-century science fantasy, but he also enlisted in the company of Carbon de Casteljaloux, a Gascon noble who appears in Rostand's play, and fought at the siege of Arras, where he was wounded in the throat, putting paid to his military career. The connections with Rostand's hero are clearly pretty tenuous and ninety per cent of *Cyrano de Bergerac* is pure invention but such is its power that the myth is firmly established and has just been given a fresh breath of life by Gérard Depardieu's marvellous performance in Jean-Paul Rappenau's film of the play.

On the south side of the Place de Cayla is the entrance to the Cloître des Récollets, a reformed order of monks who were expelled during the period of Huguenot ascendency in Bergerac but returned afterwards to convert the town's unbelievers. Today, it is the headquarters of the *Conseil interprofessionnel des vins de la région de Bergerac*, which is open to visitors.

Inside is a charming courtyard with arcades supporting wooden galleries on two sides and brick walls on the others. The galleries belong different periods, the earliest with chunky stone piers is sixteenth century; the other with elegant fluted columns belongs to the eighteenth. In fact the Bergeraçois have cheated: the eighteenth-century gallery does not belong but was brought here from another building that was being demolished.

Steps lead down to a beautiful vaulted cellar once used to store wine, where dignitories of the local wine trade dress up in medieval garb and hold initiation ceremonies. Upstairs, on the first floor, the *Conseil interprofessionnel des vins de la région de Bergerac* tests the wines of each new vintage and awards or withholds *appellation* status.

Opposite the Cloître des Récollets is the Maison du Vin which offers free tastings of the wines of the Bergerac region. The most famous of them is Monbazillac, a luscious sweet wine that is virtually unknown in Britain, although its reputation in France itself is high and it is also greatly appreciated in Holland and has been since the seventeenth century. Indeed, if we are to believe local tradition, the wines of Monbazillac were highly thought of even in the Middle Ages. The story is told of a band of pilgrims in Rome who were presented to the Pope. 'We come from Bergerac,' said their leader, and when he saw that this awoke no response in the Holy Father added, 'from Bergerac near Monbazillac'. Immediately the Pope's face lit up. He raised his hand in blessing, murmuring as he did so, 'Ah, Monbazillac – an excellent wine.'

Unfortunately, sweet wines have a bad reputation in Britain, being associated in people's minds with thin, sickly-sweet, straw coloured wines with no particular flavour. These wines have been degraded by the indiscriminate addition of sugar. Nothing could be further removed from the smooth, mellow, aromatic wines of Monbazillac which, when they have matured, take on a deep orange tint. At their best they rival those of Sauternes, which are made in the same way, although they never reach the heights of Yquem and the *premier crus* Sauternes and Barsacs. However this is difficult to prove for the best Monbazillacs are not easy to find. Those on sale in Britain are often not good examples and even in Bergerac it is not easy to track down a really good bottle. Nevertheless it is worth the effort: the best thing is to do is go to one of the local vignerons for a tasting – you will not be disappointed.

Monbazillac is made from three grapes: Semillon Blanc, Muscadelle and Sauvignon in the proportions two thirds Semillon, one sixth Sauvignon and one sixth Muscadelle. The Semillon helps to make the wine mellow and gives it in part its unusual bouquet. The Muscadelle adds a scent of musk, while the Sauvignon also contributes to the aroma and adds finesse.

Making Monbazillac is a protracted and difficult business requiring great skill on the part of the *vignerons* combined with extreme patience and an almost religious faith in the success of the outcome, for the grapes are left very late before harvesting. The *vendange* does not start until 10 October at the earliest and can go on until the beginning of December.

By this time the grapes are over-ripe and starting to dehydrate, leading to a greater concentration of natural sugar. The process is accelerated by the presence of a mould on the skin of the the grape called *botrytis cinerea*, which produces a condition known as *pourriture noble* or 'noble rot'. The skins of the grapes become mottled with grey spots and then split and wither. At the same time chemical changes take place in the grapes themselves resulting in an increase in their pectin and glycerin content. It is these transformations that help to give Monbazillac its peculiar unctuous quality.

The *vendange* is not only very late but very slow. The grapes cannot be harvested until the *botrytis cinerea* has done its work, but because the 'noble rot' does not attack all the grapes at the same time there have to be repeated pickings over a long period. To make the very finest wine the grapes have to be picked individually, a long, back-breaking business. And yet at the end of it all the yield is bound to be low because the *pourriture noble* reduces the quantity of juice that can be extracted from the grapes. Even in a good year the amount of wine produced is small, no more than thirty-five hectolitres per hectare. For this reason Monbazillac can never be a cheap wine but it compares very favorably in price with Sauternes.

When the grapes are pressed the juice has the consistency of oil, hence the cry of *pisso l'oli!*, meaning the wine will be of good quality. After pressing the juice ferments furiously, producing a frothing surface scum that looks like dirty snow. Frequent racking from barrel to barrel is needed to control the intensity of the fermentation and to keep the alcoholic and sugar content in balance. The wine begins to stabilise in February or March but even after this, unceasing care is needed if the quality is to be maintained right up to the time the wine is bottled. No wonder Monbazillac is not cheap.

The vineyards of Monbazillac run northwards from an escarpment that overlooks the Dordogne and Bergerac can be seen in the distance. On top of the ridge is the Château de Monbazillac, a beautiful piece of renaissance architecture commanding a superb view over the regimented ranks of vines. The château is maintained by the Coopérative de Monbazillac and is open to the public.

The other wines made in the Bergerac region are not in the same class as Monbazillac. The best known is a red called Pécharmant, which is reputed to be as good as the lesser wines of Bordeaux but I have not been impressed by the odd bottle I have tried. Apart from Monbazillac, my favourite is Montravel, a light, dry fruity wine with a distinctive earthy tang. The Montravel area lies about twelve miles west of Bergerac in a gently undulating green landscape of small fields and vineyards. The wine is made in fourteen communes, amongst them St-Michel-de-Montaigne where the château of Montaigne, the famous essayist, still stands and still makes wine just as it did in Montaigne's own day. Montaigne, who liked his glass of wine once wrote: 'It is not right to enjoy wine in moderation; it makes it look as though you take this gift of God for granted!'

After the horrors of the last stages of my walk to Bergerac, I was not anxious to venture on to the main road that runs south of the Dordogne to Sainte-Foy-la-Grande, about fifteen miles away. Instead I walked down through the old quarter to the river, where I found a short stretch of road running along the bank. At the end was a 'no entry' sign *sauf riverains* marking the start of a pleasant private road, lined with street lamps and bordered by riverside villas with neat front gardens. Although it was only eight o'clock, their owners were already out watering the flowers before the sun got up. The river was wide and peaceful. Wagtails flitted over the surface of the stream but otherwise it was deserted, save for the occasional fisherman, sitting hunched over his line in a shallow green punt. On the far side, houses gave way to tall poplars reflected in the placid stream. Behind them , in the distance, were the towers of the Château de Monbazillac.

After half-an-hour the road degenerated into a dirt track running alongside a perimeter fence guarding an army camp. Eventually this too petered out and I found my way barred by a pile of concrete blocks. There was a dam across the Dordogne at this point with more nasty-looking concrete slabs jumbled at its base – not a place for canoeists.

I was determined not to retrace my steps so, still wearing my pack, I scrambled up over the blocks and found at the top a narrow footpath, wide enough for one person at a time. I was now out in the country proper with maize fields on my right and poplars lining the bank on my left. After a while, the path appeared to cross the garden of a large house. I was wondering what to do when along came a man walking his dog. He assured me that this was a public footpath and that it continued along the bank all the way to Prigonrieux, about four miles west of Bergerac.

It was nice and cool in the shade of the poplars and I felt very relaxed walking there, but gradually I became aware of signs of considerable storm damage, broken branches and trees with their tops snapped off, although it was not on the scale I had seen at Creysse. I had just passed a small château when I came to a vast strawberry field. The strawberries were growing under plastic tunnels which shimmered in the distance like a lake. Two men were adjusting an automatic sprinkler system. Next door was a large apple orchard and here too there were signs of storm damage: some trees had hardly an apple left on their branches and one or two had been uprooted, yet elsewhere the crop was quite unaffected:

it was bizarre. I stopped to talk to the farmer, who was clearing away the debris. He told me that there had been a fierce local storm the week before and that he had lost half his crop. On the opposite bank was another enormous apple orchard, full of automatic sprinklers. Water was spurting in all directions, flinging rainbows into the air. It was quite a sight.

Soon afterwards I came to a field of sheep, then a small backyard full of gobbling turkeys, and then some back gardens. I had reached Prigonrieux. From here on I had to walk along the D32 from Bergerac, a minor road according to my map but still too busy for my liking. I had to keep my eye on the road ahead and take to the grass verge whenever I saw a car or lorry coming. The valley was very wide here. Flat fields stretched far away on either side with low hills in the distance. Apple and pear orchards lined the road, a nice change from maize, but even orchards can get boring if you see too much of them.

After about an hour I took a little road to the left to St-Pierre-d'Eyraud where I bought some tongue, tomatoes, peaches and a custard tart. By now it was midday and I was feeling hungry but it didn't look very promising country for a picnic. About a mile further on I found an artificial, rectangular pond, obviously dug with a bulldozer. The spoil had been piled up round the edge to make an embankment and a line of poplars had been planted. It was out-of-bounds but I reckoned that this being lunch-time, noone was likely to spot me, so I slithered down the bank, found a shady place and ate my picnic, undisturbed.

After lunch I rejoined the D32 and tramped slowly onto Le Fleix, where I stopped for a drink. Le Fleix is on a bend of the river and here I had my first sight of the Dordogne since Prigonrieux. The river bank was shaded by trees and there were benches set out at intervals under them. On my right was a high bluff, covered by trees. At the foot of the cliff was a gypsy encampment, drawn up in an old quarry. The gypsies obviously thought me quite mad to be walking, laden down by a great pack, in the heat of the day and gave me some verbal stick as I passed. I ignored them and marched on but secretly I thought they had a point. I was very tempted to stay there in the shade of the trees but there was another three miles to go before I reached Sainte-Foy and I was anxious to get on.

West of Le Fleix the Dordogne disappeared again and the road ran between vineyards, the first I had seen close to on my journey down river. It took another hour to reach Sainte-Foy, by which time it was 4.30 p.m. and I had been on the road for over eight hours.

I was staying at Le Grande, one of those pompous, old fashioned hotels, dating from the *belle époque*. My room was vast and gloomy but the bed was very comfortable and the bathroom had a bath, so I had a good soak and lay down for a rest before sallying forth in search of postcards.

Sainte-Foy-la-Grande is a *bastide* founded in 1255 by Alphonse de Poitiers, the brother of Saint Louis, and retains its original grid plan. The main square, the place Gambetta, has arcades on three sides, supporting some attractive half-timbered houses with pretty, wrought-iron balconies but is spoiled by a relentlessly classical Hotel de Ville, plonked in the middle of it. I sat down in the shade of one of the arcades at a table belonging to a rather smart *salon de thé* and ordered a pot of darjeeling. Refreshed, I went to look round the town. I liked what I saw. Sainte-Foy has a surprising number of fine, half-timbered houses, many of which are to be found in the rue de la Republique, the long thoroughfare that runs east-west through the town on the south side of the place Gambetta. One of the best is the *Syndicat d'Initiative*, a sixteenth-century building with an imposing corner turret that soars high above roof level. Unfortunately, as is the case in so many of the restored buildings of this period, and not just in Sainte-Foy, the original clay in-filling has been replaced by yellow cement. Further along the road at number 94 is a delapidated three-storey house whose façade is adorned by some remarkable wooden sculpture. The top storey has two windows flanked by debased classical pilasters; below, the first floor has a similar arrangement but the pilaster on the left of the façade has what looks like a bear, carved below the capital, while the equivalent one on the right has a bearded face. In the middle, between the windows is a strange, upside down face, like a Benin mask. Sad to say, this interesting house shows every sign of falling down and may well have done so by now.

On the corner of the rue de la Republique and the rue Victor Hugo is another unrestored house with a corner turret. The door has a pediment, supported by pilasters, containing a primitive carving of a tree with the date 1565 above it, what might be called rustic renaissance.

There are also some elegant eighteenth-century houses with wrought-iron balconies and delicately moulded pediments over the windows. These were only a few of the many treasures I spotted as I wandered through Sainte-Foy's narrow streets.

It was nine o'clock when I left Sainte-Foy, bound for Castillon-la-Bataille. My plan was to follow the left bank most of the way because the road is closer to the river on this side. At first the road ran dead straight with suburban villas on the right-hand side hiding the Dordogne, but after half-an-hour the houses came to an end and I could see the river again. Ahead of me was a high wooded bluff which forced the river to the right. As I looked a shaft of light lit up a small white château on top of the cliff and then was blotted out by clouds.

At St-André-et-Apelles I turned right onto a minor road that ran along the foot of the cliff. On my right a tree-covered bank dropped twenty feet to the river below.

I continued along this river road happily enough, with only the occasional car to worry about until I reached Eynesse, a former *bastide* of which all that remains is an entrance arch and a single street leading down to the river. On the outskirts of Eynesse was the biggest nursery I have ever seen. It stretched for a mile on either side of the road with every kind of ornamental tree – roses, beds of lavender and huge glass houses full of flowers. As I trudged along, admiring this vast establishment, a light breeze got up and rustled the leaves of the trees. It had clouded over and I smelled rain in the offing. I remembered the old sailors' saw:

> When the wind's before the rain
> Soon you may make sail again.

I hoped that it was true.

Where the nursery ended, I saw the Dordogne again but at this point I was confronted by a notice proclaiming *route barrée*. A diversion sign pointed to the left but I realised that the notice was intended for motor vehicles so I decided to ignore it and stick to the river road. Almost at once I saw the reason for the diversion: a section of the road about fifty yards long had sunk two feet, leaving a great crack at each end, and showed every sign of slipping downhill into the river. This made the route impossible for a car but I found it quite easy to negotiate: I stepped down and then up again and continued on a perfectly good road along the foot of a cliff. It was a pleasant stretch and I had it all to myself – bliss! My euphoria was short lived. A lightning flash lit up the sky and I heard a rumble of thunder, then it began to rain. I decided to take shelter under the trees at the river's edge and have an early lunch. I slipped and slithered down the bank and found a good spot near a punt chained to a tree. I was sitting there enjoying my picnic when a cygnet urgently flapped its way down river, closely pursued by a very hostile heron. I would never have believed that a swan could be seen off in this way if I had not seen it myself.

The rain soon stopped and I set off again. The river road came to an end and I turned inland. Thunder was still grumbling and suddenly there was a vivid flash ahead: it looked as though the storm was moving my way. On the outskirts of a forlorn little hamlet I found a half-built house with a large porch where I took shelter. I was just in time: the lightning and thunder increased in intensity and synchronised and rain began to hammer on the roof of the porch. The downpour lasted for about fifteen minutes then with a final flash that lit up the whole sky and a doom-like crack of thunder it was all over, the rain stopped and I was on my way again.

The thunder continued to growl in the distance but the sun came out and it was very hot again. I crossed a stretch of open country, planted with vines and came to Pessac, where I crossed to the north bank. The river was slow moving here with a large stony bank in the middle, reminding me of the Loire. A road sign said fourteen kilometres to Ste-Foy, about nine miles, but I must have done more with the twists and turns of the river.

About five miles away, up in the hills ahead of me was the Tour de Montaigne, the home of Michel de Montaigne, where he wrote his famous essays and although it meant a long detour, I was determined to see it. I struck inland and crossed a dreary tract of flat farmland until I reached the main road from Sainte-Foy to Castillon-la-Bataille. On the far side a minor road led to Moncaret where I stopped for a beer and to ask

directions. It appeared that if I continued on the same road I would find
Montaigne's tower at the top of the hill. Before leaving I had a look at the
church, which was large for the size of the village. The apse and north
transept are romanesque, the rest later. Inside there are some re-used
roman capitals and some gallo-roman sculpture from a recently excavated
gallo-roman villa on the north side of the church. I should liked to have
stayed longer and looked at the excavations but there was still some way to
go to the tower of Montaigne, let alone Castillon, so I resumed my march.

A stiffish climb brought me to the top of the hill and there, sure
enough, was a tower, alas not Montaigne's but a ruined windmill. A
glance at the map showed me that there was another two miles to go
before I reached the village of Saint-Michel-de-Montaigne, where the
true tower was to be found. I was now walking along an east west ridge
road with wide views on either side. To the left I could see the Dordogne,
winding through a wide, flat valley, bounded in the distance by low
hills; to the right a rolling, wooded landscape stretched northwards to
the horizon. In the immmediate foreground, on both sides of the road,
was row on row of well-tended vines.

It was 3.45 when I reached the village and approached the entrance to
the château. The next guided tour was at four o'clock so, while I waited,
I explored the grounds. On the north side of the château is another
splendid panorama of forest and distant hills. A solitary tower stood out
on the skyline to the north east, the Tour de Gournay, which belonged
to Madame de Gournay, a great friend of Montaigne, who published an
edition of his Essays soon after his death.

Michel Eyquem de Montaigne was born here, in the château, in 1533.
His father had only recently been enobled and came from a family that
had made its fortune in the Bordeaux wine trade.

As a young man Montaigne became a member of the Parliament at
Bordeaux and it was here he met his close friend Etienne de La Boétie
(see page 135). He subsequently became Mayor of Bordeaux and
Gentleman of the King's Bedchamber.

In 1571, at the age of 38, Montaigne abandoned his public career and
retired to his estate. This decision is recorded in a latin inscription on
the wall of his library:

'In the year of our lord 1571, at the age of thirty-eight, on the last day of
February, being the anniversary of his birth, Michel de Montaigne, being

weary of his public and the shackles of the court, and while still in possession of all his faculties, has taken refuge in the bosom of the muses, seeking there tranquility and peace of mind for the rest of his days.'

It was here, between 1571 and his death in 1592, that Montaigne wrote his celebrated *Essays*, a form which he invented. Montaigne's motto was *Que sais-je?* and in the *Essays* he takes a series of topics, *Of Sorrow*; *Of Cannibals*; *How we Laugh and Cry at the Same Thing* etc., and subjects them to a critical examination. In the process a picture emerges of a wise, sceptical, humane man, devoid of all pretension. His essay on *Liars* begins:

'There is no man who has less right to speak on the subject of memory, for I find scarcely a trace of it in myself and doubt if there is another in the world so monstrously defective.'

Although he wrote in a tower, Montaigne did not live in an ivory one but drew his examples from ordinary life. His essay *How the Soul discharges its Passions upon False Objects where the True are Wanting* begins:

'One of our gentlemen who suffered terribly from the gout and was told by his doctor to give up salted meat, used to answer, humorously, that when his suffering was at its worst he needed something to quarrel with and abusing and swearing at the sausages, ox-tongues and hams gave him some relief.'

A nice example of his sense of humour and his humanity.

In 1580 Montaigne set out on a long journey through Switzerland, Germany and Italy in the search for a cure for the stone. While he was away, the jurists of the Parliament of Bordeaux elected him mayor of the city and so, despite his resolution, he found himself drawn back into public life at a particularly difficult period when the Wars of Religion were at their height. He became a *confidant* of Henry of Navarre, the leader of the Protestants, and might well have served in his government but, by the time Henry became king of France, Montaigne had already died on 13 September, 1592. Before his death he published three volumes of his *Essays* and made important additions and changes for a new edition, published posthumously by his friend Madame de Gournay in 1595.

Most of the original château was destroyed by fire in 1885 but miraculously Montaigne's tower survived and happily is open to the public. It is a modest building which at first sight seems rather humble for such a distinguished writer but which on closer inspection admirably expresses the spirit of the man. A round, three-storey structure it is built of undressed stone and has a shallow red-tiled pepperpot roof. Inside, on the ground floor, is the chapel with, opposite the door, a niche containing the altar, above which is a a picture, after Carpaccio, of St Michael slaying the Dragon; Michel de Montaigne conquering the monster of ignorance by the light of learning one presumes. The rest of the circular wall is decorated with a painted arcade with doric columns, while the ceiling, a flattish dome, is painted a faded blue with gold stars. A stone, newel staircase leads up to a bare bedroom, furnished with an old four-poster bed, clearly not Montaigne's own. In one corner a shaft communicates with the chapel below so that Montaigne could hear mass when he was ill in bed.

The top room of the tower was Montaigne's library where he wrote his *Essays*. I cannot better his own description of this room:

'When at home I turn a little more often to my library, from which I can easily overlook my whole household. There I am above the gateway and can see below me my garden, my farmyard, my courtyard and most parts of my house. There I turn the pages now of one book, now another, without order and without plan, reading by snatches. Sometimes I reflect, and sometimes I compose and dictate my reflections, walking up and down, as at present. . . . My library is circular in shape, with no flat wall except where my table and chair stand and, being round, it offers me a view of all my books at once, arranged about me on five rows of shelves.'

Alas, those books, and there were over a thousand of them, including rare editions of ancient authors like Seneca and Plutarch, were sold off by his daughter and dispersed. Very few have been recovered, although there are some in the library of Bordeaux. What do survive are the latin and greek inscriptions carved in the wooden ceiling beams, which inspired Montaigne. I have little latin and no greek and anyway there are over fifty of them altogether, so I will transcribe just a few to suggest their flavour:

COGNOSCENDI STADIVM HOMINI DEDIT DEUS EJVS
TORQVENDI GRATIA
God has given man a thirst for knowledge to torment him
HOMO SUM HUMANI A ME NIHIL ALIENVM PUTO
I am a man. Nothing human is a stranger to me.
SUMMVM NEC METVAS DIEM NEC OPTES
Neither fear nor desire your end.

. . . which seems a fitting note on which to end this visit to Montaigne's tower.

It was a good three miles from Montaigne's tower to Castillon-la-Bataille, mercifully most of it downhill, so it was another hour-and-a-half before I limped very slowly to the entrance of La Bonne Auberge, my hotel.

I was more than ready for dinner which was taken on a first-floor terrace under a canvas awning. I was tucking into an excellent fish soup when the storm returned. Thunder boomed and the rain rattled on the awning, so that a large pool collected in the middle. One of the waiters lifted it with a broom, releasing a cascade into the courtyard below: a girlish scream, followed by a stream of abuse indicated a direct hit on one of the maids.

I turned in early but was kept awake by the noise of thunder, competing with rock-and-roll belted out by a merry-go-round organ, part of a travelling fair in the market place. Rock-and-roll won easily and it was after midnight before I finally dropped off to sleep.

Castillon is a dreary little town but my hotel was comfortable so I decided to stay a second night. This meant I could walk to Libourne, unencumbered by my heavy pack, and return to Castillon that evening by train. But first I went for a promenade along the right bank of the river to look at the Talbot monument.

John Talbot, Earl of Shrewsbury, was the English commander in the final, decisive battle of the Hundred Years War, which the

English lost. He was already an old man, some sources say he was eighty-six, when in 1452 he was summoned by the English king Edward IV to lead an army to relieve Bordeaux which the French had taken the year before. Talbot had a great reputation as an experienced and doughty fighter and when the news spread of his arrival at the head of 4000 men the citizens of Bordeaux rose against their French masters and let him in.

A French army was quickly despatched to retake Bordeaux under the command of Jean Bureau, a master of artillery. Bureau decided that Castillon was the key that would open Bordeaux and set about besieging it. He drew up his forces on the right bank of the Dordogne, just east of the town, in a triangle of land between the river and a small tributary of the Dordogne called the Lidoire. In front of his troops he built a high earth redoubt, reinforced with tree-trunks, preceded by a deep ditch. His right flank was protected by archers, stationed in the Abbey of Saint-Florent, just north of the redoubt.

Talbot with a force of about 6000 men left Bordeaux on the 16th July and marched all day and the following night, arriving at Castillon at dawn on the 17th. East of Libourne, the Earl of Shrewsbury led his men along a ridge route, north of the main road, where his advance was hidden by trees. Approaching unseen, he launched a surprise attack on the Abbey of Saint-Florent and massacred the archers to a man.

Talbot then retired to the Abbey to rest and hear mass, but in the middle of his prayers, news was brought that the French were breaking camp and in flight. Without stopping to verify the report, which turned out to be false, he called his men to arms and charged the redoubt. The result was catastrophic. Bureau's well-placed guns slaughtered the English and the remnants of the army fled in panic as the French troops emerged from behind their barricade, but most were cut down before they reached the safety of Castillon or were drowned trying to swim across the Dordogne. Talbot, fighting bravely to the last, was surrounded, dragged from his horse and stabbed to death. The next day his body was recovered by his herald: it was so mutilated that it was only recognisable by a broken tooth.

Castillon capitulated the day after and, as Bureau had predicted, Bordeaux fell the following October. It brought to an end nearly three hundred years of English rule in Gascony.

Looking at the peaceful scene today it is difficult to imagine the bloody battle that took place here over five hundred years ago with such far-reaching results for the histories of France and England. Talbot's memorial consists of a simple obelisk bearing the words:

BATAILLE DE CASTILLON
17 JUILLET 1453
MOURUT LE GENERAL
J TALBOT

A little further north, close to the main road, is another memorial commemorating the battle itself. The somewhat tendentious inscription reads:

Dans cette Plaine
le 17 Juillet 1453
Fut Remporteé la Victoire
ou delivra
de joug d'Angleterre
Les Provinces Meridionales
de la France
et termina
La Guerre de Cent Ans

Crossing the bridge from Castillon to the left bank of the the Dordogne, I couldn't help noticing that the colour of the river had changed to a murky olive, although when I had last seen it the previous day at Pessac it was still a clear dark green. I also thought I could detect, fringing the bank, something that looked suspiciously like seaweed. According to my information the Dordogne is tidal up to to Libourne but I couldn't help wondering whether the low level of the river due to the dry summer meant that the tide was pushing further up-stream than usual.

Once across the bridge I turned on to a minor road from which I had a good view of Castillon's back gardens on the opposite bank. I was soon in the country. Close by were tiny, ill-tended vineyards and the odd small house. Away to my left the hills were hazy in a morning mist. The road was straight and flat but despite this my progress was slow. My calf muscles still ached after yesterday's long trek and my left little toe was badly blistered.

At the start, the river was shallow and full of wide mud and shingle banks but these were soon replaced by willow-covered islands, separated from the shore by narrow muddy channels. A smart outboard motor-boat planed past and I noticed some big iron lighters moored on the far bank. Hereabouts there were floating landing stages on pontoons, with gangways down to them, a sure sign that the river was tidal. A little further on I saw some large, sea-going yachts moored in the stream.

After walking for two hours I reached Saint Jean-de-Blagnac, where I stopped for a beer and to look at the map. I had walked about five miles from Castillon and there was another ten to go to Libourne. My legs were still aching and I was wondering whether I should turn back. In the end I decided to walk another two miles to Branne where I hoped to find somewhere for lunch. This, I thought, would give me a rest and set me up for the last eight miles or so.

After Blagnac the road and the Dordogne parted company as the river swung northwards at the start of another great horseshoe loop. The countryside here was rather dull with endless vineyards on either side but after tramping on for another hour the Dordogne reappeared on my right, a wide chocolate coloured flood, flowing fast *up river*. My doubts were resolved: the river was definitely tidal.

Branne is a small, stone-built village, dominated by a large, ugly neo-gothic church. In the main square I found the Hôtel de France, a good old-fashioned coaching inn where I enjoyed a copious six course meal, including salmon and *gigot d'agneau* for only 160 francs. Lunch was a leisurely affair and I did not resume my journey until 2.30, rather behind schedule if I was to catch my train back to Castillon. For the first half mile I was forced to walk along the busy main road to Bordeaux, before turning right to Moulon. I was feeling rather sleepy after my big meal, the day was very hot and it was an effort to keep going, especially as the country here was flat and dull. At Moulon I took a turning to the right on to a narrow road that followed the left bank of the Dordogne but after a little way I was dismayed to find my view of the river obscured by a high embankment, presumably a flood barrier. Every so often I climbed to the top of the bank just to convince myself that the Dordogne was still there. Eventually I came to Port de Gennisac, a riverside village, where I rested for a while in the shade of a tree at the river's edge.

Beyond Port de Gennisac a long, straight road struck inland through scruffy pasture land, intersected by dykes. The sun beat down relentlessly but there was no shade. As I plodded on I became aware of a growing din ahead of me. When I got nearer I saw that it emanated from an improvised dirt track in a field to my right. A small crowd was cheering on four teenagers who were screeching round the track on 500cc motor-bikes, hurling their machines into the corners with frightening abandon. Other competitors were awaiting their turns, all of them dressed in skin-tight, designer leathers in red and black and carrying space-men crash helmets: they must have been melting inside their gear but fashion dictated that it must be worn.

I was melting myself by now and for only the second time on my journey down the Dordogne I hitched a lift for the last three miles into Libourne.

I had about an hour to wait before my train back to Castillon so I sat down at a table in the Place Abel-Surchamp, Libourne's main square, and ordered a beer. The large, open *place* is surrounded by arcades, a sure sign that it is a *bastide*. Libourne was founded in 1270 by Roger de Leybourne, who was Edward I's lieutenant in Gascony and a native of Leybourne in Kent. The square possesses a number of fine eighteenth-century town houses with some beautiful wrought-iron balconies. In the south-west corner is the Hôtel de Ville, an extraordinary gothic building of the kind one would expect to find in a northern town like Arras or Bruges but looks quite out of place in south-west France. The Hôtel de Ville dates from the fifteenth century but was woefully restored in the nineteenth.

Libourne is situated at the confluence of the Dordogne and the Isle and until comparatively recently was the most important port on the Dordogne. Freighters from England would sail right up to Libourne and load up with wines from Saint Emilion, Pomerol and Fronsac but the deeper draughts of modern ships and the increasing use of road transport led to a decline in this trade.

I finished my beer and strolled down to the river. All that remains of the high walls that once enclosed the town is the ancient fortified gateway that guarded the point where the Isle flows into the Dordogne, but the huge size of the Tour du Grand Port, the north tower of the gateway, gives some idea of how formidable these defences once were and how important Libourne was in the Middle Ages. Beyond the gateway was the Quai de l'Isle but today there was no sign of wine barrels being loaded; in fact, no ships at all. The once busy wharfs have been repaced by an *allée couverte* of pollarded plane trees in whose shade a large, excited crowd had collected. When I got closer I found that the space between the trees was filled with teams playing *boules*, cheered on by their ardent fans. I lingered on the quay, watching the fun, until it was time to catch my train. It took nineteen minutes to complete a journey that had taken me all day!

I was back in Libourne at 8.12 next morning and by 8.30 was crossing the Dordogne. My destination was St-Loubes, an undistinguished little town about twelve miles downstream which was the only place where I had been able to find a hotel within reasonable distance of Libourne. The first stretch was was on the N89, the busiest road I had so far encountered, full of fast cars and heavy lorries travelling to and from Bordeaux a mere fifteen miles away. Looking at the map I saw a small white road that followed a bend in the river, rejoining the N89 about three miles further on. It meant a detour but it seemed worthwhile to avoid the traffic. A pleasant, tree-lined country road soon made me forget the hubbub of the N89. From here I had a good view of the mouth of the Isle and the great medieval tower brooding over the entrance to the port. Gulls circled, screaming overhead, the first I had seen on my journey and in the middle of the stream, tugged at by the tide, was a round green navigation buoy. Clearly the sea was not far away.

After walking for about half-an-hour I came to a little marina with some large yachts moored alongside. Here the road came to a dead end and I was forced to take a track through a vineyard until I reached another road leading to the N89. It was marshland here, criss-crossed with water-filled dykes in one of which I saw some tufted ducks. A moorhen scuttled into the reeds as I passed.

All too soon I was back on the N89. It was horrific: an endless stream of traffic, incessant noise and choking exhaust fumes. Fortunately, there was a cycle path, running parallel to the road so I didn't have to walk on the N89 itself until I reached the village of Arveyres. On the far side was a frightening bend where there was no room for me to walk. I was forced to climb over the metal crash barrier and pursue my way along a drainage ditch. It was a great relief when at last I could turn off down a country road to Vayres.

Once again I found myself surrounded by rows and rows of well-tended vines from which hung heavy, juicy-looking red grapes. I was walking through Graves de Vayres, one of the minor *appellation controlée* wine regions of Bordeaux which produces a good red wine, comparable to all but the best of Saint Emilion. Unfortunately the annual production is minute and it is virtualy impossible to find in Britain.

Vayres is a typical small, grey Bordeaux village with a rather grand gothic church and behind it an even grander château that I was keen to visit. By now it was midday and the château did not open until two o'clock, so I walked on to Saint Pardon where there is a fine view of the Dordogne, flowing round a wide bend, lined by trees. On the bank were two fishermen, netting *écrevisses*. One of the fishermen had his car radio on playing pop music at full blast, which did not please me but after ten minutes he turned it off and went into a nearby bar. I followed him in for a beer but when I saw that they were offering lunch at only forty-two francs I decided to eat there. It was a wretched meal presented without the slightest concession to aesthetic effect. I regretted it.

Feeling uncomfortably bloated I returned to Vayres and entered the grounds of the château. The approach was through an attractive park, along a path bordered by topiary, to a classical portico with doric columns supporting a balustrade. Behind this entrance was a medieval gateway, a juxtaposition that admirably set the tone for the visit. The oldest part of the château dates from the thirteenth century but the building was badly damaged in the Hundred Years War and extensive rebuilding programmes were undertaken in the sixteenth and seventeenth centuries, so there is an interesting mix.

Once through the gateway I found myself in a courtyard: behind me, flanking the arch I had just passed through, were two thirteenth century towers, the earliest part of the château. Beyond them, completing the east side of the courtyard was the fourteenth-century keep, a massive rectangular tower with machicolation and a battlemented roof. The courtyard itself was divided into two by a low wall running from the south-west corner of the keep, creating an inner *cour d'honneur* entered through a handsome pedimented arch. On the north side of the *cour d'honneur* is the new wing built at the end of the sixteenth century by Louis de Foix. The façade is beautifully designed: on the ground floor round-headed arches alternate with flat wall spaces, articulated by pilasters with swags between them. Above, on the first floor, are tall pedimented windows, alternating with blank arcades outlined by arches echoing those on the ground floor below. Throughout, the detailing and execution are superb. Curiously the pilasters of the top floor terminate in heads some of which are supposed to represent members of the Gourgue family who set in train this rebuilding programme; others depict characters from the *commedia dell'arte*.

The château is now owned by Ghislaine and Philippe Barde, who hire out their beautiful rooms for conferences and gourmet banquets, so much of the interior is out of bounds but we were shown the so-called Salon Henri IV which has a beautiful marble fireplace adorned with a painting of the *Vert Galant*. Afterwards we went down to the magnificent vaulted kitchens. Finally we were let out onto the terrace on the north side of the house, from where there is a fine view of the formal gardens, with their topiary bushes, sweeping down to the river. The north façade of the château was destroyed by gunfire during the French civil war called the Fronde (1648–1652) and rebuilt soon afterwards. I went down to the garden and looked back at the house. Seen from here the façade appears unbalanced. The flat, castellated roof line is broken by a heavy dome, built over a projecting pavilion which is just off-centre, creating a decidedly uncomfortable effect. This is compensated to some extent by a splendidly curvacious staircase leading from the terrace down to the garden.

I spent over an hour and a half at the château and would like to

have stayed longer but there was still five miles to go before I reached
St-Loubes and I was beginning to tire.

After Vayres the vineyards disappeared to be replaced by suburban bungalows and maisonettes. I was after all only ten miles or so
from Bordeaux and this was clearly a dormitory inhabited by
commuters. The houses were every bit as dull as their English
equivalents except that all of them had shady terraces, furnished with
comfortable reclining chairs and tables where the family could take
its ease. And indeed, on this hot afternoon, to my envy, many were
doing just that.

I reached St-Loubes at 5.30, passing on the outskirts a stall selling
oysters, the first I had seen since the ones I had eaten at le Mont-
Dore.

St-Loubes looked as though it was founded as a *bastide*. It had the
typical main square with arcades on three sides but unusually they
were classical in design, perhaps eighteenth century, and there is a
classical Hôtel de Ville in the middle instead of a covered market. My
hotel proved to be a small house, beautifully furnished in period
style. My room had pink and white striped 'regency' wallpaper and a
reproduction chair, Louis XV I think. There was no bar and the
restaurant was in a separate building up the road, but Madame,
seeing my need, brought me a pot of tea on a tray – very civilized.

It was raining when I looked out of the window next morning and,
although by the time I left the hotel it had stopped, it was humid and
overcast. For the first time since my flight from Bort I had not
succeeded in booking ahead into a hotel for the night but I was
hoping to find a room in St-André-de-Cubzac, about ten miles away
on the north bank of the Dordogne. This would leave a short
eight-mile stretch next day to Bourg, at the confluence of the
Dordogne and the Garonne.

To avoid traffic I took a backroad down to Cavernes on the river.
At first it was all very suburban with boats in back-yards and the
usual cacophony of barking dogs but before long I reached open
country again. There was a mix of small vineyards, some large

orchards and arable land. In one field was a weird metal contraption, consisting of a series of horizontal, linked, wing-like pipes on tiny wheels, looking like a piece of *avante garde* sculpture or an Emmet flying machine. In fact, as I learned later, it was crop spraying equipment.

After Cavernes the road ran alongside the Dordogne, athough most of the time the river was hidden by woods. On my left were large commercial apple and pear orchards. As I walked, I gradually became aware of a steady humming noise that grew louder the further I went. The source of this din was soon evident: ahead, soaring high above the river, was a huge concrete bridge, carrying the Autoroute 10 from Paris to Bordeaux across the Dordogne. The noise I had heard emanated from an unceasing column of traffic crossing the bridge.

It would have been suicide to have tried to cross the Dordogne here but luckily I didn't have to. A hundred yards further downstream was the old bridge, a metal box construction on brick arches that still carried the old RN10 across the river and had a narrow pavement on either side of the road.

It was difficult to believe as I crossed the bridge that this wide, swirling *café au lait* coloured flood and the tiny trickle I had stepped over so easily on the Puy de Sancy were one and the same. I calculated that the river here was 680 yards wide. Just downstream of the bridge, on the north bank, was a small marina with some moored yachts. Nearby was a solitary dredger; otherwise, apart from the great sweep of the new bridge upstream the river was empty. Far away, downstream, the river merged with an opalescent sky.

St-André-de-Cubzac is a dreary place: grey, mean houses surround an enormous marketplace on one side of which was a huge advertisement hoarding promoting an international fair at Bordeaux in the style of an Indian film poster. I tramped round and round the dreary streets trying to find a room but without luck. I was just on the point of giving up and taking the train to Bordeaux for the night, when I saw painted on the wall of a house an old, faded advertisement for the Hôtel du Château at St-Gervaise, route de Bourg. I rang the number and, glory be, they had a room, *très simple*, no shower and the restaurant was closed that evening, but I was delighted to have a roof over my head and was not going to quibble.

I left St-André-de-Cubzac without regret and took the road to Bourg. The scenery here was the most attractive I had seen since Trémolat. To my right was a gentle slope covered with vines with here and there a small red-tiled roof poking above the greenery. On my left the slope continued down to the Dordogne, about half-a-mile away. Sometimes the river was hidden from view by trees but the woods were not as thick here as further upstream and usually there were long stretches clearly in view. It was wide here and the far bank was only just discernable, all beyond was lost in a grey haze.

I was in the Bourgeais, another recognized wine region of Bordeaux. There were vineyards on the Bourgeais long before they were planted in the Medoc and in the Middle Ages their wines were often blended with the wines of Graves to give them more body. They are full-bodied and fruity, similar in character to those of St-Emilion but not as fine. Like those of Fronsac and Lalande-de-Pomerol, the Bourgeais wines have recently come more into favour because of the high cost of the better known Médocs and St-Emilions. The grapes used are Cabernet Sauvignon, Cabernet Franc, Malbec and Merlot for the red wine; some white wine is also made but it is not important. There are three different *appellations* in the Bourgeais, Bourg, Côtes de Bourg and Bourgeais, but all have the same permitted minimum of alcohol of 10.5 degrees and use the same grapes, so they are almost indistinguishable, although the Côtes de Bourg is considered the best.

Apart from a brief shower of rain, I reached St-Gervaise without difficulty in fifty minutes. The village, more of a hamlet really, lies half a mile north of the main road and two miles west of St-André-de-Cubzac. On the outskirts, shouldering its way clear of a green mantle of vines was the church of St-Gervaise, a large building for the size of the village with a romanesque apse and a machicolated defensive balcony built, strangely, on the south side of the nave. The west end looked heavily restored.

The Hôtel du Château turned out to be a bar with a small restaurant at one end. My room was in a house next door. It was very primitive with only a bidet and washbasin in the corner, a large but comfortable bed and an old fashioned *armoire* that didn't contain a single hanger. The window looked straight into the street at ground level which meant that if I wished to get undressed I had to close the shutters.

I had a rest and then went out for a stroll. There was nothing much to see in St-Gervaise so I took a narrow path westwards towards Bourg, with lovely views southwards over the Dordogne. Along the way I met a nice old couple out for their evening walk who told me that I could follow this and connecting lanes all the way to Bourg. They also pointed out a circular route back to St-Gervaise via another village called St Lawrence d'Arce. I thanked them and was on the point of leaving when they called me back to tell me that there was a panorama of the Dordogne from a park behind the hotel, which they assured me was not to be missed.

Supper consisted of a *jambon* sandwich and a beer which I ate in the bar, watching the local youth playing table-top football. Afterwards I went to the park. At the south end was a belvedere overlooking the Dordogne. The old couple were right: it was a wonderful view. Below me, as far as the eye could see on either side, gentle vine-covered slopes stretched down to the river. Away to the right were six tall chimneys belonging to a power station at Bec d'Ambès, the flat peninsular that divides the Dordogne from the Garonne. Further west again, counterpointing the chimneys, stood six gigantic pylons, three on either side of the river, like sinister sentinals from the *War of the Worlds*. To the south, ill-defined in the rising evening mist was a low line of hills. A single ray of the setting sun glowed orange in the waters of the Dordogne and then was extinguished. Gradually the sun changed from amber to a deep tomato and then slowly disappeared, like the dying embers of a fire, behind a thick black cloud.

FOG: it was the last thing I had expected. A woolly cloud blotted out the landscape and visibility was down to twenty yards. It was cold and clammy and for the first time for many days I wore a sweater and my Rohan jacket. There was no question of my taking the country route, my only hope was to follow the D669 to Bourg. I made my way down the slope and found the main road without difficulty, but then my problems really began. Despite the fog there was plenty of traffic and although I could see the loom of their yellow headlights, they certainly couldn't see me. To my relief I found that there were vineyards running right up to the road and I was able to walk in the space between the ends of the rows of vines and the verge. It was a weird sensation walking in a white cocoon with only the noise of unseen lorries and cars on my right and the black twisted shapes of the vines on my left. Once I saw the yellow eyes of a ghostly tractor advancing through the vines; it reached the end of a row, turned and was swallowed up in the fog once more.

I had left the hotel at 7.30 without breakfast and I was in desperate need of something to warm my vitals but there was no sign of a bar anywhere. It was not until I reached Prignac, an hour later, that I found one, by which time I was ravenous. A hot chocolate, bread and butter and home-made jam soon revived me. By the time I had finished breakfast, the fog had begun to clear. The rest of the journey was easy and twenty minutes later I was in Bourg. It was still only 9.30.

The town is built on a bluff, overlooking the river and the first thing I did when I arrived was to make straight for the Terasse du District, from which I expected to see the confluence of the Dordogne and the Garonne. Immediately below the terasse were the red-tiled roofs of the *ville basse* and the port. Beyond was the Dordogne and on the far side Bec d'Ambès, a flat sandy spit covered with ugly warehouses and gas-containers. There was no sign of the Garonne. A hurried perusal of the map confirmed that Bourg was not the place; the junction of the two rivers was further downstream: I was devastated.

I went down to the port and wandered along the river bank where the yachts were moored, their halliards tinkling against the metal masts in the light breeze. Nothing much to see here, so I climbed back up a steep sreet to the *terasse*. On the way I passed through one of the original gateways, la porte Batailleyre. Bourg's strategic position at the mouth of the Dordogne and the natural strength of its cliff-top site made it an important stronghold in the Middle Ages. During the Hundred Years War it was the key to Bordeaux for forces advancing from the north and west and changed hands many times. The town was fortified in the thirteenth century and stretches of the original ramparts still survive along the cliff edge and to the west of the town. On the riverside of la porte Batailleyre is an inscription which gives an admirable summary of the history of the town:

BOURG
Château Gallo-Romain au IV siecle
Abbaye au VIIIs Commune au XIIIs
Filleule de Bordeaux a 1379
Ville Forte assiegé en 1294, 1295, 1388,
1406, 1452, 1548, 1569, 1590, 1653
Visitée par les Rois Charles VII, Louis XI,
Francois I, Charles IX, Louis XIII
RESIDENCE DE LOUIS XIV ET DE LA
COUR DE FRANCE DE AOÛT A OCTOBRE 1650
CHEF LIEU DE DISTRICT DE 1790–1796

After lunch I booked into the Hôtel du Commerce, a typical commercial traveller's hotel with the inevitable candlewick bedspread, and then set off walking westwards from Bourg to a point where I could see the confluence of the Dordogne and the Garonne. I was not sure how far I would have to go because it was off my map, I hoped not too great a distance: my blistered little toe, which had been troubling me for some days, was agonizing and I could only limp along.

After ten minutes I saw a notice pointing left: 'Le Pain de Sucre, Corniche de la Gironde, Panorama du Bec d'Ambès'. A winding, tree-shaded road led to the river which here was bordered by bungalows with front gardens full of flowers. Nearly all of them had a landing-stage at the bottom with a boat moored to it, one of them a large catamaran. Quite soon the road began to rise again and as it did so I saw through the trees Bec d'Ambès and beyond it the Garonne. At the top of the slope was a belvedere in front of the Château de Tayac, whose vines stretched in well-tended rows on either side of the road. The belvedere, apparently thoughtfully provided by the château, was directly opposite the tip of Bec d'Ambès. At its very end was a light buoy marking the mid-channel and beyond that a green starboard-hand buoy. On the far side of the spit I could see a stretch of the Garonne, curving gradually away southwards, inland to Bordeaux, out of sight round the bend. Beyond was a hazy impression of woods and low hills. A coaster came into view steaming down channel between Bec d'Ambès and the Isle de Cazeau, not the Médoc as I first thought. Gradually the ship cleared the point and began to steer down the Gironde to the open sea.

The water was surprisingly calm, no sign of the turbulence one might have expected at the meeting of two great rivers. Overhead, heavy slate-blue clouds shut out the sun and the waters of the estuary were the colour of pewter. As I looked, the clouds parted and a single shaft of light lit up the tip of the point, changing the surface of the water to a dazzling silver. I took this as a sign and left.

CHAPTER 9

A LA RECHERCHE DES GORGES PERDUES

The following morning I caught a bus to Bordeaux where I hired a car and drove home to Le Bel and Villeneuve-sur-Lot. I was elated to have reached the end of the Dordogne and more than ready to put my feet up but niggling away at the back of my mind was the knowledge that my journey was not finished. Ever since I had left Bort-les-Orgues on the the train I had been pondering how I could cover the stretch between Bort and Argentat. The answer was obvious: I must buy a bike and cycle down the Gorges. It was a change from my original plan which had been to walk the whole way but at least I would still be proceeding under my own muscle power. It was forty years since I had last owned a bike which explains, perhaps, why the idea did not occur to me immediately but once it had I acted quickly. I found a good sturdy model with three speeds at the local supermarket for £90. I could have bought a mountain bike with eighteen gears but I was afraid this would be too complicated for me; I wanted to keep things simple. Once I had the bike I realised I needed some panniers. These proved surprisingly difficult to find but at last I tracked down a pair that fitted neatly over the back wheel and held the same amount of gear as I had carried in my rucksack. A smaller canvas satchel fitted in front of the handlebars and held my maps and emergency rations.

I stayed at Le Bel until 15 September and then, fully restored, drove up to Brive with the bike in the boot, handed in my car and went to the station to buy a ticket for Ussel, where I intended to spend the night. Ussel is only twenty miles by road from Bort-les-Orgues and this seemed an ideal distance for my first trip. I got to the station at 6.10 p.m., with plenty of time, as I thought, before the train left at 6.30 p.m. but the queue for tickets was so long and the service so slow that by the time my turn came I had only three minutes to spare. I sprinted down the platform, down a flight of steps with the bike over my arm, along a tunnel, up another flight of steps and on to the platform. My train was just about to leave but the guard saw my frantic signals and opened the door of the guards-van. I handed up the bike, not easy because the floor of the van was at chest level, and heaved myself up the stairs into the nearest carriage. The whistle blew and the train was off.

The journey was interminable, the train taking over two hours to cover the fifty-eight miles from Brive to Ussel but all the time we were climbing and the landscape, where it wasn't obscured by trees, was getting noticeably more mountainous. By the time we reached Ussel it was dark and as I hadn't yet discovered how my dynamo worked I had to push my bike to L'Auberge, my hotel. Luckily it was not far away. By then it was 8.45 and dinner was nearly over, so I had a quick shower and went to the dining room. Dinner was *paté de campagne, moules marinières, paupiette de poulet*, a cheese board with a choice of St-Nectaire and Bleu d'Auvergne and, a favourite of mine, *tarte tatin*. Excellent value at eighty francs.

Before I left next morning, Monsieur *le patron* showed me how the dynamo worked (I had never had a bike with one before) and helped me fit the panniers, which I had taken off the previous evening –not an easy job. I cycled for about a mile and then the road began to climb. I quickly found that, what with the weight of my panniers and the flabbiness of my calf muscles, I was incapable of cycling up all but the slightest of inclines. I got off and pushed. This went on for twenty minutes, until I reached the top of the hill, then away I went down the other side; a pattern which was to be repeated many times in the next six days.

I was delighted to be back in the mountains again: the air was fresh and the scenery full of interest after the long hot roads of the lowlands with their endless vistas of maize and vines. Thick woods, oak and scots fir predominating, alternated with hay fields and cattle pastures. The road crossed the Digue, a tributary of the Dordogne and skirted a lake after which it plunged down a long one-in-six descent.

Near the bottom I saw on the left hand side of the road a belvedere. I dismounted, a little stiffly, and found to my surprise that I was looking at a magnificent panorama of the Lac de Bort, extending right up to the start of the gorges. A little way up the right hand shore I could clearly see the Château de Val on its promontory and behind it, a long way in the distance, the jagged outline of the Puy de Sancy. It was like meeting an old friend.

I reached Bort about 11.30, just under three hours after leaving Ussel. I felt tired, but nothing like as tired as I would have done if I had walked the same distance and I had averaged just over six miles an hour compared with two-and-a-half when I was walking. I was very pleased: I now knew I would finish my journey.

I stayed at the Hôtel Central, in the same room as before. Seen from my window Bort looked more agreeable than I remembered. It was a beautiful early autumn day and the low sun was lighting up the *orgues*, making them seem less oppressive than before. Below them the old town also looked less dour. After lunch I rested for an hour and then walked across the bridge into the old town. It was market day and just like last time there was a small fairground on the bank opposite my hotel. It was going to be another noisy night, but this time I really didn't mind.

It was raining when I left Bort next morning. I went up past the church and found the road which leads up the cliff face to the *orgues*. It was very steep and from the very first I had to push my bike, so progress was slow. Even so, I found the going easier than if I had been wearing a pack. It was less effort to push a bike that carried a load than carry it myself. The only problem was the pedals which occasionally turned and barked my shins. Steep wooded slopes on either hand hid the view but after half-an-hour I reached a viewing platform. Below me a solitary kite circled over the roofs of the town but unfortunately, although the rain had stopped, it was still misty and I couldn't see much. I continued upwards and after ten minutes found myself at the foot of the *orgues*, the great clinkstone columns towering high above me, then they were hidden again by trees.

It took nearly an hour in all to reach the top of the *orgues* but it was worth it. Far below was Bort, crammed into its narrow valley. Looking left, northwards, I could see in the foreground a projecting piece of the *orgues* and beyond that the Lac du Bort and, very small, the Château de Val. Opposite me, to the east, I could see the river Rhue, winding down through the mountains to join the Dordogne at the foot of the *orgues*. On a clear day, I would have been able to see all the way to the Puy de Sancy and the mountains of Cantal but it was still misty and they were lost in a haze, but I did notice, with relief, that there was clearer weather to the south, where the sun was breaking through th clouds.

It was 10.30 by the time I left the *orgues*. For a while the road continued upwards, although here it was open country, a mixture of thick woods and pastures. A herd of beautiful Aubrac, long-horned cattle, their chestnut coats shining like well-polished shoes, stared lugubriously at me as I passed. Bells round their necks tinkled pleasantly. It is said that Aubrac cattle only flourish in the mountains and that if they leave the high pastures their coats turn pale.

Ten minutes more brought me at last to the top of the long climb. From here there was a long view south and west of a hilly well-wooded plateau with almost no sign of human habitation. I mounted my bike and in twenty minutes whizzed down to St-Julien-près-de-Bort. Five minutes later I was at the Site de St-Nazaire, where the Digue meets the Dordogne. Leaving my bike I walked along a narrow stony track that led to a calvary on a headland, overlooking the confluence of the two rivers.

On all sides, heavily wooded cliffs plunged hundreds of feet to the river. Immediately below me was the Digue, emerging from its own deep ravine to flow into the Dordogne on my left. Away to the south stretched the gorges until lost to view behind a bend. The water was quite still for here the Dordogne is a lake created by the Barrage de Marèges, further downstream. There were no roads, not a solitary farm to be seen. It was a wild, grimly impressive scene.

I returned to my bike and cycled back to St-Julien-près-de-Bort where I stopped for a lemonade (no alcohol while cycling). While I was there a *chasseur* came in with a brace of pheasants he had just shot. It was the first day of the new season. Although I believe it is mistake to interfere with traditional country sports, I could not help feeling distressed by the sight of these beautiful birds. The throat of one of them was covered by lovely, iridescent pinkish feathers which the *chasseur* stroked appreciatively – it hadn't stopped him shooting them though. I quickly downed my lemonade and left.

There was a short climb after St-Julien-près-de-Bort and then, joy oh joy, an exhilarating descent of about a mile to a road junction, where I turned left. I was making for a hotel at Neuvic, about six miles due west of St-Julien-près-de-Bort, as the crow flies. Unfortunately the nearest bridge across the gorges of the Digue was at Le Moulin de Rotabourg, about three miles inland, necessitating a long detour. The road dropped steeply down the face of the gorge with numerous hairpin bends. As I sped down under a canopy of trees I caught an occasional glimpse into the gulch on my left but the Digue was hidden far below by a thick screen of trees. Most of the time, however, I was too busy concentrating on the road to see much.

By the time I reached le Moulin de Rotabourg it was one o'clock and I was feeling tired, so I was delighted to see a small restaurant on the left hand side of the road. It was built out over the ravine and a row of windows gave the diners on that side a vertiginous view. It was obviously a popular place and was nearly full but luckily they managed to find a table for me. It was a very good lunch: *salade Corrèziane*, consisting of slices of smoked duck, walnuts, cheese and lettuce; a smoky *jambon de pays*; *pintade aux pruneaux*, *pommes frites* and *haricots*, cheese and a homemade apple pie. No wine but I drank a whole bottle of Vittel. All this for only seventy francs.

It was 2.30 when I left the Auberge du Moulin. I crossed a small stone bridge that spanned the gulch and immediately found myself confonted by a long weary climb up the southern face of the gorge. It took over half-an-hour to reach the top after which I descended rapidly to the village of la Roche-Peyroux. I was back on the plateau again in open country but by now I was so tired I was hardly aware of the scenery. I cycled through a pine forest, the road verges thick with bracken, until I came to a small dam. There were men working on it, and on the north side, where there should have been a lake was a large expanse of mud. This was the Lac de Neuvic. I was nearly there.

A sign to the right directed me down a short lane at the end of which was the Hôtel du Lac. To my surprise I was met by an Englishman, John Watson, who owned the hotel, a modern building with a large restaurant and bar and a long terrace overlooking the lake. The rooms were in a separate, characterless building, rather like a motel. Mine was pleasant enough with a view across the lake but quite impersonal and I guess identical to the rest.

I spent the rest of the afternoon on the terrace. The view was beautiful, even though the water had retreated a mile or more to the middle, exposing a large expanse of mud and sand. The Barrage de Neuvic belongs to a network of dams controlling the upper reaches of the Dordogne and its tributaries, all of which are regularly inspected and maintained. It was my bad luck that it was Neuvic's turn this year and that meant draining the lake. Close to, the shore was littered with old tyres and metal mooring buoys left high and dry alongside their anchors, to which they were still attached by ropes or chains; otherwise the bottom was remarkably free of rubbish. Far away in the distance two windsurfers were darting back and forth across what water remained. As I watched a large bird of prey, with a white belly, hovered interestedly over them, decided against and veered away looking for easier prey.

I slept well that night and rose late. After a leisurely breakfast I had a long chat with John Watson. A Yorkshireman with many years' experience in the catering trade, he had first seen the Hôtel du Lac four years ago. It had originally been built as a casino in the 1940s and the rooms were a later addition. Impressed by the beauty of the setting, John Watson felt sure that the hotel had great potential and made an immediate offer. Since then, with the help of his wife Sally he had worked hard to build up trade to its present very successful level.

I asked Mr Watson if he knew any other hotels close to my route down the Dordogne: I had been able to find only one, Hôtel Fabry at Pont du Chambon but it was too far to reach in one day. He was very helpful and told me that some English friends of his ran a bar-restaurant at Sérandon, which had some rooms, and there was another further down river at Chalvignac. He rang his friend at Sérandon who said yes he had a room but warned that five *ouvriers*, who were working on the dam, were staying there and that as my room was over the bar it might be rather noisy. I didn't care: I reckoned I could put up with the noise for one night.

It was 10.30 by the time I left. Much later than usual, but I wasn't worried: the Barrage de Marèges, which I was off to see next, was only eight miles away and Sérandon a mere two miles further on, so I knew I had plenty of time.

To begin with I had to back-track over the dam and through the pinewood. The road I had found so tiring yesterday seemed easy enough that morning and I quickly found myself at the turning that led to the dam. Soon I was speeding down an increasingly steep slope through a gloomy forest of fir trees. Quite suddenly, I came out into the open and saw, on my left, a small, grey château with pepper pot corner towers, the Château de Marèges. The road continued past an enormous electricity sub-station and through the village of Marèges. The houses were all new and looked like alpine chalets. Presumably they were built for the workers at the sub-station. After Marèges the trees closed in again and the descent became still steeper with numerous hairpin bends. I had my brakes full on to keep control. I was beginning to wonder what had happened to the dam when I saw on my left a viewing platform built out from the edge of the cliff. I dismounted and looked over the edge.

I was looking straight down on top of the barrage, a hundred feet below. High wooded cliffs hemmed in the dam on either side and at first I didn't realise the huge scale of the construction until I noticed a toy car parked in the forecourt of the hydroelectric station at the foot of the massive retaining wall. The sheer face of the dam drops three hundred feet to the bed of the Dordogne, filling the narrow gorge as if it were a natural extension the cliffs. None of the later dams has quite this simple grandeur. After Marèges their design was modified and all have gigantic sluices projecting from the front of the retaining walls.

Impressive though I found the *barrage*, I was not sorry to leave the gloomy enclosed gorge, although I was certainly not looking forward to the climb back to the the village of Marèges. In fact, it did not take as long as I expected and in twenty minutes I was out into the sunshine again. At Marèges, I turned left and started southwards to Sérandon. It was a lovely ride along a quiet country road with no traffic to worry about. The countryside was beautiful: on either side were mountain pastures where long-horned Aubrac cattle grazed. In one field a circle of these handsome beasts stood in the shade of a huge umbrella-like oak tree. On my left an undulating wooded landscape fell away towards the Dordogne, hidden in its gorge. A long way in the distance was the blurred outline of the mountains of Cantal.

It was 12.30 when I arrived at Sérandon. I soon found my hotel which could well have been a *Routier*. To the left of the entrance was a small bar where local farmers and workmen were drinking *pastis*; on the right a simple restaurant with red-and-white checked tablecloths. I quickly drained off a beer and sat down to a simple lunch.

My room on the first floor back was large enough to contain two double beds, on one of which I dumped my gear. It had a washbasin, a bidet and the usual huge *armoire*. But the best thing was the wonderful view from the window, the same that I had seen on my ride from Marèges.

I spent most of the afternoon dozing or listening to the BBC World Service but at four o'clock I ventured out to look at a small romanesque church that I had passed on the outskirts of the village. It was at the foot of a hill, surrounded by fields where red Aubrac cows were grazing. A path led through a triangular church yard, shaded by pollarded plane trees, to the south porch, but the door was locked. The church was built of a local grey stone and had a slate roof with, at the west end, a two-stage belfry. The lower half was square and covered by slates; above it was an opening covered by an octagonal pointed roof. There was a second, smaller belfry, perhaps a lantern, over the east end. At roof level the corbel ends had carved heads with leering faces. One had a hand in its mouth, suggesting toothache. At the west end was a deep, recessed arch of unusual size for such a small church. Round the outside of the arch were strange, primitively carved figures: one was dancing, another wore what looked like a bag at its waist, probably meant to represent a purse. Easier to make out were a peacock, a fox, a cow, a sheep and two strange four-legged animals, with human heads, facing each other.

Inside the arch were more carvings in blind arcades on either side. On the north side a bearded man was depicted riding a horse or a donkey, holding what looked like a thin tube and followed by sheep: Christ's entry into Jerusalem, or Christ as the good shepherd perhaps? The next arch showed two figures sitting either side of a round object: Adam and Eve and the forbidden apple? On the south side was a figure riding side saddle on a horse. The rest of the sculpture was too worn to decipher. It was an interesting collection to find in a small church in such an out-of-the-way place.

I returned to the hotel and asked in the bar if anyone knew who had the key to the church. A big man called Po-Paul, with an enormous belly wobbling under a tight orange T-shirt, at once set off to scour the village for it, but returned empty-handed. I was upstairs in my room, preparing to go down to dinner, when there came an urgent knock at the door. There was Po-Paul with the keys.

The inside of the church was completely bare. It was embarrassing after Po-Paul had taken such trouble to obtain the keys and I had to pretend to be interested but it was difficult when every bit of furniture had been stripped out. One thing I did notice: it looked as though the original intention had been to cover the vault with a tunnel vault and the springing of the vault was still visible but for some reason, probably cost, a wooden ceiling had been substituted. Otherwise all I could find was a capital in the apse with three monstrous heads, with leering mouths, supported on puny legs.

Back at the hotel I was buying a drink for Po-Paul when an Englishman, whom I had seen dining at the Hôtel du Lac with a pretty auburn-haired girl, came in. He recognised me and invited me to join him in a glass of champagne. It turned out that it was his birthday and he had been celebrating all day. He owned the Hôtel Moderne at Neuvic and invited me to stay. I thanked him and explained that I had to be on my way next day down the Dordogne, then made my escape to dinner.

The *ouvriers* were very well-behaved and I passed a peaceful night until five o'clock, when I was woken by the noise of rain drumming on the roof. I went back to sleep but when I awoke it was still raining. By nine o'clock the rain had eased enough for me to don my waterproof and set off for the Hostellerie de la Bruyère, fifteen miles away, near Chalvignac on the opposite side of the Dordogne. Ten minutes later I was hurtling down a steep, twisty road with dark woods on either hand. Suddenly, as I rounded a bend, I saw the Dordogne, flowing through a narrow ravine far below. It was a nasty shock for it meant I had taken a wrong turning on the outskirts of Sérandon and was on the road to Champignac. There was no help for it, I would have to retrace my steps. It took a quarter of an hour to trudge back to the crossroads just ouside the village and by now it was raining hard again. It was a bad beginning.

Two miles of easy cycling on the flat brought me to the start of the Route des Adjustants, the first road in the Gorges de la Dordogne that runs alongside the river and famous for its views. Right at the start of the route is a viewing platform called the Belvedère de Gratte Bruyère. I parked my bike and clambered up a slippery rocky outcrop at the top of which was the belvedere. Through the driving rain I could just see, 1700 feet below, the river Sumène emerging from a ravine opposite to flow into the Dordogne. Away to my left, fold on fold of tree covered slopes, their crests lost in the low-lying cloud, marked the unseen passage of the river. To the right the gorge widened and the Dordogne became a lake again, this time held back by the Barrage de l'Aigle. On either side the cliffs fell sheer to the waters edge and it was difficult to believe that there could really be a road down.

I had been looking forward to the journey along the Route des Adjustants and enjoying its spectacular views; I certainly hadn't visualised myself cycling down it in pelting rain, nor had I expected the slope to be so steep. I had the brakes full on but even so I felt that the bike was running away from me. In the end I dismounted and walked down; even then the bike, with its heavy panniers, was tugging me along like a puppy on a lead. The road followed a ledge down the cliff face and there was a steep drop on my left down to the Dordogne. Most of the time I couldn't see the river and when I did it was wreathed in mist and low cloud, a dreary scene.

It took forty minutes to reach the bottom where there was a small bridge, the Pont des Adjustants across another small tributary of the Dordogne, the Triozoune. A short climb brought me to a junction with the main road from Neuvic to Mauriac and twenty minutes later I was crossing the Pont de St-Projet to the left bank of the Dordogne.

There followed a long, long climb up the narrow valley of the Abiou under a canopy of dripping trees. There was nothing to see but greenery, I was soaking wet, cold and bored. It was another hour before I reached the plateau and was able to remount my bike. By then I was desperately looking for a bar where I could get a hot drink but there was none and in the end I cycled on to the Hostellerie de la Bruyère.

The hotel was set in a large park, planted with fir trees under which were scattered inviting-looking garden tables and chairs. I was quartered in a big old-fashioned house of the kind you would expect to find in a town rather than the middle of the mountains. My room was vast and, as the heating was not turned on, rather cold. I stripped off and had a shower. My top half, which had been protected by my waterproof, was reasonably dry but my Rohan slacks, underpants and socks were dripping wet. Worse still, when I opened my panniers, I found they were not waterproof and the contents were soaking. I managed to find a pair of slacks, a shirt and some dirty underpants that were still dry and thus attired I went to lunch.

The restaurant was in a separate chalet-style building and had a fake stone fireplace. Despite these unpromising surroundings I had a very good meal: the main course was a delicious, rib-sticking *coq-au-vin* made with a generous quantity of wine. It was just what I needed after my trek in the rain and I returned to my room in much better fettle.

When I looked out of my window next morning the rain had stopped but the hotel was wreathed in mist. I packed my still sodden gear and set off gingerly down the road to the Barrage de l'Aigle. The fog was on the uplands and as the road began to descend it began to clear. Soon I was speeding down a zig-zag road with rugged cliffs above and below me. In fifteen minutes I was down at the *barrage* and crossing the road that runs along its top. I parked my bike by the electricity sub-station on the right bank and climbed a flight of steps up to a viewing platform at the top of a rock overhanging the dam.

Although not the largest of the great *barrages* of the Dordogne the grandeur of its setting makes L'Aigle by far the most impressive. The gorge is wider here than at Marèges so the aspect is less gloomy. From where I was standing I could see across the dam, with its great concave curves, to a grim-looking cliff face opposite, so sheer that it was almost bare of trees. A thousand feet below was the Dordogne, its black waters flecked with foam as they swirled down a narrow gulch. Further down river I could see the village of Aynes, small stone houses crammed into a narrow stretch of land just wide enough for a single village street and behind the houses some pastures. Above the village loomed the tree-covered rock face of the gorge. On my side the the view was limited by a projecting cliff. Upstream, behind the dam was the still lake framed by high wooded slopes.

I recrossed to the left bank and cycled down to Aynes. The houses were for the families of men working on the dam and date from 1940s but they are built from local stone in the traditional manner with fish-scale roofs and white shutters and they are very attractive; so much so that most of them now are holiday homes.

After Aynes, for the first time since le Mont-Dore, the road ran on the flat alongside the Dordogne making cycling easy and enjoyable. Four miles downstream at Spontour was another suspension bridge across the Dordogne. Below the bridge were moored some pleasure boats and a *gabare*. Before the dams were built and turned the upper Dordogne into a series of lakes, the river was only navigable from St-Projet downwards. Spontour and St-Projet were the first villages on the upper reaches where *gabares* were used to ship the timber products of the region downriver to Bergerac and Libourne. Even so, the stretch between St-Projet and Argentat was one of the most difficult on the whole Dordogne, full of rapids, islands and hidden obstructions that required enormous skill to negotiate – not surprisingly the *gabariers* of these villages were some of the most courageous and respected of the whole river.

Spontour presented me with a choice of routes. My destination was Hôtel Fabry, *au rendezvous des pecheurs*, on the edge of the Dordogne at Pont du Chambon. To get there I could either cross the bridge and take a long detour northwards, via St. Merd-de-Lapleau; or I could climb a very steep hill on the left bank to Auriac and down to the Hôtel Fabry from there. My Michelin guide advised the first route but I decided that this was too long and opted for the second.

It was 10.45 when I started my climb and the sun was full out. At the beginning the road wound backwards and forwards above Spontour and I kept catching glimpses of the river through the trees but eventually it was lost to sight. On either side of the road a dense beech forest blocked out the sun and made it so chilly that I was forced to don my jacket. Occasionally the road came out of the trees and for a moment the sun was hot, then it plunged back into the trees once more. Eventually I had climbed so high that the beech woods were left behind, to be replaced on my left by a craggy red cliff and on my right by a steep slope thickly covered with oak trees. At 11.30 I stopped at a waterfall for a drink but it was another half-an-hour before I emerged on to the plateau and saw meadows and cattle once more. The road continued to climb up to the village of Auriac where at long last I was able to mount my bike again. Before setting off, I looked back, over the top of the woods I had just left behind, across the undulating plateau to Mauriac and beyond, in the far distance, the mountains, stretching all the way from the Plomb du Cantal in the south to the Monts Dore to the north east: it was a marvellous panorama.

Auriac was a typical mountain village with some nice stone houses and fish-scale roofs but I didn't stop to explore. From there it was downhill all the way, sweeping round curve after curve through a dark forest until once again I saw below me water glinting through the trees. A moment later I came to the Pont du Chambon, rattled across the bridge and stopped at the Hôtel Fabry. Ten minutes later I was sitting down to lunch.

It was the kind of simple, beautifully cooked meal that the French do so well; Elizabeth David would have loved it. The first course was a perfect *omelette aux fines herbes*, straight from the pan and still runny. This was followed by a trout cooked in butter, served with boiled potatoes. The cheese course was a creamy *cabecou* and a piece of *cantal* and I finished with a ripe Williams pear. It was the best meal of the whole trip.

It is a small hotel, a restaurant really, with rooms, but very comfortable. My room, on the first floor, had a beautiful view out over the Dordogne. The wallpaper had a kind of paisley design in grey-blue and the curtains and bed cover were a plain ice-blue. The bathroom had tiles of a similar colour. The only discordant note was a large, sexy mirror on the cupboard opposite the bed, which I tried to avoid looking at.

At one end of the hotel was a little triangular garden and here I spent the rest of the afternoon, in the shade of a tree, reading and looking at the lake. It was a beautiful autumn afternoon, the sun lighting the undersides of the trees, the outline of the wooded crags on the opposite side of the Dordogne wreathed in mist and no sign of life except for wagtails dipping over the surface of the water. It was difficult to believe that the next day would be my last in the mountains.

According to the Michelin Green Guide there are no views of the Dordogne between Pont du Chambon and the *barrage* de Chastang and they recommend another long detour on the right bank via Marcillac-la-

Croisille and St-Martin-la-Meanne. After studying my map I decided that the left bank route looked much shorter and more interesting, so I ignored their advice and set off across the bridge.

It was a chilly morning and I was wearing my jacket but the sun was shining and the morning mist was clearing rapidly from the lake. The first short stretch was along the river bank. After about ten minutes I stopped to take a last look at the graceful suspension bridge, the little grey hotel and above them both the high wooded hills, splashed with red patches amongst the green where the bracken and heather had already changed colour.

The road began to climb and I was forced to dismount. It was the start of another long trudge upwards like the one to Auriac, but the woods were not so thick here and there were frequent views down to the lake. The treetops were still robed in mist and it was cool so I kept my jacket on even though by now I was sweating profusely. After about a quarter-of-an-hour I came to a gap in the trees and saw on the far side of the Dordogne a magnificent crag with the river curving round its base from left to right. I was looking at the Roc de Charlus, a famous landmark at the start of one of the most difficult passages of the Dordogne. Before the valley was drowned the Roc would have towered even higher over the river and must have been a frightening sight to the *gabariers* in their frail craft.

I plodded slowly on for another twenty minutes when the screen of concealing trees parted once more to reveal through a wedge-shaped cleft a staggering view of the Dordogne nine hundred feet below. Ten minutes later I came to yet another gap and yet another view, this time back towards Pont du Chambon. Unfortunately I was looking into the sun and there was still some mist below so I couldn't actually see the bridge but I was sure that on a clear day I could have done – so much for the Michelin Green Guide!

I had been pushing my bike laboriously upwards for just over an hour when I emerged from the woods and saw ahead of me the village of Bassignac-le-Haut. Once again Michelin had missed out. Not only is Bassignac itself, with its old stone houses and fish-scale roofs, worth a second look but there is an outstanding panorama from the road beyond, looking across the roofs of the village to the cliffs on the far side of the Dordogne and beyond them miles of open country stretching away into the far distance.

Bassignac proved not to be the top of the climb. I toiled on for another twenty minutes before I was able to mount my bike. It had taken me an-hour-and-a-half to cover six miles. Away I sped down to Darazac where I turned right on to the road to Chastang. It was rather nondescript country here, stony, infertile uplands, succeeded by birch woods and bracken and then scruffy pastureland but after three-quarters-of-an-hour I saw on my left the beautiful lake of Servières-le-Château. I skirted the lake and took a turning on the right leading to the *barrage*. A short climb was followed by a hair-raising descent down a zig-zag cliff road with snatched views of the Dordogne below through a screen of trees. Just before I reached the dam I saw a notice advertising a belvedere at the side of the road. I parked my bike and slithered down a steep path to a platform built out from the edge of the gorge. To my astonishment I found myself looking northwards at the face of the dam at a level just below the crest. It was a remakable vantage point: the massive retaining wall and huge sluices seemed to fill my whole field of vision creating an overwhelming sense of the sheer size and strength of the dam and I was filled with admiration for the French engineers responsible for this magnificent construction..

Leaving the belvedere I continued on to the dam itself, arriving at 11.28 a.m. precisely. My journey down the Dordogne was over.

EPILOGUE

ONE MORE TIME

I was back at Chastang in June of the following year, this time with Sybil. We had decided to spend the last three days of our summer holiday at Pont du Chambon before boarding the auto-train at Brive. We had left Le Bel just after lunch, driven east to Cahors and then struck north-eastwards across the Causse de Gramat. I had forgotten how barren this stretch of country is with its stony fields, tumbledown dry stone walls and stunted oak-trees, although it has its admirers, Freda White amongst them. Beyond the town of Gramat the landscape was less arid, there were pastures and the trees grew tall and straight. I had just noticed a sign to Loubressac, when we came to the edge of the ridge and saw below us the valley of the Bave and directly opposite, on its hill, the grim red hulk of Castelnau-Bretenoux. It looked even more sensational than I remembered and Sybil, who had not seen the castle before, was also very enthusiastic. We drove down into the valley and up to the entrance but could not get into the castle itself which had been taken over by a large school party. Instead we strolled round the walls enjoying the views.

From Castelnau we drove to Beaulieu, where we stopped for a quick look at the church, and then on to Argentat and up the river road to Chastang. We followed my route across the plateau to Bassignac-le-Haut and then down through the woods to Pont du Chambon.

There was a hidden agenda in our decision to stay at Hôtel Fabry. Although I had travelled the whole length of the Dordogne, because I had not been able to find anywhere to stay at Messeix, I had missed out the Gorges d'Avèze, the only place between La Bourboule and Bort-les-Orgues where the gorges are accessible, and I was determined to make good this omission.

We decided to take the following day easy, so after breakfast we drove across the bridge and up to Auriac where we shopped for a picnic. From there we descended to the *barrage* de l'Aigle, then up again through the woods to Chalvignac, across the plateau and down once more to St-Projet, across the bridge and along to the beginning of the Route des Ajustants, where I knew there was a rough track down to the water's edge. We bumped along until we found a grassy space under a tree big enough to give shade to both us and the car, unloaded our folding table and chairs, spread out our picnic and settled down for the afternoon.

It was extraordinary what a difference the sun made to the scene. The wooded cliffs that had looked so forbidding when I had peered at them through the rain now revealed a sombre magnificence when seen sil-houetted against a clear blue sky and reflected in the clear waters of the Dordogne. Apart from a noisy flotilla of canoes that passed us, the gorge was eerily quiet: no traffic and no sign of life except for a solitary buzzard circling lazily over the lake. It was infinitely relaxing.

We left our picnic site at four o'clock and climbed up the Route des Ajustants to the Belvedère de Gratte-Bruyère, where I took another look at the confluence of the Dordogne and Sumène. Of course, on this bright, sunny day, the view was superb but somehow I couldn't help thinking that it had lost something of the awesome grandeur I remembered.

We continued on to Sérandon and thence to the Hôtel du Lac at Neuvic. It was a very different scene from the last time I had been here: the lake was now full and where before there had been old tyres and stranded mooring buoys, children were paddling and windsurfers capsizing. There was no sign of John Watson but Sally was giving water ski-ing lessons, towing learners behind a smart white motor boat.

We sat on the terrace, eating ice-cream, and admiring the dedication of the French to their leisure activities. There were the usual pretty girls with beautifully cut hair and wearing the latest fashionable swimwear, sitting in sports cars doing nothing in particular, while hunky youths, dressed in Bermuda length surfing shorts, hung about teasing them. Everywhere there were tiny tots, running, screaming and splashing, pursued by harassed mums. Meanwhile, their fathers sat on the terrace sipping beer. Sybil was much taken with the scene and thought that Neuvic was an ideal place for a family holiday.

The quickest way to the Gorges d'Avèze from the Pont du Chambon is to pick up the main road at Mauriac and drive north, via Bort-les-Orgues, to Tauves, where the road to the Gorges d'Avèze begins, a total distance of about fifty miles.

The first part of the drive was the same as the previous day but after Chalvignac, instead of turning left to St-Projet, we went right to Mauriac, where we stopped to buy our picnic. It was market day and we drove round for some time looking for somewhere to park. Eventually we found a place in the market square near the twelfth-century church of Notre-Dame-des-Miracles. While Sybil went off to do the shopping I took the opportunity to nip into the church and have a quick look round. The interior was rather austere with a tunnel vault and ambulatory with radiating chapels. The best part was the west porch which has a tympanum depicting the Ascension, surrounded by signs of the zodiac. Unfortunately there was not time for more than a very superficial visit: I must go back.

There was the usual traffic jam in Bort, aggravated by the fact that it was lunchtime and the locals were all desperate to get home. We reached Tauves at 12.30 and turned left on to the narrow country road that leads to the gorges. We drove as far as the village of Avèze, where I got out, shouldered my day pack and started walking, while Sybil drove on to wait for me on the far side of the gorges.

The road up here on the plateau was flat with rough pasture on either side. It was stony soil and there were abandoned fields overgrown with bracken. A mile or so ahead of me I could see what looked like a dark green hedge but as I got nearer I realised it was the tops of trees growing in the gorge. Beyond, on the far side of the gorge was a cluster of houses, probably Chomadoux, one of the hamlets I had passed through on my way to Messeix.

On the plateau there was a mixture of trees – accacia, holly, silver birch, oak and apple – but as the road began to descend oaks and firs began to predominate. The further down I went the steeper it became.

On one side I was on a level with the roots of massive trees that soared high above me; on the other I looked down on the tops of scots firs growing lower down the slope. As the road zig-zagged downwards the trees seemed to crowd in, blotting out the sunlight. All I could see was a narrow wedge of blue, the width of the road, high above. Occasionally there was a gap in the trees with a view across the gorge to pastures on the far side, then the trees closed in again.

I had been on my way down for half-an-hour when I heard the sound of running water. I stopped and peered down through the trees but could see nothing. I carried on and a few minutes later thought I could just see sunlight glinting on water a hundred feet below. At last, forty-five minutes after I had started my descent, I emerged from the shadow of the trees into the valley bottom, over four hundred feet below the plateau.

I stood on a small road bridge and looked down at the Dordogne. Upstream only a short stretch of the river was visible, emerging from a dark, rock-strewn gulch, but downstream it raced through a fresh green meadow before disappearing into the trees again. If lunch hadn't been waiting for me, I would have liked to explore a little way down the river but there wasn't time, so I began my ascent.

This side of the gorge faces south east and the woods were less dense, so that stretches of the road were quite sunny. I was soon quite hot but the slope was less severe and I made good progress. For some time I could see the Dordogne, like a strip of silver foil, through the trees, then a bend in the road hid it from view. As I climbed I noticed that there were more deciduous trees here than on the other side, where they were nearly all scots fir. An orange butterfly fluttered past me and then I was out of the gorge and walking on the plateau once more. Another bend and there was Sybil waiting for me. She had found a splendid place for a picnic nearby, under the shade of an oak tree, with a wonderful view eastwards to the Monts Dore. It was a hazy day but I could still make out the jagged crest of the Puy de Sancy where my adventures had started just under a year ago

We opened a bottle of St-Pourçain, and toasted the indisputable end of my long journey down the Dordogne.

But I still haven't finished Proust.